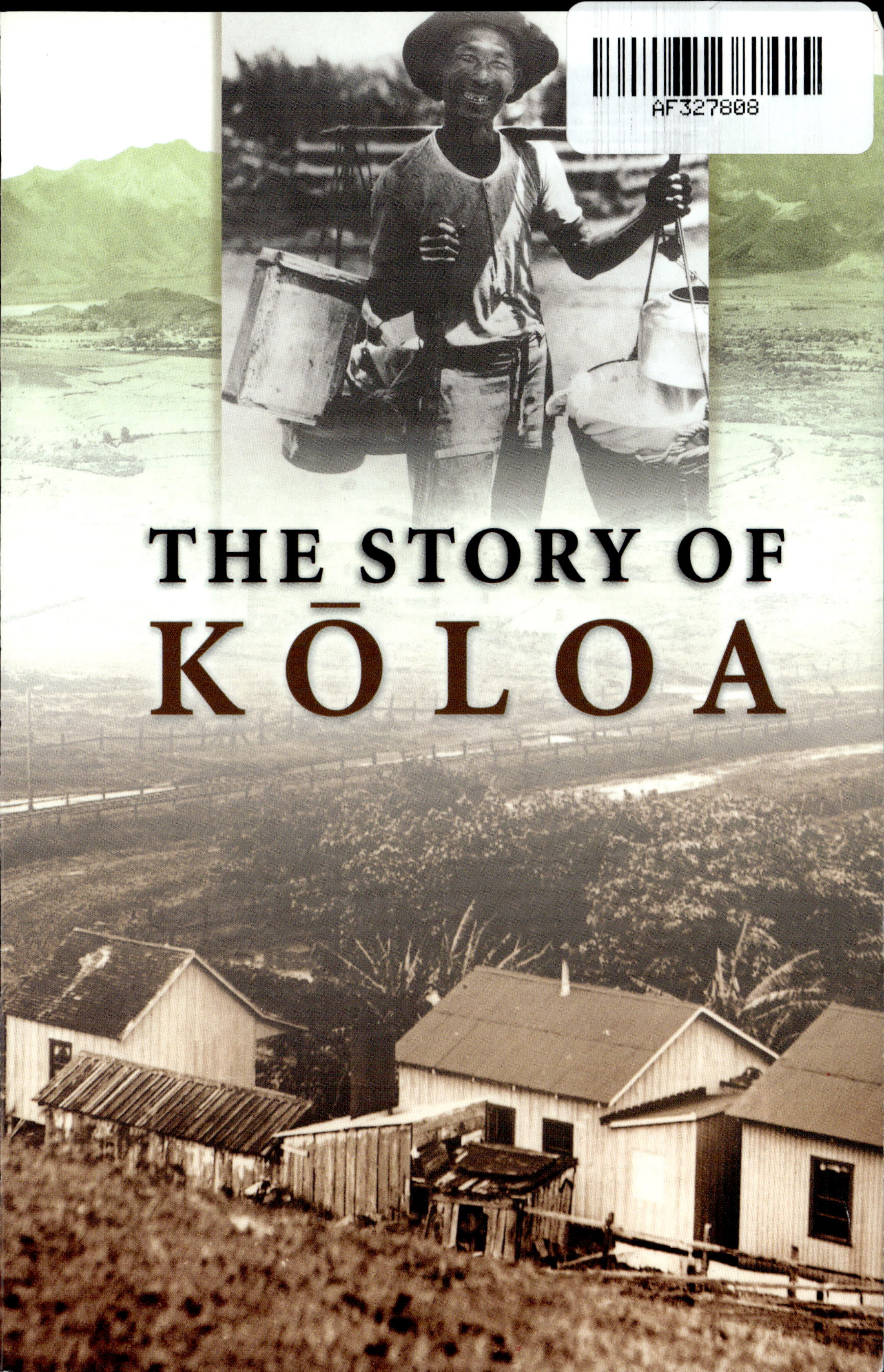

THE STORY OF
KŌLOA

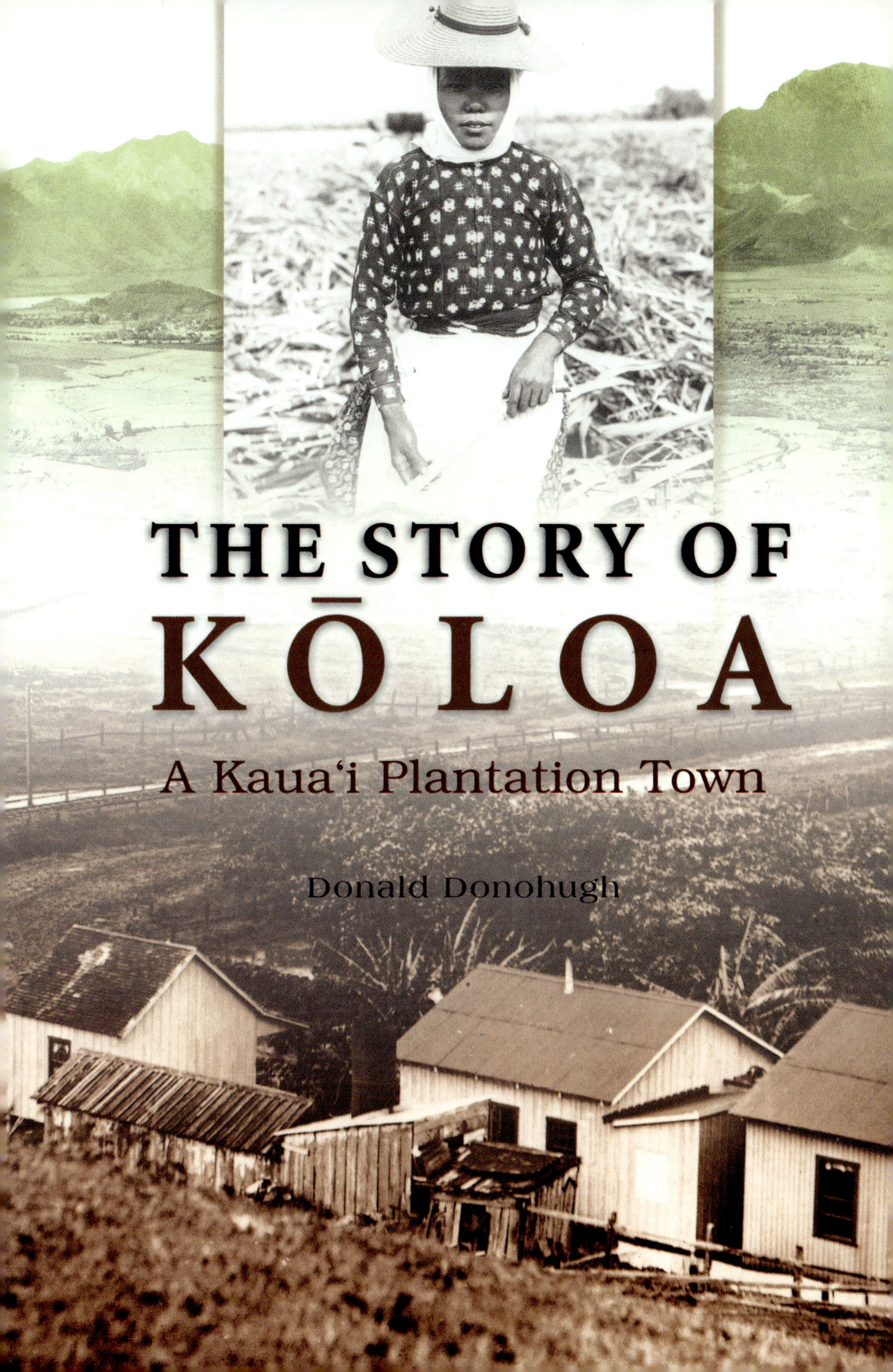

THE STORY OF
KŌLOA
A Kauaʻi Plantation Town
Donald Donohugh

Softcover ISBN 1-56647-449-3
Hardcover ISBN 1-56647-507-4

Library of Congress Catalog Card Number: 2001088535

Design by Sistenda Yim

First Printing, August 2001
Second Printing, October 2002

Mutual Publishing
1215 Center Street, Suite 210
Honolulu, Hawai'i 96816
Ph: 808-732-1709
Fax: 808-734-4094
Email: mutual@lava.net
www.mutualpublishing.com

Printed in Taiwan

*"The history of Kōloa
is in many ways Hawai'i's history in microcosm."*

Carol Wilcox, *The Kaua'i Album*

Table of Contents

	Acknowledgments	*ix*
	Introduction	*x*
(1)	"Beautiful Kaua'i"	*1*
(2)	An Island Is Born	*4*
(3)	The Polynesians Arrive	*8*
(4)	Culture and Customs	*19*
(5)	Contact, Conquest	*33*
(6)	Sandalwood and Whales	*50*
(7)	Puritans in Paradise	*66*
(8)	Tall Cane	*83*
(9)	Sojourners and Settlers	*111*
(10)	Plantation Life	*141*
(11)	By The Wind Grieved	*168*
(12)	A Tour of Kōloa and Po'ipū Today	*188*
(13)	References	*273*
(14)	Bibliography	*280*
(15)	Index	*289*

Acknowledgments

Mahalo ā nui loa to the following individuals: Abraham Keli'i Aka; Grace Blake; Marvin Brennecke, M.D.; Peter W. Dease; Gabriel I; Louis Jacintho Jr.; Tadao Kawamoto; William "Pila" Kikuchi; Val Knudsen; Catherine Lo; Karl Lo; Barbara Waterhouse McCord; Eric "Iki" Moir; Toyo Nishida; John Plews; David Pratt; Barbara Robeson; Warren Robinson; Phil Scott; Leilani Souza; and Robert T. Watts.

Appreciation, as well, to the staffs of: Bernice Pau'ahi Bishop Museum Archives; Hawaiian and Pacific Collections, Hamilton Library, University of Hawai'i at Mānoa; Hawaiian Mission Children's Society; Hawai'i State Archives; Hawai'i State Public Library System; Kaua'i Community College Learning Resource Center; Kaua'i Historical Society; and Kaua'i Museum.

My warmest aloha to those above and the many others in Kōloa and elsewhere who also shared the stories of their lives and of their ancestors—without all of you this story could not have been written.

Introduction

Kōloa is a small town on the southern shore of Kaua'i, itself a small island within the Hawaiian chain. The entire archipelago is only a tiny group of dots near the center of a map of the Pacific Ocean. Yet these islands have had far more than the share of history their size would warrant.

Nearly everyone is aware of what happened at Pearl Harbor on December 7, 1941. Far less is known about many other places in Hawai'i where events have occurred that, while less dramatic, have proved over time to be nearly as meaningful.

Kōloa is one of these places.

Polynesians first arrived in the Hawaiian Islands, sailing their double-hulled voyaging canoes, nearly two thousand years ago. Theirs was a society without writing, so accurate accounts of their incredible migrations and history for centuries after they settled are unavailable. Only shadows remain in legends and chants passed down orally through the generations, illuminated by suggestions from surviving cultural traditions and clues provided by archeology.

Captain James Cook first sighted the previously uncharted "Sandwich Islands" in January 1778, and named his fortuitous discovery in honor of the Earl of Sandwich. In view of all that was to result, many consider this the single most significant event ever to occur in Hawai'i. The first Hawaiians to encounter Westerners paddled out to Cook's ships in canoes launched from the Kōloa shore. Thus the written history of Hawai'i began with this episode at Kōloa. Cook and subsequent voyagers kept journals and logs but their accounts are of the voyages and the men who made them. They tell little about Kōloa.

It was not until 1835 that the first Christian missionaries settled in Kōloa. That same year the first sugar plantation in the Islands was started, barely a stone's throw away from the mission station. Thus, missionary reports, letters, and diaries exist that convey something of the history of Kōloa at the time. Sugar plantation documents also exist from that year on. Yet neither the missionaries nor plantation officials intended to write a history of Kōloa, so their records reveal little about the lives of either the Native Hawaiians or those from other lands who settled there.

Plantation workers were brought to Kōloa from many parts of the world to plant, tend, and harvest the fields of sugar cane. They had been selected because it was thought they would be hard workers and inexpensive. Most of the new arrivals spoke only their native languages and could neither read nor write. Fortunately, in the twilight of their lives, many of them told their stories to their children and grandchildren, who have preserved these precious fragments of history.

Excellent histories of Hawai'i as a whole have been written. While most are concerned primarily with events taking place on the more populous island of O'ahu, some do mention Kōloa. Over the years many travelers have passed through Kōloa and, in some cases, their diaries and letters are available in archives and family collections. These private sources provide just enough information to awaken one's interest.

The author has known Kōloa for over half a century. During these years he came to know numerous Kōloa kūpuna, or elders, and heard their stories before they passed on. Many of their children and their children's children have graciously shared the remembrances of their parents and grandparents. Contemporary residents have added to the record when their recollections were stirred by old photographs and family memorabilia. Several have graciously translated letters and other documents from various languages. In this sense, memory has been able to reach back more than a hundred years. It is primarily from the verbal accounts of those who came to Kōloa in the early years, and the recollections by their offspring of the tales they had been told, that this chronicle has taken form.

Together, these sources offer enough to tell much of the story of Kōloa. Yet it has never been written. This work began with a request by the Kaua'i Historical Society for a pamphlet on historic Kōloa. From that beginning it grew to its present scope. Undoubtedly gaps remain, and we hope readers will help fill such gaps with additional information recovered from family records in dusty attics and old trunks.

For the moment, however, let us enjoy what we do know.

KAUA'I
Nā Pali Coast
Hanalei
Kīlauea
Anahola
Koke'e
Kapa'a
Mt. Wai'ale'ale
Wailua
Mānā
Waimea Canyon
Kekaha
Lihu'e
Waimea
'Ōma'o
Hā'upu Range
Kalāheo
Lāwa'i
Hanapēpē
Kōloa
'Ele'ele
Po'ipū
W E
0
5
10 Miles

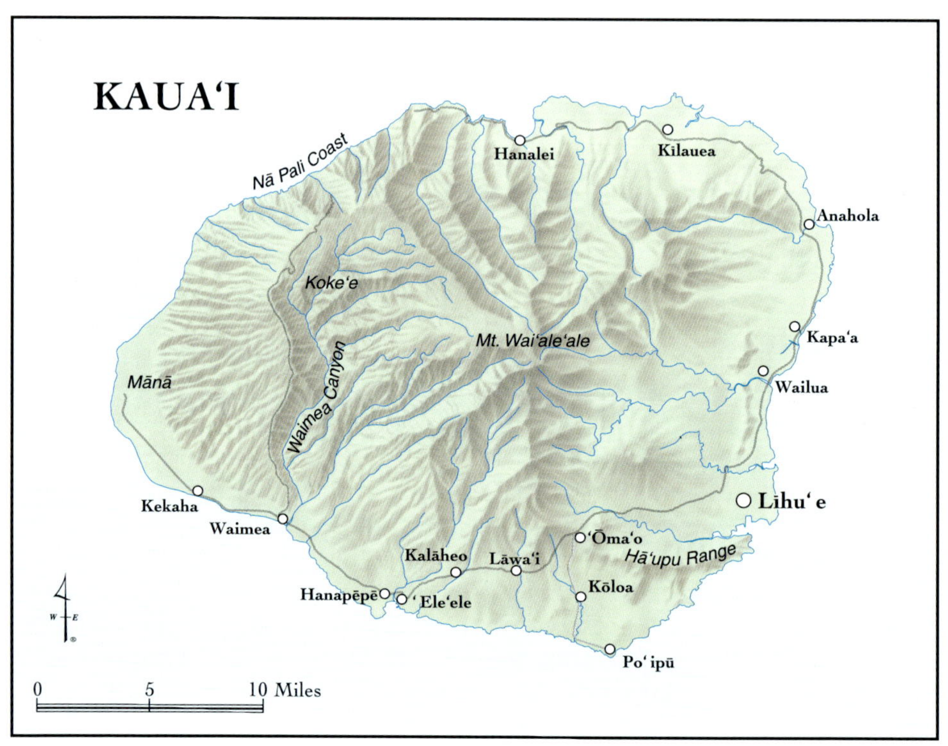

Kaua'i Map

"Beautiful Kaua'i"

Maika'i Kaua'i
Maika'i Kaua'i hemolele i ka mālie
Kupu kelakela ke po'o o Wai'ale'ale
Kela i ka lani kilakila Kawaikini
Ka no ka helekua linohau Alaka'i . . .
—mele kahiko

Beautiful Kaua'i
Most beautiful Kaua'i in serene perfection,
Rising from the sea to the summit of Wai'ale'ale,
She flowers in the heights of Kawaikini,
Her majesty radiates in splendor from Alaka'i . . .
—ancient chant

Few islands on earth can compare with Kaua'i. Fields of green growing in red earth sway in the trade winds. Waterfalls shimmer down emerald mountains and rainbows arch over verdant valleys. Spires of ancient volcanic ridges soar into the sky. Crescents of white sand, punctuated by points of black lava rock, fringe the shore. White-tailed tropic birds swoop in the unseen thermals of the vast multi-hued Waimea Canyon. Surrounding all this is the sapphire sea.

Kaua'i is the oldest of the major Hawaiian Islands, so nature has had time to etch its mountains, shape and color its canyons, form hanging valleys, and drape a lush green over all. Hawaiians of old referred to it as "Kaua'i Kilohana," or "Superb Kaua'i." It has more beaches, rivers, and waterfalls than any other Hawaiian Island and is well deserving of its contemporary sobriquet, "The Garden Island."

Archeological evidence indicates that the first Polynesians who settled on Kaua'i chose the north shore, where water from rain and streams was readily available for their crops. Later on, as their numbers increased, they developed incredible skill in building irrigation systems, and then preferred the south shore, where Kōloa and other settlements were to appear.

Here, the coast was more sheltered from the impact of winter storms generally blowing from the northwest. The early Polynesian settlers could fish and paddle their outrigger canoes safely along the shore and from village to village throughout most of the year. Trade winds carried sufficient rain to the southern uplands, from which the intricate irrigation systems brought life-sustaining water to the plants vital to their lives and culture. The abundant sunshine of the south shore also favored their crops.

Near the center of this shore was a huge marsh fringed by tall sugar cane that grew wild. This marsh was the most impressive feature of the local landscape, and Hawaiians called both the marsh and the land around it Kōloa.

Looking out to sea from the hills above Kōloa, the Hawaiian settlers were accustomed to seeing only the island of Ni'ihau anchored in the distance. One day in 1778, they saw two cloud-like apparitions moving slowly along the horizon. As recounted, Captain Cook had come upon the previously unknown Sandwich Islands while heading north in search of the fabled Northwest Passage, which geographers of the day believed must cross the top of the North American continent. The next day Cook's two ships, the *Resolution* and *Discovery*, approached close to Kaua'i, rounded the headland at Makahū'ena, and coasted west along the southern shore. Paddling out in their canoes from Kōloa, Hawaiians saw for the first time Western men. The sailors aboard the ships gazed down upon the Hawaiians in almost equal awe. Cook continued along the southern coast and the next day set foot on the gray sands of Waimea.

After Cook came other mariners, whalers, and missionaries who established stations at both Waimea and Kōloa, and elsewhere on the island. The early commerce of Kaua'i centered in Kōloa, however, and this is where the sugar industry of

Hawai'i started. Yet, as intimated before, the history of Kōloa did not begin when the two strange-looking ships were sighted.

To appreciate the story of Kōloa fully, we have to go back before written history began, back before the Polynesian migrations that brought them to these islands, back to the formation of the islands themselves. Only then can we view it in the context of Kaua'i as a whole, including the island's position in the archipelago as it relates to the geological and cultural history of all the Hawaiian Islands.

Let's start at the beginning common to every volcanic island—its birth.

An Island Is Born

No one knows when the formation of the Hawaiian archipelago began because its earliest elements lie deep on the ocean floor or have been subducted under the Aleutian Trench. More is known about those islands that are still above the surface of the ocean and accessible to scientific study. From them we have learned how—if not when—the archipelago itself was first created.

The atoll now at the northwestern end of the chain came into being about 30 million years ago when a column of lava thrust up from the mantle of the earth near the middle of the huge Pacific tectonic plate, melting its way through a thin spot in the crust. Molten lava emerged hissing and boiling onto the ocean floor through this "hot spot" some three miles down. The sea mount this formed grew slowly until the volcano that was to become Kure Atoll rose from the dark sea into the bright sun. A fringing coral reef began to form around it. Then, over millions of years, the volcano which had soared thousands of feet above the sea subsided and sank beneath the surface once again. As the coral continued to grow waves made sand of it. A circle of sand, an atoll, is all that now remains.

The Pacific tectonic plate has continued to move northwest over this "hot spot" at three to four inches a year. As weak spots in the crust were melted through, magma flowed forth intermittently to create a series of islands in a northwest-to-southeast direction over millions of years. The process is still continuing. Seventeen miles southeast of the island of Hawai'i, eruptions from the ocean floor are forming Lo'ihi, a sea mount already 8,000 feet above the seabed. When it breaks the ocean surface thousands of years from now, there will be one more island in the chain.

The Hawaiian archipelago now consists of 132 islands stretching for 1,523 miles from the northwest to the southeast. The eight major Hawaiian Islands comprise the last 400 miles of the archipelago. Of these, Kaua'i and Ni'ihau are the oldest. Kaua'i is the fourth largest. By the time these two rose from the sea many of the islands to the northwest had subsided, and were eroded to little more than rocks and shoals.

Kaua'i emerged from the ocean as a great shield volcano, a term Western vulcanologists use because the dome shape resembles the round fighting shields of early Germanic tribes. Erosion on the Nāpali coast on the northwest side has revealed some of the oldest lava flows, which date from 4.2 to 5.6 million years ago. Core drilling elsewhere confirms the age of the major part of the island as about five million years. Kaua'i and its small satellite Ni'ihau emerged from the surface of the sea together but are now separated by a shallow channel 17.2 miles wide.

Kaua'i then underwent a period of volcanic quiescence for the next 1.5 million years. During this time erosion took its toll. Wind, rain, and streams sculpted the island, while waves and winter storms attacked its northern shores. Coral reefs formed in coves and bays around the island. Because the Hawaiian Islands lie on the edge of the latitudes that favor coral growth, the reefs did not grow into a continuous fringe as they do in warmer waters.

Major geologic events occurred during this dormant period, however. The summit of the great shield volcano, which once soared 10,000 feet into the air, sank and formed a crater, or caldera, nearly 13 miles across. The southern flank of the volcano collapsed, creating the Makaweli depression. A second collapse of the southeast flank created the Līhu'e basin and left the Wai'ale'ale scarp standing high against the sky. On the southwest, a huge fault broke open, giving birth to Waimea Canyon. The Waimea River and other streams flowing in further eroded the canyon to greater depths. Elsewhere, alluvial fans formed the floors of Hanalei and other valleys. The lava in the central caldera had puddled during the last phases of the eruption, limiting seepage of water through these layers and thus creating the great Alaka'i Swamp within the crater. Most of the remaining volcanic rim crumbled, leaving only the eastern ridge with its two prominent peaks, Wai'ale'ale and Kawaikini. A massive tilt lifted the southwestern shore to form the dry plains of Mānā, backed by ancient sea cliffs.

Then, about 3.6 million years ago, a second series of eruptions began on the southeastern two-thirds of the island, spreading aprons of lava over the areas of Kōloa and Līhuʻe. Cinder cones from this series dot the land today. About half a million years ago these eruptions ceased. The island grew quiet after Kaluahonu Crater, near the Hāupu Range, smoldered and died out.

The reason we had to go back to the formation of the island to tell its history and that of Kōloa now becomes apparent. These secondary lava flows were to have a profound effect upon life in Kōloa by making much of the land relatively level. The deep valleys with streams coursing their depths that characterize windward Kauaʻi did not form here, for two important reasons. The first is the marked difference in rainfall between the two sides. Trade winds from the northeast bring moisture gathered from thousands of miles of "fetch" across the ocean. As the humid winds rise over the island, most of the moisture is precipitated on the northeast shores and the windward slopes of the mountains. By the time the trade winds sweep down to the south shore, they leave behind only a third of the rain there that falls on the north shore. Even so, this would have been enough for the streams and rivers to erode deep valleys were it not for the second factor. The hard *pāhoehoe* lava of the secondary flows that spread over the region is relatively impermeable, causing the water courses to run close to the surface. Because erosion has not been so effective on the *pāhoehoe* lava, the soil in most places is rocky and relatively shallow.

After the secondary lava flows ceased, the forces of nature continued to sculpt the island. Crashing waves from winter storms tore at the northwest shore to form cliffs that plunge 2,000 to 3,000 feet into the sea—the dramatic Nāpali coastline. Although much larger when first formed, Kauaʻi is now some 30 miles in diameter. Winter waves have reduced the northwest-southeast diameter to 25 miles, but Kauaʻi is still nearly circular and 553 square miles in area. Niʻihau, formed of softer substance, fared worse from these fierce winter waves. The northwest half of the island is entirely gone, ending abruptly in cliffs.

Life came slowly to Kauaʻi. The first forms to take hold must have been the tiny spores of ferns, mosses, and lichens borne by the jet stream sweeping out of Southeast Asia. The small seeds of orchids and other plants probably arrived that way, too. Insects tossed about by storms may have come next. Sea birds, and migratory land birds blown off course by severe storms, arrived. Some bore seeds of plants such as grasses and sedges embedded in the mud on their feet, or sticky seeds of various plants and trees caught in their feathers. From time to time larger floating seeds arrived in rafts of plant material, or by themselves.

The coming of life to Kaua'i—and the other Hawaiian Islands—did not happen as rapidly as the above may suggest. If the number of known indigenous plant species is divided by the time involved, the results suggest that only one species became successfully established, on average, every 30,000 to 40,000 years. Yet they flourished on Kaua'i, turning the island green while coral reefs grew quietly around it.

Thus favored by nature and time, Kaua'i—and the area that was to be called Kōloa—awaited the human voyagers who were to come.

Chapter Three

The Polynesians Arrive

How the first Polynesians came to Hawai'i has always been cause for speculation, and perhaps even something of a mystery. Their wide dispersal throughout the Southeast Pacific had astounded early European explorers.

The first serious attempts on the part of Westerners to solve the enigma took place late in the nineteenth century, when the myths, legends, and other oral traditions of the Hawaiians were translated into English. These were found to be allegorical for the most part. They emphasized chiefly genealogies and exhibited many parallels in content with the traditions of other Polynesian groups. Western scientific minds sought more solid evidence about the Polynesian migrations and were not satisfied with these.

A second phase of study took place at the start of this century. The Hawaiian language was analyzed using the new science of comparative linguistics. Common elements were identified from such widely scattered regions as Madagascar, the Philippines, Indonesia, and Melanesia. Indonesian root words were especially prominent. Later studies revealed the Polynesian language spoken by Hawaiians was more closely related to Marquesan than to any other. This linguistic evidence gave the first suggestion of a migratory pathway.

The tools of physical anthropology were applied in two distinct stages. Early studies of physical type and morphology demonstrated a remarkable similarity among all Polynesians, indicating a common origin. One remarkable finding that emerged from these studies, termed the "founder effect," suggested that each island group had been colonized by a small number of people. This reinforced the hypothesis that only one voyaging canoe had arrived and settled each group. More recent studies, made possible by sophisticated computer analysis, statistically compared the vast body of skeletal measurements accumulated over the decades. Results showed Hawaiians to be more closely related to Marquesans than to other Polynesians. These findings corroborated earlier linguistic evidence as to a probable migratory path, but the details were still far from being understood.

Archeology became a systematic study in Hawai'i and the Pacific in about 1950 when radiocarbon dating was developed as a powerful investigative tool. Traditional methodology in archeology relies heavily upon the study of pottery to arrive at relative, but not absolute, dates based on stylistic change. Since there was no pottery in Hawai'i these dating methods, known as seriation, were attempted on fishhooks and other materials but with limited success. Archeologists also applied other methodologies to the study of unearthed artifacts, eventually learning many details to fill gaps in the migration story. Though much superior to more traditional methods, radiocarbon dating provided only ranges of time, not precise calendar dates. In the 1980s, hydration-rind dating of volcanic glass chips (produced when tools were made) added more accuracy to dating archeological sites, especially when the two technologies were used together. Even more sophisticated techniques have been applied with notable success during the last decade. Thermoluminescence and single-grain optical luminescence, for example, have moved the probable date of Polynesian arrivals in Hawai'i back from the first radiocarbon estimates of approximately A.D. 450 to as early as A.D. 100.

Although a great deal of racial mixing has occurred since contact with the outside world over the last two or three centuries, DNA profiling (genetic fingerprinting) is now being utilized in some areas of the Pacific to shed light on interisland migrations that occurred in the distant past.

These are the major fields of scientific investigation that have been pursued. As a consequence, the general outline of Polynesian migration and settlement is now apparent, although many details are as yet unknown.

The Polynesian migration epic starts with the movement of another distinct group of people in the distant past. During the last ice age, when the ocean was about 300 feet lower than it is now, Negroid hunter-gatherers from Africa and Madagascar were able to cross over nearly continuous land bridges as far as Australia and New Guinea. Over the next 10,000 years or so they settled New Guinea and the Bismarck Archipelago. These dark-skinned people, whom we now call Papuans and Melanesians, were agriculturalists and warriors, not seafarers. Subsequent short sea journeys brought them only as far as New Britain.

About 30,000 years ago, lighter-skinned people with physical features resembling those of modern Mongoloid populations moved down into Southeast Asia and the Malay Peninsula. At the same time, Caucasoid groups moved east through India, keeping south of the Himalayas, and also arrived on the Malay Peninsula. There the two groups intermixed, becoming the Austronesians, the distant but direct ancestors of the Polynesians. Here they developed skills in horticulture, fishing, and seafaring. A unique type of pottery known as Lapita, from a site in New Caledonia, has helped unravel early phases of their history. Lapita pottery shows stylistic development from Southeast Asia to Fiji, and onward to Samoa and Tonga, the Western Polynesia heartland and stage for future dispersals eastward. But Lapita pottery disappears from the archeological record farther east for unknown reasons, though clay suitable for ceramics is found on many Polynesian islands, including Hawai'i.

As their seafaring skills developed on the Malay Peninsula and surrounding area, these Austronesian ancestors of the Polynesians learned to build and paddle outrigger canoes. They added sails, which enabled them to explore the islands of Indonesia. The prevailing winds in the Malay-Indonesia region blow from the southeast, causing currents from the same direction. But due to meteorological effects now well-known, winds would shift to come from the west for up to twenty days at a time. Small exploring groups apparently chose such times to sail eastward with the prevailing wind. When the winds returned to normal out of the southeast, the explorers were able to return to their home islands by dead reckoning. If suitable islands were found to the east, they returned to settle them.

By 2,000 B.C. or soon thereafter, their Proto-Polynesian descendants had reached New Guinea, the Bismarcks, and the Solomons, encountering the Melanesians already settled there. A degree of mingling occurred over the next several centuries, resulting in some interchange of seafaring skills, because the Melanesians afterwards were able to settle islands to the east as far as Fiji. The Proto-Polynesians did not remain but moved on. It is presumed this was due to conflicts with the entrenched Melanesians as well as a greater susceptibility to malaria, to which the Melanesian peoples were more resistant. The Proto-Polynesians arrived in Tonga and Samoa by about 1200 B.C.

These islands were free of malaria and beyond the reach of the Melanesians.

It was here, in Tonga and Samoa, that this group of people truly became Polynesian over the next thousand years. Their seafaring skills were further developed in journeying from island to island. There is clear evidence they acquired the skills necessary for long-distance voyaging about the same time. To sail between Tonga and Samoa, they built twin-hulled voyaging canoes capable of carrying people and cargo on a platform affixed between the hulls. These were remarkable vessels of plank strakes surmounting huge hollowed-out logs, lashed together with sennit (braided coconut-husk fiber). Built exclusively for extended seafaring, the canoes attained lengths of 70 to 100 feet and had two masts. They were not used for coastal or short interisland trips because they were relatively unwieldy as well as cumbersome to beach and launch. The V-shaped hulls acted as keels to reduce leeway, and the vessels were steered with a large oar. Sennit was used for the rigging and the sails were made of tightly woven pandanus leaves. The sails evolved into a distinctive crab-claw shape that allowed the vessels to be sailed closer to the wind. Although the Polynesians learned to tack into the wind with these sails, they were able to make headway against it only with difficulty. Thus, most of their voyages were either on a reach (nearly at a right angle to the wind) or running before the wind.

The Polynesians also studied the stars, named some 150, and relied extensively on them for navigation. The bearings on which the stars rose and set at various latitudes were memorized, and zenith stars or constellations helped them locate the more important island groups. For example, Orion's belt was the zenith constellation for Samoa; later Sirius was used for Tahiti, and Arcturus for Hawai'i.

With these skills the Polynesians could sail far from the sight of land. On overcast nights, even a glimpse of a star or constellation was enough to orient them. During the day, they used the sun and knew its declination with the season. They could distinguish swells coming from a long distance due to trade winds from swells produced by local winds, or distorted by land nearby but over the horizon. The voyagers also understood different cloud formations and knew, from as far as 100 miles away, which ones indicated land. They were familiar with the seasonal directions of migratory birds and especially observant of land and shore birds heading home near the end of day. From drifting objects they could tell when land was near and in which direction it lay.

In contemplating this remarkable development of Polynesian navigational skills, it is imperative to view their world as it was to them: primarily aquatic. On all of the hundreds of inhabited islands, most Polynesians lived close to the ocean. Many were upon it daily in small outrigger canoes to fish or trade with other coastal villages. The ocean held little fear for them; indeed, it was a pathway. People of the Western world at that time were largely land-bound and looked upon the ocean as a barrier. This mind-set led some early European explorers and even later investigators to believe Micronesia and Polynesia had been settled by accident. Some discoveries undoubtedly were fortuitous, but most were the result of intentional exploration. One also has to consider the fact that from Southeast Asia to all the islands of Oceania, no voyage of over 300 miles was required if one excludes New Zealand, Hawai'i, and Easter Island.

As their skills improved, the Polynesian voyagers apparently repeated the pattern of easterly exploration and return over longer and longer distances. They carried coconuts for both food and drink; brought water in gourds and bamboo joints; caught rain in finely-woven mats; preserved breadfruit and taro by drying or fermentation to last a month or more; and cultivated the sweet potato, which keeps at sea for weeks. The Polynesians carried dried fish, trolled at sea with lures, and built rudimentary fireplaces on the deck platforms using rock and coral. In short, they were at home upon the ocean and had the means to stay at sea for well over a month in vessels that could carry 30 to 40 persons and as many tons of cargo.

As population pressure, perhaps combined with a sense of adventure, pushed them on, Polynesians settled the islands they found to the east of Tonga and Samoa. The Societies, Cooks, and Australs presumably were settled first, but archeological evidence for this is scant due to the tectonic submergence of these islands. There is substantial evidence that Polynesians arrived in the Marquesas, some distance northeast of the Societies, by 200 B.C.

Life was hard in the Marquesas. There were few coral reefs to fish and little level land to cultivate. The deep valleys allowed scant sunlight to reach their crops. It is probable these factors, with overpopulation, were reasons the Marquesas became a major dispersal point a century or two after settlement. They were apparently convinced no more islands lay to the east of what we now call the Tuamotus because voyaging canoes that had gone beyond either failed to return or found no land. They were aware, however, of the annual northward migration of a small land bird, the kōlea or golden plover, as the sun moved north; and its return when the sun moved south. This meant land lay somewhere to the north. Every year, golden plovers still migrate from the Marquesas and islands south to Hawai'i and then beyond to the Arctic.

The details of the first successful voyage to Hawai'i will always remain conjectural. One or more canoes apparently set out from the Marquesas about A.D. 100 heading north on the path of the plover. They brought women, domestic animals, plants, and everything that was required to settle the land certain to be there.

There is no way of knowing how many canoes embarked on this voyage. In addition to the anthropometric and DNA evidence favoring the arrival of only one canoe, there is one other factor in support of the single-canoe hypothesis. The difficulty of maintaining contact between vessels on the high seas through the vagaries of wind, dark nights, and storms is not appreciated by most. European navigators, who made their voyages of discovery in groups of ships, had written instructions, used the same charts, and could determine latitude accurately, although longitude less so. They possessed compasses and at night showed lights protected by glass from wind and rain. But most important, they had predetermined points of rendezvous to gather after being separated, which they often were. Polynesian voyagers had none of these advantages.

The journey following the golden plover would be more than 2,400 miles. At first, prevailing winds and current from the southeast would have set their canoes to the west; at the equator they would have been set farther to the west by the equatorial current. Above the equator, the northeast trades and current would have set the voyagers still farther to the west. By continuing to pursue their northerly heading, the voyagers would have been lined up by these forces of nature on a direct course to Hawai'i.

On one magical night during the latter part of the voyage, a star fixed in the heavens first came into view. The Polynesians called it *hōkūpa'a*, the "steadfast star," the North Star. By then their food may have been almost gone and their water low. They knew they had come too great a distance to return with these essentials depleted. They also would have known the Marquesas were too far upwind for their vessels to return. Perhaps they saw this strange star as an omen, and it may have given them courage to carry on.

The earliest habitation site excavated thus far in the Hawaiian Islands is located at South Point on the island of Hawai'i.

It is far from certain the colonizers landed there first. However, if we assume the voyagers were approaching from the southern quadrant, the tall peaks of Mauna Loa and Mauna Kea, almost 14,000 feet high, would have been sighted first. The theoretical distance at sea from which they can be seen is an incredible 700 nautical miles. Factors such as atmospheric diffusion, refraction, ocean haze, and others reduce this distance to less than half of that, even on an apparently clear day. The venerable *American Practical Navigator*, first written by Nathaniel Bowditch two hundred years ago and referred to by mariners simply as "Bowditch," contains tables for the distances that landmarks can be seen from sea level under various weather conditions. The next highest peak in the islands, about 10,000 feet, is Haleakalā on Maui. Given the same conditions of visibility, the voyagers would have had to sail some 200 miles farther north with the two peaks of the island of Hawai'i constantly visible on their starboard hand before Haleakalā, or any of the summits on the other islands, came into view. Either that, or miss the islands entirely, which we know they did not do. So in all probability, the voyagers sighted the island of Hawai'i first, made their way toward it and landed there.

The second phase of Polynesian migration to Hawai'i took place nearly a thousand years later. The island of Raiatea in the Societies became a second center of dispersal about A.D. 1000. Polynesians living there referred to the island as *Hava iti*, following a long tradition of naming one island in each group "Little Java." To this day the various cognates throughout Polynesia, such as Savai'i in the Samoas and Hawai'i in the Hawaiian Islands, refer somewhat mystically to their ancient ancestral home. For reasons not known, but probably not unlike those of the Marquesans before them, a canoe or small fleet of canoes sailed north from Raiatea about that time, prepared to settle any islands they found. Authorities are of the opinion that when the newcomers arrived in the Hawaiian Islands they promptly set about conquering the Marquesans already settled there. This belief holds that some may have fled, as suggested by archeological finds on Necker and Nihoa, and the rest became the working class under the new rulers.

This scenario leaves important questions unanswered. According to the "founder effect" and DNA analyses in support of it, each distant island of Oceania most likely was settled by the occupants of a single canoe. Furthermore, although the number of passengers aboard voyaging canoes was reduced to conserve food and water as long as possible, nearly half of those on board were women. There is no reason the voyage from Raiatea would have been different. The theory fails to explain how some two dozen Raiatean men, weary from a month or more at sea, were able to conquer the Marquesan settlers who had been multiplying for nearly a thousand years and by then occupied all of the major Hawaiian Islands. Instead, one might postulate that the new arrivals included one or more chiefs of higher lineage who would be accepted as rulers. Or perhaps one or more *kahuna* among them would have been perceived as possessing great *mana* or spiritual power. At least one navigator was almost certainly aboard, which would account for the Tahitian navigational terms that became part of the Hawaiian language.

Yet, there must have been another factor greater than these that propelled this small group of newcomers to positions of dominance in Hawai'i. In all likelihood, after some 900 years in isolation, those living in Hawai'i had lost immunity to outside diseases, while the Raiateans had maintained theirs by continued voyaging from island to island. Perhaps what was to happen to Hawaiians upon contact with the West happened to their Marquesan forebears. Among the casualties of the onset of epidemic diseases would have been a weakened social structure, affecting the resident Marquesans and their faith in their own institutions. That the new arrivals were unaffected by these diseases would have been perceived as evidence of their superiority in ways we cannot hope to fathom, and this also would have increased their influence. To this observer it would appear that a combination of such factors would account for the linguistic, anthropometric, and other evidence far better than the presently held theory of simple conquest.

The Hawaiian *menehune* are mythical little people legends describe as having preceded the Polynesian settlers. Long before the voyage postulated above, the Raiateans had become fearsome warriors. They conquered many of the nearby islands including Tahiti, whose vast commoner class referred to themselves as *manahune*. The Raiateans adopted this term for them as one of derision. The Marquesans, including those who long before had migrated to Hawai'i, had no such word in their language.

The earliest Hawaiian legends about *menehnue* refer to them as lower in status, not stature, and as having prodigious strength. When the first European explorers asked who had built certain *heiau*, fishponds, and irrigation ditches, all hundreds of years old and their origins by then lost, it was natural for Hawaiians to reply that workers or *menehune* built them. It seems all but certain that these were the Marquesans who had arrived earlier, referred to by this Raiatean term. Westerners are apparently responsible for the myth of tiny men who labored through the night performing stupendous feats. Western mythology is replete with small people doing such things and must have had some influence on the Hawaiian tellers of tales. Since no other objective evidence, including skeletal remains, has ever been found of small humans the myth of the *menehune* is just that—a myth—but a delightful one.

Now turning from myth to presumption, this book is about Kaua'i, and Kōloa in particular. The date Polynesians first inhabited Kaua'i is unknown. Undoubtedly there were exploratory excursions as well as fishing trips and other expeditions from the island of O'ahu, where archeological findings support permanent settlement about A.D. 300. The only evidence available at present for the earliest settlement on Kaua'i comes from radiocarbon analysis of the remains of individual fires unearthed in Hanalei Valley. They date to approximately A.D. 700. But there have been very few "digs" on Kaua'i, so it may be presumed Hawaiians were established on the island perhaps as early as A.D. 400. The pattern of settling the windward sides first where rain and stream water for crops was abundant, then moving to the southern shores as the population increased, probably would have been replicated on Kaua'i. Thus, the best estimate for settling the Kōloa area would be approximately A.D. 500.

With the resurgence of interest in Hawaiian culture and history since the 1970s, legends of back-and-forth voyages are becoming more familiar, especially those to and from Tahiti about A.D. 1200 to A.D. 1400. Unfortunately, while it is accepted they were technically possible, little concrete evidence exists to support voyages to Tahiti and back; what evidence there is would suggest they did not take place. For example, the scarcity of large shellfish in the Hawaiian Islands meant that traditional Tahitian fishhooks could not be made. Early Hawaiians adapted to the scarcity by making two-piece bone hooks that were actually superior. The basalt adze developed in Hawai'i about A.D. 700 was also better than those in the Societies. In addition, Hawaiians devised a weighted cowrie-shell lure with a hook to catch octopus in deep water, freeing them from the limitation of spearing octopus in shallow water. No traces of these or any other original Hawaiian artifact have been found in the Society Islands. Alone among the Polynesians the Hawaiians made salt in quantity by evaporating sea water, a skill developed around the middle of the millennium. They used this salt both to flavor food and to preserve fish. Elsewhere in Polynesia food was dipped in salt water for flavoring, and fish were preserved by drying in the sun—a method not nearly so effective as salting. Hawaiians also originated the walled fish-pond well before A.D. 1000, another feature missing in the Societies. Patrick Kirch, perhaps the most eminent archeologist specializing in Polynesia today, has stated that Hawaiians had developed a unique culture by A.D. 1000, yet none of the concepts that made it unique had counterparts in the Society Islands.

It is intriguing to speculate that arrival of the Raiateans about A.D. 1000 may have brought an infusion of voyaging skills to the original Marquesan settlers of Hawai'i, who by then would have lost them. Two-way trips to Tahiti then could have been possible for a century or two before the navigational skills were again forgotten. But if return trips to the Societies did take place, the supporting evidence one would expect to find is not there. The legends of back-and-forth trips do fit the needs of Hawaiian culture and religion, however, as the purpose was to retrieve a sacred image, or drum, or to bring a chief of higher lineage from Tahiti.

Surprisingly, the evidence is scant for the second Polynesian migration to Hawai'i from Raiatea. Enough is there to persuade but little more. Three petroglyphs on Maui depict sails uniquely Tahitian in design, and this rock art has been dated to approximately the thirteenth century. There is also linguistic evidence mentioned, such as Tahitian words for the lunar calendar and navigational terms. The surge of *heiau*-building in Hawai'i in the thirteenth century suggests the introduction of new rituals. There are other indications, but not many. Together they constitute enough for experts to agree this second migration did take place as described.

No voyaging canoes were present in Hawai'i when Captain Cook arrived, although large double canoes were seen. Beaglehole, Cook's biographer, notes these "double canoes were not the great structures of the Society Islands." Possessing the ability to build double canoes, skilled craftsmen would have little difficulty producing voyaging canoes. It was the lack of navigation skills that restricted Hawaiians to their own islands. Cook noted in his journal that inhabitants of the "Sandwich Islands" had no knowledge of the navigational skills necessary for long voyages, although he had observed these skills in several other island groups. Cook speculated they had been lost because the Sandwich Islands are so isolated in the Pacific Ocean.

Working from drawings of double canoes by John Webber, the artist with Captain Cook, careful descriptions, and petroglyphs, a replica of an ancient voyaging canoe was built in 1974 on the island of Hawai'i and named the *Hōkūle'a*. Mau Piailug, one of the last in the Pacific who still knew the traditional navigational skills described above, was found in Micronesia and agreed to guide the *Hōkūleʻa* on a voyage from Hawaiʻi to Tahiti. The trip from May 1 to June 4, 1976 was successful. On the return a young man from Honolulu, Nainoa Thompson, came along to learn the art. He has since passed on this knowledge to others, the Polynesian Voyaging Society has been formed, and more voyaging canoes have been built and sailed to other Pacific islands.

Hawaiians were to have most of a millennium after the second migration to develop their social organization, customs, and legends before strangers about whom they knew nothing would change their way of life forever.

Culture and Customs

"**U**nfortunately, none of the foreigners who came to Hawaii in the early period, or the missionaries who followed them soon after, had any adequate understanding or appreciation of the native culture or considered it, or any important part of it, worth preserving." This quotation, from the definitive three-volume *The Hawaiian Kingdom* by Ralph S. Kuykendall, is typical of those encountered in the works of historians who endeavor to learn about Hawaiians before contact with the outside world. All have had to face the fact that in a culture without writing there are no documentary sources such as historians are accustomed to using.

This limitation makes difficult the portrayal of life in pre-contact Kōloa . By summarizing what is known about Hawaiian culture in general prior to contact, however, valid inferences can be made about the lifestyles of Hawaiians living there before the arrival of Europeans.

Among the sources are legends and myths Hawaiians had passed on orally for centuries as chants or mele. Many of these were written down by a small group of Hawaiian students at Lahaina Luna Seminary on Maui in the early 1830s. One, David Malo, wrote a series of articles in the 1840s based upon the mele and additional information gained from older Hawaiians. These were assembled and published in his seminal work *Ka Moolelo Hawaii*, translated as Hawaiian Antiquities. A few years later, using similar sources, Samuel Kamakau amplified Malo's writings through serialized newspaper articles. Although Kamakau criticized Malo for attempting to show similarities between the ancient

Hawaiian way of life and Christianity, Kamakau failed to mention or recognize the effect of those Christian influences on himself.

The problems of interpreting legends and myths are much greater than many realize. The information they contain relies upon human memory and repeated oral transmission over centuries. There is abundant evidence that oral traditions were altered to suit the particular audience, chanter, place, and occasion. Sound patterns and body language are missing from the written records, creating another source of ambiguity. The *'ōlelo*, or text, contains word formulas whose meanings were often less than clear to a listener of the time, and to all since. Many of the symbolic associations were and still are open to subjective interpretation. Most important, the *kaona*, or layered meanings, that give the chants much of their mystic quality remain largely hidden to this day. While oral traditions are far from perfect, they do reveal something about the early Hawaiians: their love of natural beauty, respect for nature, and awe at the mystery and magnificence of natural forces; and their deep interest in gods, chiefs and heroes.

The first Hawaiian to write about the old ways from his own observations was John Papa Ii. An associate of the young Liholiho or Kamehameha II, he was born in 1800 when many of the old ways were still being followed. He recorded his memories from youth in *Fragments of Hawaiian History*. The fact that his observations were firsthand lends them credibility, and his integrity is evident throughout his writings.

The accounts of Cook and other early explorers should not be regarded lightly, as some historians have been wont to do. If their observations about Hawai'i sometimes seem superficial, it must be remembered they faced language barriers and interpreted situations and events in the context of their own culture. Despite such limitations, many of their observations show a keen seaman's eye for detail. The drawings that early Western artists made have proved especially valuable.

The letters and journals of the first missionaries were strongly slanted. Hawaiians, in their view, were not to be understood as fellow human beings but "barbaric heathens" to be taught righteous ways. One exception was Reverend William Ellis of the London Missionary Society, who visited Hawai'i in 1822 and 1823. He was fluent in Tahitian and had no difficulty communicating with Hawaiians. He was also empathetic and perceptive with regard to their customs. Unfortunately, his writings are not voluminous because of his relatively short stays. In contrast, the American missionaries lost a marvelous opportunity to record the Hawaiian way of life during a critical period of change.

Their perceived arrogance aroused the ire of one man, originally from Sweden, who was married to a Hawaiian lady of rank. He understood and respected Hawaiian ways and was himself fluent in the language. Abraham Fornander wrote his monumental work *Account of the Polynesian Race* during most of the decade of the 1870s. While many of his suppositions are challenged by modern scholarship, his work chronicling Hawaiian history from the dim past to the present performed a valuable service in countering missionary bias.

Nearly a hundred years after Fornander, modern science began to shed new light on pre-contact Hawai'i. The findings of cultural anthropologists who studied remote Polynesian islands, although not directly applicable, furnished insights and offered new perspectives. The most valuable information has come from archeology. Using modern techniques, much has been learned from middens, or accumulated habitation refuse, on and under the earth in Hawai'i.

In this chapter I will try to summarize from these varied sources what is known about pre-contact Hawaiian culture, and by inference that of Kaua'i and Kōloa. As far as we can ascertain, regional differences on any one island and between the islands themselves were not so great as to preclude the effort.

Although early Hawaiians lived near the coast, preferring that topography, most of their sustenance came from inland. As noted before, the first settlers were attracted to the wet windward sides of the islands where ample water from streams and rainfall easily provided for their crops. As long as the population remained small, there was no need for land divisions or a chiefly polity. Probably about the fourth century A.D. the first settlements were made on the leeward sides of one or more major islands where extracting a living from the land was more difficult. Here, irrigation systems had to be constructed, in due course bringing the first boundary divisions and the beginnings of the chiefly system.

In the society that evolved, the four largest islands—Kaua'i, O'ahu, Maui, and Hawai'i—were each regarded as *mokupuni*. The word *moku* means island and *puni* means surrounded, as by ocean. Smaller islands were satellites of the nearest large island and politically part of it, such as Ni'ihau to Kaua'i, and the three islands of Moloka'i, Lāna'i, and Kaho'olawe to Maui. The land of each *mokupuni* was controlled by an *ali'i nui*, or high chief, who derived his position through lineage. Starting about the fifteenth century, warfare began to alter this hereditary pattern. As a consequence, a high chief might not rule over an entire island, or his dominion might include a portion of a nearby large island. Each *mokupuni* was divided into *mokuʻaina*, or districts, which were usually defined by natural land barriers. The high chief appointed lower chiefs called *aliʻi ʻai mokuʻaina* to oversee each district. It is important to note that chiefs controlled the land and associated irrigation water rights; there was no ownership of land, in the Western sense, in the ancient Hawaiian way of life.

Within each district were land divisions called *ahupuaʻa*, ruled by a still lower order of chiefs called *aliʻi ʻai ahupuaʻa*. Each *ahupuaʻa* was roughly triangular in shape with its apex in the mountains, extending to the shore or seaward edge of the reef. Ideally, these land units were formed so that each contained adequate proportions of natural resources to make the inhabitants self-sustaining, or nearly so. Most *ahupuaʻa* consisted of three zones: the coastal plain and valleys up to about 1,000 feet, the uplands, and the rain forest. From the forest zone came trees for canoes, house posts, religious images, and other purposes. The *olonā* plant grew there, the inner bark of which provided the strongest cordage. Below the forests, in the upland zone, bamboo, *ti*, and *pili* grass for thatching houses grew almost unattended where rainfall was sufficient. In the coastal plain and valleys, *kalo*, or taro, was cultivated in irrigated pond fields near streams. Sweet potatoes, yams, and sugar cane were grown in both coastal and upland areas. Coconut palms, pandanus, and other useful species thrived nearer the shore. The shore and reefs provided fish, shellfish, and edible seaweeds. Fishing was controlled by the chiefs of the *ahupuaʻa* and their *konohiki*, or overseers, which helped prevent serious reduction of the stock nature had provided.

The name *ahupuaʻa* comes from the markers erected near the shore at the boundaries of these land divisions. An *ahu* is an altar, in this case a pile of stones, and *puaʻa* means pig. A pig's head carved from *kukui* wood was placed on top of the ahu to mark the boundary. All *ahupuaʻa* were named and their boundaries carefully defined, usually with reference to natural land features such as mountain ridges or streams. Ranging in size from 100 to 100,000 acres, there were roughly 1,000 in all the islands. In the larger *ahupuaʻa*, smaller strips called ʻili were recognized.

The *aliʻi ʻai ahupuaʻa* chose lesser chiefs to be their *konohiki*, or agents. The primary task of the *konohiki*, assisted by *luna*, or foremen, was to organize planting and harvesting, enforce water and fishing rights, and to collect tribute. The *konohiki*, after giving a portion to his own chief, passed the remainder on to the high chief of the *mokupuni*.

There were five traditional districts on Kauaʻi: Puna, Kona, Nāpali, Haleleʻa, and Koʻolau. These were changed by the Territorial

Legislature in the early 20th century when the population centers of Kōloa and Līhu'e had become established. Kōloa District was formed from a part of the old Kona District. The eastern boundary of Kōloa District runs from Mount Kāhili across Kōloa Gap, then along the Hā'upu ridge to the shore. The western boundary follows the eastern edge of Hanapēpē Valley. The town of Kōloa is approximately in the center of Kōloa District. The seven traditional *ahupua'a* in Kōloa District were not changed: from west to east they are Wahiawa, Kalāheo, Lāwa'i, Kōloa, Weliweli, Pā'ā, and Māhā'ulepū.

Archeological evidence indicates the Kōloa area was forested to the shore before the arrival of Polynesian settlers, who cleared land for agriculture by burning. Rainfall is less on the leeward side of Kaua'i, as mentioned before, and in most places the soil is shallow. For these reasons, and because the Kōloa streams flow near ground level, inhabitants built some of the most sophisticated irrigation systems in Hawai'i for their taro and other crops. With fishing and other food sources, the agricultural system supported a pre-contact population of about 4,000 in what is now Kōloa District.

Political and social organization was tied closely to the land and its use. Traditionally, the high chief attained his rank through lineage, which extended back to the gods. Thus, the people under his dominion believed he could intercede with the deities on their behalf. After contact, high chiefs were frequently referred to as *mō'ī*, or "kings," following European practice. The lower chiefs appointed by the high chiefs to control the *moku'aina* and *ahupua'a* were also usually ranked by their lineage. These appointments were not permanent. When a high chief died, his successor redistributed control of the land to his own followers.

High chiefs issued *kapu*, quasi-religious prescriptions and proscriptions believed by the people to be derived through his authority as spokesman for the gods. These *kapu* constituted the main framework by which the people were governed. The penalty for breaking a *kapu* was often death. The high chief also pronounced *kānāwai*, or decrees, on more secular matters on his own authority. The distinction was often blurred between *kānāwai* and *kapu*, however, because the high chief was believed to speak for the gods even when he did not invoke them. The Polynesian word *kapu* is now used throughout the world, usually in the form "taboo."

Each high chief assigned a chief of lesser rank to act as his prime minister or *kālaimoku*, literally "manage island." He also selected a chief to be his principal advisor, or *kāhuna nui*, and one to be the high priest or *kāhuna po'o*. Men not necessarily of chiefly lineage but skilled in various arts and professions such as healing, canoe-making, forecasting the weather, or interpreting omens were chosen to fill these functionary positions and were also known as *kāhuna*. A *kāhuna lapaʻau*, for example, was one who used prayer, rituals, and herbs in healing. A *kāhuna kālai waʻa* was a skilled canoe maker, and a *kāhuna kilokilo* observed the skies for omens.

Below the tiers of chiefs and *kāhuna* were the common people, or *makaʻāinana* (watchers of the land). They were the farmers and fishermen and forbidden to trace their genealogy. At the bottom were the *poʻe kauā*, or outcasts. They lived apart, on land that was *kapu* to others and usually the least productive. A main function of their group was to provide members for human sacrifices. A messenger from the high chief or priest would come to the edge of their land to demand one of them for this purpose. They would decide who was to be sacrificed and the victim was led off to his fate.

Every element of ancient Hawaiian life was governed by religion. All significant undertakings began and ended with appropriate rituals. Hawaiians believed all of creation was pervaded by gods who were to be placated by incantations, offerings, and rituals. The interconnectedness is reflected in one of their creation chants, the *Kumulipo* (source of life), which linked a chiefly family to the gods and deified the stars, plants, animals, and some inanimate natural objects such as rocks.

The Polynesian settlers brought with them their four primary gods. Kāne was the provider of life substances in nature and took many forms. As one of them, he was the maker of heaven, earth, and all things that filled them. As another, Kāne opened springs of fresh water in dry areas by plunging his staff into the ground. Kū was the god of war and also had many forms. His *heiau* were the most elaborate and human sacrifices were performed at them. Lono was the god of peace and fertility of plants and people. He often took the form of a pig and in this aspect was known as Kamapuaʻa. He also assumed the guise of a fish, the *humuhumu-nukunuku-ā-puaʻa*, whose snout resembles that of a pig. Lono was the patron of sports and of the annual *Makahiki*, a four-month period of festivities and sports when tribute was paid to the chiefs. The priests and people prayed for rain and abundant crops in *heiau* built for Lono. The fourth god in order of importance was Kanaloa, who ruled the oceans and ocean winds.

Countless demigods and demigoddesses also populated the Hawaiian universe. Among them was Pele, the goddess of fire, who is perhaps the best known today. Many of these were once chiefs and chiefesses who had been deified by their descendants after death. Family gods occupied the lowest level in the Hawaiian pantheon. Each extended family worshiped its own family gods who were their ancestors who had been similarly deified. Thus elements of ancestor worship were woven into the animistic patterns of Hawaiian religion.

Heiau were temples or places of worship presided over by *kāhuna pule*, who conducted the rituals. The largest *heiau* had walls of stacked lava rocks and one or more platforms within covered by smooth pebbles. On these platforms were located the *'anu'u* or oracle tower; *hale mana* or spirit houses (*mana* is the spiritual power possessed by gods and chiefs); an altar, carved images, a drum house, and houses in which the *kāhuna pule* lived. The large *heiau* were of several types. Two of the most important were *heiau luakini*, where human sacrifices were performed; and *heiau pu'uhonua*, or places of refuge. If a person who had broken a *kapu* were successful in reaching one of the latter, after undergoing appropriate rites of purification he or she could return home unharmed. Other forms of *heiau* included small shrines built near agricultural and fishing sites. Worship of appropriate deities took place there and of family gods in the men's sleeping houses, without the mediation of *kāhuna pule*.

As for their daily life, Hawaiians lived simply and in harmony with their surroundings. Their dwellings were thatched structures designed primarily for protection against inclement weather. Most activities, including cooking and eating, took place outdoors when the weather permitted. The floors of their houses were raised platforms of medium-sized lava rocks on which small pebbles were layered. Then *pili* grass was strewn about and covered with *lauhala* mats, plaited from the *lau*, or leaves, of the *hala* tree. The house framework consisted of posts set in holes dug around the periphery. Rafters and tie beams were bound to the posts with sennit cordage. The roof and walls were thatched with either *ti* leaves or *pili* grass, which had to be renewed every two to five years depending upon its thickness and the weather. Although there was only one low door and rarely a window, those inside could easily part the thatch for light or air. Usually members of an extended family, or *'ohana*, occupied the house. A large or important family lived in a *kauhale*, or group of houses, consisting of separate structures for sleeping, cooking, eating, and other activities.

The residences of chiefs were elaborate compounds. There was a sleeping house for the chief; a men's eating house containing an altar to the family gods; a women's eating house; a menstrual house for women; one or more storehouses; a canoe shelter; and a roof over the *imu*, or oven dug into the ground. The sleeping houses had a fireplace in the center for warmth on cold nights. Charcoal from the *imu* was customarily used instead of wood to reduce smoke. Fire was made by rubbing a stick in a grooved piece of soft *hau* wood. The dust this made soon ignited and the flame was nurtured with coconut husk fiber.

In the Kōloa area, as elsewhere, Hawaiians did not cluster in villages but lived in scattered hamlets. They built their houses, many with rock foundations as described above, along Waikomo Stream, near the taro fields, or along the shore. Today, almost anywhere from the town of Kōloa to the ocean, rock ruins can still be seen on land not cleared for sugar cane or other development. Some rock walls were house sites, others were pigpens, boundary markers, or part of the extensive irrigation system fed by Waikomo Stream. Some *'auwai* or watercourses are relatively intact, as are many of the low rock walls that defined their *lo'i*, or taro patches.

Lamps provided light inside the houses at night. Whether halves of coconut shells or carved of stone, they were filled with oil pressed from *kukui* nuts and had wicks of *tapa* cloth. A kind of candle was also made from *kukui* nuts. Ten or twelve husked nuts were skewered on a sliver of palm frond, and the top nut was lit. Each nut burned for several minutes and then ignited the one beneath it. Time at night was measured by the number of nuts burned. Torches for outside use were made of several such *kukui*-nut candles bound together with cordage and then wrapped in dried *lauhala*.

Clothing was not a major concern in the mild climate of Hawai'i. Until the age of eight or so, children did not ordinarily wear anything. From that age on a *malo*, or loincloth, for males and a *pā'ū*, or skirt, for females were customary. These were made of bark-cloth or *kapa*, "the beaten thing," more commonly known as *tapa* as derived from Tahitian. The same material served for bedclothes and numerous other purposes, utilitarian as well as ceremonial.

Women, often assisted by their daughters, made all of the *tapa* for domestic use, including clothing. The source of most bark was the paper mulberry tree, or *wauke*, grown in moist upland areas or cultivated around the houses and taro fields. Saplings about an inch in diameter and six to ten feet tall were cut off close to the ground. Using her thumbnail or a sharp rock, the *tapa* maker slit the bark lengthwise in order to peel it off, then scraped away and discarded the gray outer layer. Using a rounded mallet she pounded the white inner bark on a flat rock or wooden anvil until the fibers began to separate. Following an intricate process involving soaking in salt and fresh water between beatings, she could overlap and pound together several strips of the inner bark to form a large sheet. The finished sheet was allowed to dry in the sun and then decorated.

For ordinary clothing, the creamy white *tapa* was commonly used undecorated. *Tapa* for bedclothing or other purposes might be decorated in various ways, depending on the whim and skill of the maker. She might choose a mixture of *kukui*-nut oil and soot for a black pigment, or *kukui* tree bark crushed in oil or seeped in water for a rich brown. A skilled artisan knew how to extract a rainbow of colors from plants and other sources, and produce an array of patterns and designs. These she applied with a variety of tools including stamps, liners, and brushes made from pandanus keys. Sometimes *tapa* was scented with leaves, ferns, or even berries. After use, soiled tapa could be washed by weighing it with stones in a stream of clear water for a day or so. Oil-based dyes were not affected, nor was the *tapa* if handled carefully, but water-based dyes would fade, requiring re-dyeing.

A number of early visitors, including David Samwell, surgeon's mate under Cook, and Charles Clerke, Cook's second in command, wrote clear accounts of *tapa*-making describing these ancient methods.

Most of the common people were farmers; relatively few were fishermen. The first settlers, it is believed, brought 28 food and other useful plants with them. Otherwise, there was little in the islands except roots and a few greens to sustain the new arrivals. Scholars are of the opinion that, together, both immigrant groups had some 32 plants available to them which they would have brought. Apparently some did not survive the voyage or failed to thrive once they were planted. Not all were for food; some were fiber plants for clothing and cordage, and others for medicine, utensils, and other purposes.

During the millions of years before the Polynesian settlers arrived, the endemic plants of Hawai'i had evolved to achieve an environmental balance. No plant interfered significantly with the growth of another, and there were no land animals or other predators to destroy them. Thus, many of the endemic species had lost the defenses they may have had in their lands of origin, allowing more aggressive introduced species to take over except in remote mountain regions. Pigs, brought by the Polynesians, rooted and ruined many areas of endemic vegetation. Their introduced chickens scratched and ravaged more. Rats, believed to have stowed away on the voyaging canoes, raided the nests of endemic birds. In time the combined effects were catastrophic. It is estimated Polynesian settlers destroyed more than half of the endemic plant species. Looking back today, one wonders if perhaps a few thoughtful Hawaiians might have pondered what would happen to them when the inevitable contact was made with the outside world. This wholesale destruction of endemic plants, which had lived and evolved in isolation, was a harbinger and symbol of their own fate in the future.

In the Society and Marquesas Islands the staple food was breadfruit, propagated from shoots that had to be watered frequently and carefully nurtured. Probably only a few survived the long journey to Hawai'i. Since breadfruit requires at least seven years to mature, it may have been many years before enough trees were productive for breadfruit to be an important part of the Hawaiian diet. Hawaiians adapted to the lack of breadfruit by shifting to taro as their main food. One often hears that breadfruit is scarce in Hawai'i because it does not grow well at this latitude, but the largest collection of breadfruit cultivars in the world is at Kahanu, near Hāna on Maui. Most breadfruit trees are productive only about four months of the year. Where it is the staple, Polynesians have developed techniques to ferment it in pits as a paste that will keep for months, called *masi* in the Samoa-Tonga group, *mahi* in Tahiti, and *ma* in the Marquesas. Interestingly, only Hawaiians pound taro into a paste similar to breadfruit paste, allow it to ferment the same way, and eat it the same way.

The best taro is grown in flooded *lo'i*, or pond fields. Hawaiian farmers developed a complex system of interconnected fields and depended upon *'auwai*, or watercourses, of fitted stones to bring water from streams and springs. The farmers created the taro fields by first leveling the land into terraces separated by walls of packed earth, then trod the mud on the bottom of the ponds to pack it and minimize water seepage. Sluice gates positioned at strategic intervals allowed the proper amount of water to enter the ponds and then flow onward to lower ones.

Taro was planted by slicing off a portion called a *huli* from the top of the root or corm, leaving the leaf stems intact. Leaves grow rapidly in the sun above the water, as do roots from the *huli* in the rich soil. Taro matures in six months to a year after planting and can be left in the ground a few months longer before it deteriorates, providing, in a sense, its own storehouse.

Taro farmers often used the walls of their *lo'i* to plant sugar cane, bamboo and *ti*. The latter was prized for its leaves, which had many uses; the roots could be eaten when other food was scarce. Sugar cane was peeled and chewed, a delicacy enjoyed by everyone. Many taro ponds were stocked with small fish and fed food scraps. Hawaiian farmers also grew dry-land taro, more accurately called upland taro, in cleared areas near the lower forests where rainfall was adequate. They recognized and experimented with mutants of both kinds of taro under various conditions to see if their characteristics were desirable. Hawaiian farmers were growing some 300 varieties of taro at the time of contact, and were the most skilled taro cultivators in the world.

Other than feet and hands, the only agricultural implement was the *'ō'ō*, a hardwood stake about three feet long. It usually had a point at one end and sometimes a blade at the other.

The sweet potato and yam (two different botanical families), which required little tending and grew above the irrigated areas, were two other principal crops. Bananas were also cultivated in gardens or flourished along streams with little care. Like other Polynesians, Hawaiians had neither beasts of burden nor the wheel, so they carried produce home from the upland gardens by means of carrying poles on their shoulders with nets suspended at the ends.

Kava, or *'awa*, was an important drink on social and cere-monial occasions. It was made from the *Piper methysticum*, a shrub that grew with little tending when planted in areas of abundant moisture and partial sun. Portions of the roots were pounded or chewed, water added, and the fibrous residue removed by straining. *'Awa* numbs the mouth and has a slight tranquilizing effect when consumed in quantity.

Men did most of the farming; women assisted only in plant-ing sweet potatoes and yams. Men also were responsible for most of the food preparation and serving. Although fish was often eaten raw, and small amounts of other foods were broiled on hot coals or boiled in large bowls using heated stones, most food was cooked in an *imu* or underground oven. Because it was laborious, an *imu* was usually prepared every two or three days toward dusk when it was cool. First, a large hole two to three feet deep was dug in the ground and lined with rocks. A fire was built on the rocks and allowed to die down. The heated rocks were spread out with a stick, then a thick layer of *ti* or banana leaves was laid on top. Meats (pig, chicken, and dog), fish, and vegetables (taro, yams, sweet potatoes, breadfruit, and arrowroot tubers) were separately wrapped in bundles of *ti* leaves and placed in the *imu*. More leaves were spread on top, and finally a heavy *lauhala* mat. After steaming for several hours the food was uncovered and served on wooden plat-ters or bowls in family style and eaten with the fingers.

Throughout Polynesia taro is cooked and eaten in chunks. As mentioned before, only in Hawai'i was it pounded into a paste, called *poi*, for consumption. After being baked in an *imu*, the taro corms were scraped and pounded with a shaped stone on a slab of wood carved for that purpose. Traditionally, men performed this task except on Kaua'i. The usual taro pounder, conical and rela-tively heavy, was carved for use with one hand which requires the strength of a man. On Kaua'i, many pounders had handles shaped like either a ring or a stirrup, permitting the use of two hands. For this reason, it is believed that on Kaua'i women did much of the pounding. Some of the pounded taro paste was left in a semi-dry state that would keep for a few weeks. The portion to be consumed was watered and pounded further, then allowed to stand in bowls for a few days to ferment to the point Hawaiians considered *poi* to be the tastiest.

Hawaiians who specialized in fishing were highly skilled. They were experts in the use of nets of various types as well as many different kinds of traps, spears, hooks, lures, and poisons. Men fished near the shore or far out to sea in outrigger canoes. Women gathered shrimp from the streams, collected mollusks and edible seaweeds on the reefs, and caught small fish with traps in shallow streams and along the shore. Farmers and fishermen traded with one another any surplus produced.

One of the more sophisticated methods of obtaining fish was the building and maintenance of *loko*, or walled fishponds, which were unique to Hawai'i. Most were constructed of rocks on a shallow reef with one or more *mākāhā*, or sluice gates. These were double wooden gates that faced the ocean. The outermost was solid and could be opened to allow seawater to come in with the rising tide and then closed to retain the water. The innermost was a grate made of straight wooden poles set vertically about half an inch apart. Smaller fish would enter with the incoming tide to graze on algae on the bottom of the fishpond. The depth was kept shallow to allow enough sunlight for the ample growth of algae. As the fish grew larger, the gates kept them in and predators out. Hawaiians did not rely entirely upon the small fish that entered on the tides. To stock their ponds, fish they knew would thrive in the ponds were caught elsewhere by net to supplement the tidal stock. Catching the larger fish in the ponds was simpler than it might seem. At each outgoing tide the fish would gather at the grate trying to get out and could be taken by hand.

The finest example in Hawai'i of a *loko kuapā*, or walled fishpond, is the huge 'Alekoko Fishpond near Līhu'e. This is also called the Menehune Fishpond because of the myth that *menehune* built it in one night. It is truly a remarkable feat of engineering. It was constructed over a thousand years ago by cutting off a loop of the Hulē'ia River with a dike 900 yards long that is faced with stone where the current otherwise would erode it.

In the Kōloa area there is another famous pond, the Nōmilu Fishpond near Lāwa'i. It is a sunken volcanic cone over 20 acres in size fed by freshwater springs as well as saltwater seeping under the sand. This seepage made the water brackish, which hindered breeding. Hawaiian fishermen solved this problem by bringing in various species of fingerlings netted elsewhere. The small fish thrived and were harvested when grown to full size.

Outrigger canoes not only served for fishing and travel between islands but also as the main mode of transportation along the coast when burdens were considered too heavy to carry on foot. Canoes were made from a single log of koa, a hardwood similar to mahogany, with built-up sides and an outrigger attached to one side for stability. A typical canoe could carry one to six persons. Although they could be paddled or sailed far out to sea, Hawaiians preferred to remain within sight of land. Considerable interisland trade and travel took place but mostly between islands near enough to be seen. As a consequence, journeys to Kaua'i were relatively few due to the distance from O'ahu and the hazardous channel between the two islands. This, and other cultural and historical differences, led Edward Joesting to title his magnificent history *Kaua'i: The Separate Kingdom.*

As alluded to briefly before, Hawaiians were the only Polynesians to manufacture and use salt in quantity. It was produced by allowing seawater to evaporate from shallow ponds located on flat areas near shore. The most famous salt ponds in Hawai'i are near Kōloa at Hanapēpē, the only place in the islands where salt is still made this ancient way. Every summer, the descendants of those who have inherited rights to these plots, the *Hui Hana Pa'akai o Hanapēpē*, can be seen working them. During Cook's visit, Lieutenant James King described saltmaking at Hanapēpē as it is done today, noting that salt was obtained there to preserve many casks of pork for shipboard use. Cook also mentioned salt from Hanapēpē in his journal, describing it as "brown and dirty." This color is deliberate, as the salt was mixed with ocherous red earth called *'alaea.* Hawaiians still regard this traditional mixture as much tastier than ordinary table salt.

In old Kōloa all was not work such as farming, fishing, and salt- or *tapa*-making. The lives of the people were relaxed and full of fun and good humor. The splendor and pageantry of ceremony was enjoyed by everyone. Nearly every day, and particularly during the four months of *Makahiki* each year, the able-bodied enjoyed sports and games. Prominent among these activities was surfing, the sport of chiefs, and at night the chiefs played *kōnane*, a game like checkers, by lamplight. Hawaiians were fond of music and hula evolved in these islands, a dance form unique to Hawai'i that was elevated into an art form with religious connotations. Their art was also expressed in carving of wood and stone, plaiting mats and twining baskets, *tapa*-making, tattooing, and decorating the simplest items of everyday use.

Without doubt, their most spectacular art in Hawai'i was feather work. Items such as *kāhili* (feather standards), lei, and brightly colored capes, cloaks, and helmets for their chiefs evidenced remarkable talent. The brightest red, yellow and other feathers were plucked from birds captured by professional hunters who smeared sticky gum on the branches where the birds fed. Skilled artisans tied the feathers to networks of cordage to create the capes, cloaks, and helmets. Birds that survived the ordeal were released to grow more feathers. Feather work is widely believed to account for the relatively low number of native forest birds in Hawai'i today. In fact, their scarcity is due to the introduced animals that destroyed their habitat or ate their eggs, and to diseases introduced by foreign birds to which the indigenous species lacked resistance.

This, in brief, reflects something of what is known of Hawaiian culture at the time Captain Cook discovered Hawai'i for the Western world. The same customs and way of life almost certainly prevailed on Kaua'i and on its southern shore in the Kōloa area. The old ways would never be the same after this first contact with the outside world.

Chapter five

Contact, Conquest

In the early dawn of January 18, 1778, Midshipman James Ward was the lookout high up in the rigging of *H.M.S. Resolution*. Suddenly he shouted "Land!" His captain, James Cook, saw through his long glass that it had "the appearance of being high land." Then another sighting was made farther to the east. Cook was aware no land was known to be there, and that he might be on the verge of his greatest discovery.

This was Cook's third voyage of exploration into the Pacific. He had been directed by the Lords of the Admiralty to find the Pacific entry to the Northwest Passage, believed to link the Atlantic and Pacific oceans across the top of the North American continent. He well knew that if such a route did exist it would be icebound and unusable, but orders were orders. The result would be that he searched for and did not find something that did not exist, a navigable Northwest Passage, but he did not search for and found something that did: the Hawaiian Islands.

Cook was in command of an exploring expedition sailing in two ships, the *Resolution* and *Discovery*. He was in charge of the former and Captain Charles Clerke of the latter. Departing England on July 12, 1776, they had passed a fleet of 65 ships in Plymouth Sound bearing a division of Hessian soldiers being sent to suppress the American revolution.

Cook knew Tahiti well from his first two voyages. Thus, he sailed around the tip of Africa to Tahiti, there to gather stores, prepare for the next leg of the trip, and await the most propitious time to venture north. He left Tahiti on November 2, 1777, touched at Raiatea and Bora Bora, then set a course due north.

His plan was to continue north until encountering the westerlies which had been used by the Spanish for more than 200 years, then close the coast of North America. He had no way of knowing that his northerly course from Tahiti was the same one the second group of Polynesian voyagers had taken hundreds of years previously, and that he would encounter the same islands they had. Seven weeks out on the day before Christmas he discovered and named Christmas Island, an atoll where his crew obtained turtles but not the water needed. Cook continued northbound until his lookout shouted "Land!"

Spanish galleons had traversed the Pacific from Panama to Manila since 1566 and had passed by Hawai'i, both north and south, never suspecting the Islands were there. Some believe the Spanish had in fact discovered the archipelago, citing the presence on their charts of islands off the west coast of America and the inaccuracy of determining longitude at that time. It was not until Cook himself proved the accuracy of the Harrison chronometer on his second voyage that the calculation of longitude became precise. There is no reliable evidence the Spanish had discovered the Islands. If they had known of their existence, it is unlikely they would have passed up such an ideal place for rest and revictualing, especially with water and fresh foods, midway on their voyages.

Cook's description of the discovery of Hawai'i and landing at Waimea on Kaua'i seems almost perfunctory, given the magnitude of the event and all that was to follow:

> In the morning of the 18th, an island made its appearance, bearing northeast by east [O'ahu]; and soon after we saw more land bearing north and entirely detached from the former [Kaua'i]. Both had the appearance of being high land. At noon the first bore northeast by east, half east, by estimation about eight or nine leagues distant . . .
>
> We had now light airs and calms, by turns; so that at sunset were not less than nine or ten leagues from the nearest land [Kaua'i].
>
> On the 19th, at sunrise, the island first seen [O'ahu] bore east several leagues distant. This being directly to windward, which prevented our getting near it, I stood for the other [Kaua'i], which we could reach; and not long after discovered a third island [Ni'ihau] in the direction of west-northwest, as far distant as land could be seen. We had now a fine breeze at east by north; and I steered for the

east end of the second island, the nearest part being two leagues distant.

Cook's journals are preserved in the British Museum. Although J.C. Beaglehole, his biographer, did an admirable job of editing them for publication, the originals and the log of the *Resolution* make fascinating reading. Cook set a course for the closest "high land" on Kauaʻi, the head of the Hāʻupu Range. As his entry above indicates, the ships were unable to tack well into the prevailing trade wind from the northeast. When Makahūʻena Point came into view, he altered course more to the west. William Ellis, surgeon's mate on the *Discovery*, sketched this part of the coast as the ships approached. The land features are easily recognizable, and the distance from shore when the sketch was made can be estimated as about five miles. Cook then coasted west along the south shore.

> At this time [afternoon of the 19th], we were in some doubt whether or no the land before us was inhabited; this doubt was soon cleared up by seeing some Canoes coming off from the shore towards the Ships. I immediately brought to, to give them time to come up. There were three and four men in each and we were agreeably surprised to find them of the same Nation as the people of Otahiete [Tahiti] and of the other islands we had lately visited. It required very little address to get them to come along side . . .
>
> These people were of a brown color, and though of the common size were stoutly made . . They seemed very mild and had no arms of any kind . . .

This is a fascinating point. The men who paddled out to his ships were from the Kōloa shore; the first Hawaiians to encounter Westerners were from the locality that is the topic of this book. As Cook continued west in search of suitable anchorage he described the south shore of Kauaʻi from a distance of "half a league" (approximately two miles). His observations of Kōloa were the first by a Westerner. According to the log of the *Resolution* he was off Ka-lae-kīʻki Point near the western boundary of Kōloa District when darkness overtook them.

> Night now put a stop to any further researches and we spent it standing off and on. The next morning [January 20, 1778] we stood in for the land, and we were met with several Canoes filled with people, some of them took courage and ventured on board. In the course of my several voyages, I never before met with

the natives of any place so much astonished as these people were upon entering a ship. Their eyes were continually flying from object to object . . .

They were in some respects naturally well bred, or at least fearful of giving offense . . . [but] they endeavored to steal everything they came near . . . We soon convinced them of their mistake . . .

Cook noted in his journal that the people knew of iron, and referred to it as *hamaite toe*. The Hawaiian language, as spoken on Kaua'i, was close to Tahitian. Cook, and many in his crew, were familiar with Tahitian, so it is understandable he would have recorded the words in Tahitian. In Hawaiian this becomes he *maika'i ko'i*, which means "good for adze(s)." The term differs from that used in the native accounts below, but both pertain to practical uses and two or more Hawaiian terms, each related to a usage, are certainly conceivable. Moreover, the former was recorded while the latter relies on memory over decades before it was written.

We bore away to leeward . . . at the distance of about a mile and a half from shore . . .we passed divers villages . . . we could also discern several plantations of sugar cane and plantains . . . At nine o'clock, being pretty near the shore, I sent three armed boats under the command of Lieutenant Williamson to look for a landing place and for fresh water. I ordered him that if he should find it necessary to land in search of the latter, not to suffer more than one man to go with him out of the boats . . .

The order not to permit the crews of the boats to go on shore was issued that I might do everything in my power to prevent the importation of a fatal disease into this island, which I knew some of our men labored under, and which, unfortunately, had been already communicated by us to other islands in these seas. With the same view, I ordered all female visitors to be excluded from the ships . . . . I wished to prevent all connection which might, too probably, convey an irreparable injury to themselves, and through their means to the whole nation . . .

About noon Mr. Williamson came back and reported that he had seen a large pond behind a beach near one of the villages, which the natives told him contained fresh water; and that there was an anchoring ground before it . . .

Cook then was in Waimea Bay. Here he would water at a lagoon in the Waimea River near shore and visit the village of the same name. He soon learned this, but was yet to find out that during the winter onshore (*kona*) winds and storms occur, making this a dangerous lee shore.

> Between three and four o'clock I went ashore with three armed boats, and twelve marines, to examine the water and to try the disposition of the inhabitants, several hundred of whom were assembled on a sandy beach before the village. The very instant I leaped on shore, the collected body of the natives fell flat upon their faces . . .

As they lay prostrate the Hawaiians repeatedly murmured "Erona." Only later did Cook realize that he was being greeted as Lono, one of their four primary gods who had gone away and promised to return.

> As soon as we landed a trade was set on foot for hogs and potatoes, which the people of the island gave us in exchange for nails and pieces of iron, formed into something like chisels. We met with no obstruction in watering; on the contrary, the natives assisted our men in rolling the casks to and from the pool and readily performed whatever we required. Everything thus going on to my satisfaction and considering my presence on the spot as unnecessary, I left the command to Mr. Williamson, who had landed with me, and made an excursion into the country, up the valley, accompanied by Mr. Anderson [William Anderson, surgeon] and Mr. Webber [John Webber, artist]; the former of whom was as well qualified to describe with the pen as the latter was to represent with his pencil . . .

Cook's party walked about half a mile inland, on a path that is now Ala Wai Road, to approximately where the Waimea Higashi Hongwanji Temple is now. The Hawaiians they passed along the way flung themselves prostrate upon the ground and muttered "Erona" as had those at the beach.

Webber sketched this inland part of Waimea village and a nearby *heiau*, both of which have become famous for the detail they reveal. He undoubtedly added the background mountains later, because they bear no resemblance to the actual topography. Cook's description of the *heiau*, which he referred to by the Tahitian term *marae*, probably relying on Anderson's notes, is surprisingly accurate. He described the walled enclosure, the oracle tower, carved images, sacred structures, the drum house, and graves of chiefs. He also noted the agriculture in the area was well-ordered, with tidy fields of taro and other crops.

The Hawaiian version of the coming of Cook was gathered from the accounts of those who had been there at the time by seminary students at Lahaina Luna School on Maui in the early 1830s. Reverend Sheldon Dibble compiled and later published them in abbreviated form in his *History of the Sandwich Islands*. In 1867, Samuel Kamakau also described the event using these sources, in addition to versions passed down orally by the people of Kaua'i and told to him and Malo at that later date.

> The inhabitants of Waimea awoke, saw the ships *Resolution* and *Discovery*, and many asked what those things were. Others replied that they were trees moving about on the sea. Some were terrified and shrieked. All were astonished as the trees moved on the sea, a floating forest. A kahuna declared that the larger ship was the *heiau* of Lono with an oracle tower and altar.
>
> The chief sent some men to see what the wonderful things were. When they drew near and saw how much iron there was along the side of the ship, they commented excitedly to each other about how much dagger material there was. They called iron *pāhoa* because that was what they used for the blades of their *pāhoa* or best fighting daggers. When the canoes returned from the ships, the excitement became intense and the shouting grew louder. Those who had gone out to the ships said the men had white foreheads, sharp noses, wrinkled skin [their clothes] and three-cornered heads [their hats]. The men aboard the ships speak in a confused tongue [a language other than their own]. . . and [those who smoked pipes] breathed fire from their mouths . . . they have doors in their bodies into which they thrust their hands and draw out knives, bells, and pieces of iron . . .

As mentioned, Cook observed that Hawaiians were familiar with iron. When questioned further, they said driftwood and other debris containing nails and bolts occasionally washed up on the shores of Kaua'i. This iron was highly valued for adzes, knives, and fishhooks. Cook saw two pieces of iron in the hands of Hawaiians, who said it had come from the east upon the ocean. After Cook's death, Lieutenant James King returned to Waimea where a Hawaiian brought aboard an iron bolt. The man requested that it be made into a *pāhoa*, saying he had extracted it from a piece of driftwood.

Iron was so important to Hawaiians it is worth a brief digression to discuss how it came to the Islands before contact. Historians differ but most conclude that iron came from Japan. This belief may have arisen because of the dark blue current that sweeps up the eastern coast of Japan and then flows east toward Hawai'i. The Kuroshio or "Black Current" had been known to Europeans as early as 1650 when it appeared on a chart drawn by Bernhardus Varenius. More to the point, James King described the current in *A Voyage to the Pacific Ocean* published in 1784 after he returned, which received wide publicity in England. The Hawaiian accounts that the driftwood containing iron came from a generally eastern direction were overlooked.

More is known today about oceanography, and ocean currents have been charted with satellite-tracked drifters. All but the largest floating objects are affected more by wind than by currents. In the case of Hawai'i, the distinction is unimportant because trade winds from the northeast cause a constant current from the same direction. An almost stationary area of high pressure, called an anticyclone because the "gyres" in the northern hemisphere rotate clockwise, lies between the 30th and 40th parallels northeast of Hawai'i. This is the source of the trade winds. As they approach the equator, the trades veer steadily west because of the earth's rotation and produce the North Equatorial Current. It is this current that swings north near the Philippines as the Kuroshio Current. Off the east coast of Honshu, the Kuroshio Current turns eastward as the major part of the North Pacific Current. What James King did not know was that most of this current's force is lost about a thousand miles west of the Hawaiian Islands in a great eddy that flows south to join the North Equatorial Current and return to the Philippines.

South of the equator an almost mirror image of this phenomenon takes place. Spanish galleons leaving Panama for the Philippines caught the steady trades coming from the southeast below the southern "horse latitudes." These "horse latitudes," about 30 degrees both north and south of the equator, acquired this odd name because they characteristically have variable winds: rainfall is so scant that horses often were thrown overboard to conserve water. On their return trips, the galleons had to get above the northeast trades to the northern "horse latitudes." This is why the Spanish missed Hawai'i in both directions. The weather is generally good in the "horse latitudes," so when storms do occur they are unexpected. The archives in Seville list the names of the many galleons lost on these Pacific voyages over the two centuries preceding Cook's arrival. When one foundered northeast of the Islands, the floating wreckage would have been carried by the trade winds and current the few hundred miles downwind directly to Hawai'i.

Cook saw only three islands but was told of the others. He named the group in honor of his patron John Montagu, Earl of Sandwich, the First Lord of the Admiralty. The Earl's title did not survive as the name of the Islands; today he is remembered for the sandwich he invented in order not to have to leave the gambling table to partake of a formal meal.

In his journal, Cook referred to Kaua'i as "Atooi" and William Bligh of *Bounty* fame, then a lieutenant under Cook, assisted him in charting the south coast of the island and did the same. Others who kept written records used this spelling or "Atoui." While this may seem strange to us, if we bear in mind that the people of Kaua'i had retained the Tahitian "t" instead of the "k," and we substitute a "k" for the "t," the sound comes closer to the familiar pronunciation "a-koh-ee." The "i" should be pronounced as it is in English, not Hawaiian, which gives us "a-koh-eye." The "a" occurred because Hawaiians listed their islands from windward to leeward and the recitation would end with Kaua'i: "a" means "and," so they were saying "and Kaua'i." If the "a" is subtracted we are left with "koh-eye," close to our present pronunciation.

Cook's journal also tells how he learned Waimea Bay could at times be treacherous, experiencing what would later become known as a *kona* or onshore storm. It came up suddenly, with strong winds, rain, high seas, and a formidable surf on the beach. Cook immediately ordered the *Discovery* to anchor farther out to avoid the danger of running aground on the lee shore of Waimea. He used an additional (bower) anchor on the *Resolution* and spent a day and a night struggling to hold anchorage. As suddenly as it had started, the *kona* storm abated and the trade winds from the northeast resumed. Cook seized this opportunity to weigh anchors and move farther out, but shifting winds and currents made it difficult to clear the Bay. When he finally did, it was nightfall. All during the night the *Resolution* was swept by the current nearly to the west end of Kaua'i. Cook struggled for four days to return to the vicinity of Waimea in order to contact the *Discovery*, because he wanted both ships to take on more water there. He was finally able to signal Clerke from a distance.

Neither ship could regain Waimea Bay against the trade winds, so Clerke joined Cook off Ni'ihau. They searched for a suitable landing there but failed to find one. Although the surf was running high, a party of one officer and 20 men went ashore. They found little water but did obtain a supply of yams and salt. Unable to make their way out to the ship again, the landing party was forced to remain on the island two nights and one day. When the surf finally abated somewhat they were able to return to the ship but lost most of the supplies in the surf.

Lieutenant Williamson wrote of this experience ashore, "ye extreme reservedness of the party excited so great a curiosity in the women, that they were determined to see whether our people were men or not, & us'd every means in their power to provoke them to do that, which ye dread of punishment would have kept them from."

Preparing to leave the Islands, Cook lamented that "the very thing happened that I had above all others wished to prevent," referring to the communication of sexually transmitted diseases. From the recorded descriptions of the ships' surgeons and others, this was mostly gonorrhea, to a lesser extent syphilis, and to an even lesser extent both in the same person.

On February 2, Cook left the island group and resumed his northerly course for the westerlies, then to the coast of North America and on to the Bering Sea and beyond. He found no navigable passage. As the Arctic winter approached he decided to return to the Islands and arrived off Maui eight months after he had departed. From the Hawaiians who paddled out and came aboard ship he learned that venereal disease had spread as he had feared. One of his visitors was an important chief from the island of Hawai'i, Kalani'ōpu'u, who was at the time making war on Maui. One member of the chief's retinue, a young warrior who was his nephew, quietly watched the strange white men and spent the night aboard. Cook noted him, and we will hear more of Kamehameha.

The ships anchored at Kealakekua Bay in the Kona District of the island of Hawai'i. Word had spread from island to island that Captain Cook was Lono. Landing at Kealakekua, he was greeted the same way as he had been on Kaua'i. It was there that Cook met his death in an altercation over a stolen ship's boat. Parts of

Cook's remains were recovered, placed in a coffin, and, with the guns of both ships booming and the crews standing in silence, committed to the waters of Hawai'i.

The last entry in Cook's journal could have been his epitaph. "The discovery of these islands was in many respects the most important that has hitherto been made by Europeans throughout the extent of the Pacific Ocean."

There were no more visits by foreign ships until 1786, but from then on one or more visited the Islands every year. By 1800, nearly all of the seafaring nations of the world had been represented. The ships that came to Kaua'i stopped at Waimea because the belief had grown since Cook's visit this was the capital of Kaua'i, even though the principal residence of the high chief was at Wailua. This belief also was to influence the missionaries. The ships calling at Waimea not only brought seeds of many useful plants, and domestic animals such as sheep, goats, and geese, but also fleas, mosquitoes, and centipedes, which were unknown in the Islands before then. They also brought diseases other than the sexually transmitted ones Cook's men had left behind.

The most influential of the visiting sea captains was George Vancouver. He had been a midshipman under Cook in 1778 and 1779, then returned in command of his own expedition in 1792. On this visit he stopped at Waimea and met Kaua'i's future King Kaumuali'i, who was then twelve years old. On subsequent visits to Hawai'i in 1793 and 1794, Vancouver spent most of his time at the island of Hawai'i, where he formed a friendship with Kamehameha. Vancouver presented him with cattle from California, which was the start of the ranching industry in Hawai'i. He also gave Kamehameha several other domestic animals as well as many seeds and cuttings of useful plants.

During his last two visits, Vancouver completed the most thorough survey and charting of the Islands done to date. He had spoken out against the sale of arms to Hawaiians, refused to sell arms himself, and tried to bring peace and reconciliation to the Islands being devastated by Kamehameha's conquests. The latter, however, was intent upon obtaining control of all the Islands. He also was aware that this would come to naught if a well-armed foreign power endeavored to take over the Islands. Having enjoyed good relations with Great Britain, Kamehameha had Vancouver agree to take the Islands under British protection, an action that was later rejected by the British government.

In 1793, Vancouver visited the south coast of Kaua'i, stopping at Waimea. He walked inland and described an unusual watercourse named *KīkīaOla*, which means "flow of Ola."

According to legend, Ola is the name of the chief who ordered its construction. This is the major and almost only example of cut and dressed stone found in the Hawaiian Islands, an art that had been lost for centuries. Less than a hundred feet of the top of the ditch wall is visible today because of thoughtless road construction. Vancouver described the height of the stone wall as twenty-four feet above the level of the river, with a base twenty feet thick. He did not venture beyond this point, but noting it brought water from an intake on the Waimea River, concluded it was of considerable length. He observed the residents using the top as a pathway to the interior, and that the rocks used to build it were quarried seven miles away. Since Hawaiians did not have the wheel, the rocks had to be dragged or rolled on logs that distance. They were shaped by pecking and grinding with stone implements. Small wonder Hawaiians invoked the myth of the *menehune* to explain it, thus bestowing its alternate name "Menehune Ditch."

Despite Vancouver's advice, Kamehameha continued to acquire arms and war supplies with the intention of conquering all the other islands. Vancouver had given Kamehameha a Union Jack, which he flew over his own residence for years. During the War of 1812, some Americans informed Kamehameha that flying the British flag was stirring ill feelings, so he had the first Hawaiian flag designed. It incorporated the Union Jack in one corner, with red, white, and blue stripes representing each of the major islands in the manner of the American flag. This continues today as the flag of Hawai'i. The Union Jack represents the influence of Great Britain during these early times.

Over the next few years Kamehameha continued to pursue his quest to unify the Islands under his own rule. He had started as chief of one district on Hawai'i. Gathering foreign arms in the 1780s, he formed an association with other chiefs loyal to him and took approximately one-third of that island. By 1795, he had conquered all of the Islands except Kaua'i and Ni'ihau. Later that year he commenced preparations to take these also. He assembled foreign advisors, ships, and weapons, and built canoes. A shrewd trader, he continued to acquire all he deemed useful for his purposes from foreigners. By 1796, he had assembled a fleet of 1,500 canoes and 15,000 warriors, 600 of whom were armed with muskets. He also had 14 cannon and 40 swivel guns.

That year was perhaps the most dramatic in the history of Kaua'i. King Kaumuali'i was sixteen years old and untried in battle. He had only a fraction of the population and resources of his opponent. Kamehameha and his forces set sail from Wai'anae on the northwest shore of O'ahu to cross the 70-mile channel to

Kaua'i. Almost always tumultuous, the channel was worsened by a storm. Many of Kamehameha's canoes swamped and capsized. Reluctantly, he ordered those still afloat to turn back.

Over the next few years Kamehameha devoted himself to building large *peleleu*, double canoes difficult to capsize. Eventually he had 800, which together could carry thousands of warriors. He also obtained 21 schooners, either by purchase or by having them built by resident European shipwrights. He desperately desired dominion over all of the Islands and pressed his preparations.

By 1802, Kamehameha's armada was ready. He stayed for a year at Lahaina, Maui, then at Ka'a'awa on the north shore of O'ahu, stripping both islands of supplies. Joesting states that "Accounts vary somewhat, but it is agreed he commanded an army consisting of about 7,000 Hawaiian men and 50 Europeans." That number was nearly a third of the total population of Kaua'i. Most of Kamehameha's warriors had muskets, and he was well-supplied with cannon and mortars. Kamehameha sent threats to Kaumuali'i from both Maui and O'ahu, and passing ship captains told Kaumuali'i of the mighty forces of Kamehameha. The young king was filled with fear and a feeling of futility.

While Kamehameha was still on O'ahu in 1804, an epidemic decimated his army, so the invasion of Kaua'i never took place. This epidemic is given short shrift by many historians, although its effects were profound. Kamehameha himself was seriously ill and came close to death. The illness and the loss of so many close friends changed him appreciably, altering the course of Hawaiian history in ways not yet analyzed. On Kaua'i (including, of course, Kōloa), it meant thousands of young men lived who otherwise would have been slaughtered. It also meant the people of Kaua'i were not ruled by Kamehameha—for a time—and that their beloved Kaumuali'i continued to govern—also for a time. Kamehameha had lost most of his wisest and trusted chiefs. Their counsel and able assistance were missed in his rule from that date on. The younger chiefs Kamehameha appointed to take their places were untrained and inexperienced, and most led dissolute lives with little concern for the welfare of the people.

The cause of the epidemic has not been agreed upon, and the theories put forward have been little more than guesses by those not in the medical profession. The author feels qualified to offer his opinion as a physician certified in internal medicine, with graduate education in tropical medicine (master's degree), public health and epidemiology (master's degree), and a fellowship in infectious disease. Years of experience in underdeveloped areas, on Pacific islands and elsewhere around the world, enables me to interpret accounts of non-professionals whether they are patients or observers. Although the cause is apparent immediately to any physician with this or a similar background, enough information and guidance will be provided here so the reader can come to his or her own conclusion.

Briefly, this is what is known about the epidemic. Hawaiians called it *ma'i 'ōku'u,* and such an epidemic they had never before experienced. The *Hawaiian Dictionary* defines this term as a dysenteric disease that caused people to squat almost constantly at stool. It had a high case-rate mortality of approximately 50 percent. After reviewing the available evidence about Kamehameha's troops, Joesting stated: "The destruction to his forces was greater than any he could have suffered in battle. His forces were so depleted, particularly through the loss of dedicated and trusted chiefs, that the invasion of Kaua'i became an impossibility."

Although all available accounts were written after the fact by those who had not witnessed it, Robert Schmitt made an exhaustive review of this material in 1970. As a statistician, and primarily concerned with the number who died, he remarked upon the wide range of estimates that had been made. Noting general agreement that the epidemic was severe, he concluded: "If, as seems likely, the epidemic was limited to O'ahu, the death toll was probably well under 15,000 (out of perhaps 35,000 or 40,000 on the Island at the time)." He was uncertain about its spread to other islands. We may assume it did because the reports agree the disease had spread rapidly on O'ahu, and many would have fled O'ahu to escape, carrying the disease with them.

All reports but one tell of the epidemic and do not describe the malady itself. The one description of the disease was written by Samuel Kamakau in 1867 after interviewing firsthand witnesses. His account appeared later in *Ruling Chiefs of Hawaii.* Kamakau's reliability can be assessed by a critical review of his other writings. His accuracy was often limited by his sources, and in this instance nothing is known about sources except there were several. Kamakau's bias on religious matters is well-known, as is his bitterness about certain matters in his later years, but neither apply here. The most appropriate appraisal can be made from the chapter *'Oihana Lapa'au* in *Ka Po'e Kahiko: The People of Old,* in which he describes the sicknesses of early Hawaiians and their treatment. In this it is apparent he was a reliable recorder of details about diseases as recounted by others. When he had witnessed an illness himself, e.g. smallpox, he was amazingly accurate. But Kamakau had one failing: he was not forthright about bodily functions he considered distasteful or disgusting. When describing enemas, for example, he wrote "they were given below" and the results were referred to by euphemisms. With this one proclivity in mind, here is his description of *ka maʻi ʻōkuʻu:*

> At the end of this time [of mobilization] the pestilence appeared called *ʻōkuʻu.* It was a very virulent pestilence, and those who contracted it died quickly. A person on the highway would die before he reached home. One might go for food and water and die so suddenly that those at home did not know what happened. The body turned black at death. A few died a lingering death, but never longer than twenty-four hours; if they were able to hold out for a day they had a fair chance to live. Those who lived generally lost their hair . . .

Most historians have proposed typhoid fever as the cause. At the time Kamakau wrote, diseases were identified and named according to their clinical aspects; little or nothing was known (even by physicians) about specific bacteriologic causes. Typhoid fever was not distinguished from other diseases until 1837 when William Gerhard coined the word "typhoid," which means "resembling typhus." The giants of microbiology, Pasteur, Koch, and Lister, were born about that time; Gerhard could only say typhoid fever was caused by an "infectious principle."

For comparison with Kamakau's account, a clear description of a person suffering from typhoid fever is required. This is more difficult than it might seem. Most of the modern medical literature has been written in developed countries where typhoid fever is rarely seen (400 cases annually in the U.S.) Further, the descriptions are mixed with data from laboratory tests and other technology. We are fortunate that Sir William Osler, the finest physician of the late 19th century, emphasized clinical observation apart from such other data in his capacity as a professor of medicine at Johns Hopkins. He had a great deal of experience with typhoid fever and wrote the clearest description known in his 1892 text, *The Principles and Practice of Medicine.* Osler had the added advantage of being able to follow untreated cases through their natural course.

In summary, this is what Osler wrote: during the first week there is an increasing lassitude, a rise in temperature to high levels accompanied by chills, a headache which gradually becomes severe, and abdominal discomfort. Constipation is characteristic in adults, but a mild diarrhea may occur in children. In the second and third weeks these symptoms worsen and may be accompanied by a "rose spot" rash on the abdomen, and by disorientation and delirium. During the fourth week, patients begin to convalesce. Complications cause death in approximately one percent of cases.

Osler's description agrees with others based upon observations made at the bedside of untreated patients, without laboratory and other data. These were the conditions under which Hawaiians witnessed the disease. None bear any resemblance to that of Kamakau. So typhoid fever can be dismissed as the cause of the epidemic.

What follows can be done by the reader. A methodical approach must be based upon the characteristics of the disease that are generally agreed upon: it was a *severe diarrhea of sudden onset*. For the greater part of this century, physicians working in underdeveloped areas have relied upon the manual *Control of Communicable Diseases*. It was written by world authorities on infectious disease precisely for that purpose and is published in a format that fits into one's pocket in the field. It is accompanied by a CD-ROM easily accessed by computer when the physician returns to more tech-friendly circumstances. Contact the American Public Health Association, 1015 Fifteenth Avenue NW, Washington D.C. 20005. Following the simple instructions for the use of the CD-ROM, the keyword "diarrhea" gives 91 possible causes, but when the word "acute" (of sudden onset) is added in a Boolean search, nine principal causes appear: cholera, *Escherichia* coli infections, shigellosis, campylobacteriosis, giardiasis, cryptosporidiosis, salmonellosis, yersiniosis, and viral gastroenteropathy. Of course, these are not given either there or here in the order of their probability, but a clinical description of each is provided so the physician can assess probabilities for the situation at hand. Before the word "severe" is added to the search, the degree of severity may be modified to take into consideration what is known of the resistance to infectious diseases the Hawaiians possessed at the time. Or the actual case-fatality rate reported by observers may be used. Either way, adding this term to the search, only one disease remains: cholera.

Cholera is caused by the bacterium *Vibrio cholerae*, which is most commonly transmitted in an endemic area by drinking contaminated water. It can also be transmitted by eating poorly cooked food, but rarely from person to person by hand-to-mouth means. The organism is capable of living in various foods for an extended period. It can remain alive for a somewhat shorter time in coastal salt water, fresh water, and in brackish estuaries. Most epidemics in underdeveloped areas begin with the introduction of contaminated food and then spread through contaminated water.

Belaboring the point further would be inappropriate. We can conclude with some certainty that *ma'i 'ōku'u* was cholera. Speculation on how it may have reached Kamehameha's troops would be futile. All that can be said is that Bernice Judd in *Voyages to Hawai'i Before 1860* recorded the arrival at Honolulu of many ships from many lands before the epidemic.

In any event, Kamehameha called off the planned invasion of Kaua'i and his canoes were left on the beach to rot. In that same year, he transferred his headquarters from the island of Hawai'i to Honolulu, which had become the center of commerce because of its fine harbor.

Kamehameha spent months at Waikīkī seeking solace, as Hawaiians are wont to do, from the land. He labored in the taro ponds with his hands in the rich earth until his depression lifted. Then, once again, he began preparations to invade Kaua'i, but it was evident that his zeal for conquest had abated. In 1810, Kaumuali'i came to Honolulu at some risk to himself to talk with Kamehameha. He offered to cede Kaua'i and Ni'ihau. According to Kamakau, Kamehameha replied, "Return and rule, but if our young chief Liholiho [Kamehameha's son] makes you a visit, be pleased to receive him." Kaumuali'i understood the meaning of this and agreed to a nominal annual tribute acknowledging Kamehameha's sovereignty. Kaumuali'i learned of a plan by some of Kamehameha's chiefs to poison him and promptly returned to Kaua'i.

There he pondered his situation. He still did not trust Kamehameha and sought outside sources of help to little avail. Kamehameha's advisors were mostly English and he considered himself to be under British protection. Kaumuali'i looked to the United States but the War of 1812 had brought about a decline in American influence.

Kaumuali'i's uneasy situation prevailed until Kamehameha's death on May 8, 1819, when his son Liholiho became Kamehameha II. Ka'ahumanu, who had been Kamehameha's favored wife, declared it was the wish of Kamehameha I that she "share the domain together" with Liholiho, and a dual reign of the Islands ensued. She anticipated trouble from the chiefs of Kaua'i with Kamehameha gone, and undoubtedly conferred with Liholiho over this. Apparently on an impulse, he visited Kaua'i in 1821. The channel was stormy and his men pled to turn back, but Liholiho ordered them to continue. On Kaua'i he was received warmly by Kaumuali'i and had what appeared to be a friendly visit with him at Waimea. Almost certainly under instructions from Ka'ahumanu, Liholiho kidnaped Kaumuali'i and took him to Honolulu. Kaua'i never saw its last high chief again. He died in Honolulu in 1824.

Liholiho left on a trip to England in 1823 and both he and his queen succumbed there the next year to measles. Ka'ahumanu had assumed total power during his absence. When word of Liholiho's death was received in 1825, she became regent with the nine-year-old boy who was to become Kamehameha III. It had been the wish of Kaumuali'i that the chiefs of Kaua'i retain control over their lands upon his death, but Ka'ahumanu did not assure the chiefs his wish would be carried out. The Kaua'i chiefs suspected, probably correctly, that she had other plans and were uneasy. They had been loyal to Kaumuali'i and some were loyal to his son Humehume. Others shifted their allegiance to Ka'ahumanu, and the rest were discreetly absent on other islands.

In 1824, Humehume, with the chiefs and followers who were loyal to him, launched a rebellion. It began with a poorly organized attack on Fort Elizabeth in Waimea, which was garrisoned by Ka'ahumanu's troops. The defenders of the fort were caught asleep. With the numbers at his command, Humehume's forces easily could have seized the fort with its muskets, ammunition, and cannon. They badly needed these weapons because they were armed only with spears, daggers, and slingshots. Humehume and his soldiers were driven off and retreated to Hanapēpē Valley. The warriors in the fort sent a ship to O'ahu requesting reinforcements, and Ka'ahumanu promptly dispatched an army from O'ahu and Maui of over a thousand men armed with muskets. Her army pursued and attacked the men under Humehume. In a battle on the eastern ridge of the valley, the insurgents were overwhelmed and most were slaughtered. Humehume fled. Later he was found drunk, wandering aimlessly in the hills. He was captured and taken to O'ahu. The surviving rebel chiefs were removed from Kaua'i and dispersed throughout the Islands.

Ka'ahumanu divided the lands of Kaua'i and Ni'ihau among chiefs from other islands who had been favorites of Kamehameha and were as loyal to her as they had been to him. She appointed Kaikio'ewa governor of the two islands, replacing Kanoa. Kaikio'ewa was Kamehameha's cousin, and had been a distinguished warrior chief under him. Kaikio'ewa governed both Kaua'i and Ni'ihau through the newly appointed chiefs.

Thus, the complete conquest of the Hawaiian Islands, which Kamehameha had sought for so long while he lived, was accomplished five years after his death by those who had been loyal to him in his lifetime and remained loyal to his memory afterwards.

Chapter six

Sandalwood and Whales

The first Hawaiians to engage in trade with the outside world were from Kōloa. The event took place off Makahū‘ena Point, and Cook recorded this in his journal of January 19,1778:

> seeing some Canoes come off from the shore towards the Ships, I brought to give them time to come up. . .they exchanged a few fish they had in the Canoes for any thing we offered them, but valued nails, or iron above every other thing . . .

Cook also observed stones in the bottoms of their canoes, which the visitors were prepared to offer in a more forceful way if necessary. But when friendly trade began these were thrown overboard.

> As soon as we made sail the Canoes left us, but others came off from the shore and brought with them roasting pigs and some very fine Potatoes . . .we again found ourselves in the land of plenty.

From that first encounter, this chapter will describe how Kōloa was involved in various forms of trade with many nations until sugar became dominant. The types of trade will be presented in four phases: trinkets for supplies, the fur trade, sandalwood, and whalers. These are not phases in the sense they occurred sequentially, but overlap considerably; in fact, at one point around 1820, all four kinds of trade were taking place at the same time.

At Waimea, Cook obtained water from the lagoon behind the sandbar at the mouth of the river. Most of the other supplies he took aboard there, obtained in exchange for nails and similar items, came from nearby areas, including Kōloa.

After Cook, the next ships to visit Kaua'i were the *King George*, commanded by Nathaniel Portlock, and the *Queen Charlotte*, under George Dixon. They arrived off the southern coast together in 1786 and anchored at Waimea, following Cook's example. They obtained water, "Cocoa-nuts," sugar cane, and taro in exchange for pieces of iron. Returning to Waimea at Christmas that same year, they celebrated with a feast of roast pig. The crew mixed their ration of rum with coconut milk, Dixon noted in his journal, "which pleased more on account of its novelty than from any other circumstance." Afterwards, the ships took on a large quantity of water and supplies brought in from the surrounding area. Kōloa contributed to this trade with hogs and vegetables which were brought overland suspended from carrying poles on the shoulders of the Kōloans.

From then until the end of the century, ships came to Waimea nearly every year for water and provisions. During these years sea captains learned, as had Cook, that the exposed anchorage at Waimea was dangerous when *kona* winds came up, threatening to hurl their ships onshore.

This weather phenomenon deserves explanation because it was the major reason for the decline of Waimea as the favored port of Kaua'i, and the rise of Kōloa Landing to take its place. Hawai'i has only two seasons, not four as in temperate climates. Summer, *kau*, lasts five months from May through September; winter, *ho'oilo*, constitutes the other seven months, from October to April. The word *kona* means leeward, the opposite direction from which the trade winds blow. A kona wind, therefore, is one that comes from the southwest quadrant, opposite the usual northeast trade winds. *Kona* winds originate in storms between Hawai'i and the equator and are drawn north over the Islands by areas of low atmospheric pressure at higher latitudes above Hawai'i.

Kona conditions are less frequent at Waimea and elsewhere in the Islands during the summer months when the trade winds are stronger. The usual result on the southwest coast of Kaua'i is a gentle onshore wind or merely a cessation of the trades; *kona* storms with strong winds are rare in the summer months. Thus, the usual problem sailing ships faced when anchored at Waimea Bay during summer *kona* conditions was difficulty in clearing the bay because of the uncertain winds and the frequent tacking required to clear the headlands on either side.

It is during the seven months of winter that *kona* winds can be dangerous. The storms that spawn them are much more common, more severe, and the opposing trade winds are weaker. The result on the southwest coast of Kaua'i may be onshore winds reaching velocities of 30 knots or more. A modern sailboat can work its way out of the bay under these conditions, but not ships of the eighteenth and nineteenth centuries. Nor could ships of that time remain safely at anchor. The anchors used then were the stock type, essentially unchanged from those developed by the Greeks in 600 B.C. which did not hold well in the sandy bottom because of their relatively small flukes. A modern stockless or Danforth anchor today would hold under most circumstances. Thus, ships of that time often could not clear the bay or remain at anchor. They were in peril of being blown onto the "lee" shore, so-called because it lay downwind or to leeward, where they would be pounded to pieces in the high surf produced by the wind.

At the first hint of a *kona* wind, prudent seamanship then required clearing the bay at once for the open sea. Ships of that era had to sail close-hauled and try to beat into the teeth of the wind, but they were unable to sail closer than 60 or 70 degrees from the direction the wind was coming from. Each time they tacked they lost way, and were blown some distance towards shore. Although the headlands on either side of Waimea Bay do not project far out into the ocean, they do restrict the room to maneuver, making frequent tacking necessary, as described.

For ships anchoring instead off Kōloa Landing the situation was quite different. All captains had to do was hoist sail and set an eastward course on a "broad reach," meaning the wind is coming roughly 120 degrees from the direction the ship is headed. This is the most favorable course relative to the wind for any sailing ship and produces a speed greater than that of the wind itself. No tacking is required. Ships leaving Kōloa Landing easily cleared Makahū'ena Point to the open ocean.

By the turn of the century ship captains knew of the tiny protected indentation, not yet called Kōloa Landing, with its shelving rocky shore ship's boats could beach upon. Yet it took them nearly another two decades to realize their ships could anchor offshore of this small landing and, if a *kona* wind came up, they could sail away without difficulty.

First one ship, and then another, called at Kōloa Landing. They obtained ample provisions there, and a small waterfall on Waikomo Stream near shore was an easy place to get water. In the hills above Kōloa firewood was plentiful, as was *olonā* cordage for shipboard use. In upland areas, yams, sweet potatoes, and sugar cane were grown. Salt was made in the salt pans around Kōloa Landing, supplemented when necessary by salt brought overland from Hanapēpē. Because of the level land, hogs and chickens could be raised in numbers almost without limit. Melons and squash almost covered sandy Punahoa Point just down the coast. The waters off Kōloa yielded more fish than the ships could consume, so much of it was salted and stored away for future use. Most important was the magnificent irrigation system that had been constructed at Kōloa. It made the area dominant in the production of taro and other products. By that time, the many seeds and cuttings given to the Kōloans were producing bountiful yields and a wide variety of fresh fruit and vegetables were proffered in trade. Irish potatoes grew exceptionally well around Kōloa.

It was in this way Kōloa entered its first phase of commerce; and ships were not lacking. The position of Hawai'i in the mid-Pacific was ideal for participation in the trans-Pacific trade of many nations with the Far East, primarily China and the East Indies. Paradoxically, Hawai'i looked west to the East, and east to the west coast of America.

Meanwhile, the threat of invasion by Kamehameha lessened, although the anxiety of Kaumuali'i did not. When the latter acknowledged Kamehameha's suzerainty over Kaua'i and Ni'ihau in 1810, the conquering chief turned his attention away from war to consolidate his kingdom. In the words of historian Gavan Daws, "For Kamehameha, the agreement with Kaumuali'i marked the end of war and thoughts of war." Steps Kamehameha then took facilitated the involvement of all Hawaiian ports in trade with the outside. In peace, Kamehameha proved to be as able as he had been in war.

Kamehameha's first major act as ruler of all the Islands was directed toward the ownership of land. Before contact with the outside world the concept of individual ownership of land was unknown. In the traditional Polynesian system of land tenure, the absolute power of the *ali'i nui* was of primary importance. As described before, the high chief only *controlled* the use of land until his death, whereupon "title" or control passed to a successor. Kamehameha had learned the difference of the Western system from visitors and declared all land in Hawai'i belonged personally to him.

Kamehameha then appointed chiefs loyal to him as governors of each major island and mandated a flow of authority from him through his chiefs to the lowest *maka'āinana*. This authority was in a form also previously unknown in Hawai'i. Under the traditional system, as described, a high chief issued *kapu* that carried the power of the gods the chief represented, and he also declared *kānāwai*, or secular decrees, on matters of less importance. But both were at his whim, and laws, as known in the West, did not exist in traditional Hawai'i. Kamehameha changed this by proclaiming a system of statutes that bound the Islands together and applied to all of his subjects. He instituted methods of enforcing these laws and ensured that justice was swift and certain.

Kamehameha had also learned a great deal about commerce with foreigners from bartering for muskets, cannon, and armed sloops. Widening his interest, he had achieved a monopoly on all foreign trade by the time of his death in 1819. There were advantages for the foreign traders in the way Kamehameha exercised his authority in matters of trade. He became the one to whom all traders turned, and he assured them of fairness by appointing agents to accompany them in their negotiations. He mandated that his subjects produce the goods foreign merchants desired, which assured an adequate and steady supply. He also provided pilots for the safety of merchant ships as they entered and left Hawaiian ports.

By the time Kamehameha began to institute these reforms, the commerce of Hawai'i with the outside world had expanded from simple bartering supplies for trinkets with the captains of visiting ships. In exchange for food, water, and other supplies, foreign traders offered Hawaiians cloth, furniture, tools, utensils, and many other items. Kōloa Landing participated fully in this growing trade.

Hawai'i became involved in the fur trade in 1786 when four ships stopped in Honolulu for supplies, including salt to preserve the pelts. China wanted furs but little else from the West. In exchange, China offered porcelain, tea, and fine fabrics coveted by the nations of Europe and the former colonies in America. The two nations that engaged initially in the fur trade were Russia and England. Russia obtained furs from the Aleuts in Alaska and from Indian trappers along the northwest coast of America. From there south to San Francisco, England acquired furs from the local Indians. Firearms and other commodities were offered by both nations in exchange. When goods from China were sold in Europe and New England the profits were large, but the limited quantities of furs restricted the trade.

The stimulus that led to expansion of the fur trade occurred serendipitously. Charles Clerke, who had assumed command of both the *Resolution* and *Discovery* after Cook's death, stopped at Waimea on Kaua'i for supplies before heading for North America to continue the search for a Northwest Passage. Along the latter coast he discovered a seemingly inexhaustible source of furs in the coastal waters: the fur seal, sea otter, sea lion, and sea cow. These were easily taken by his crews, and he stowed some pelts aboard. On the homeward passage the two ships, by then under the command of James King following Clerke's death, stopped at Macao. The Chinese were delighted with these new furs, which the English sold for extraordinary prices.

Then the United States entered into the growing fur trade. Following the Revolutionary War, the economic condition of the new nation had become desperate. New Englanders rebuilt their merchant marine only to find transatlantic trade had been rendered nearly impossible. Britain would not trade with its previous colonies, and traffic with former ally France proved unsatisfactory for several reasons. Merchants of the new nation were eager to trade wherever a dollar could be turned and looked to the Pacific, where they found the fur trade.

At first, the sources of furs were closed to the Americans. Spain governed the entire coast south of San Francisco until the Spanish colonies won their independence in the 1820s. To the north, British fur traders were dominant through the Hudson's Bay Company. From Sitka, Russians governed the Aleutians, Alaska, and that part of the northwest coast not claimed by England. Canny Yankee traders soon discovered the Russians could not guard this long stretch of coast to which they claimed title. The Americans also learned that supplies received from Russia by the far-flung outposts of the Russian-American Company were irregular and insufficient. These outposts were grateful for any supplies the American trading ships could bring them. The Russians exchanged the furs obtained from the Indians for provisions, and the United States was in the fur trade.

The British hold on the old "Oregon country" loosened when England became embroiled in the Napoleonic wars. Taking advantage of the situation, American fur traders extended their range farther down the coast from Alaska. Soon, the Americans were rivaling both Russia and England in this form of commerce. In Hawai'i, all ports that could supply the Americans and other traders en route to and from China were caught up in this new wave of prosperity. Kōloa Landing became the main port of Kaua'i involved in the fur trade. The one difficulty encountered in this three-point trade circuit was minor. China opened only one port, Canton (now Guangzhou), and insisted ships first stop for clearance at Macao and then make their way up the Pearl River to Canton. The Treaty of Nanking, which would open other Chinese ports in 1842, was still in the future.

Although the desire of China for furs seemed inexhaustible, all three nations engaged in the trade were to learn the sea mammals were not. By 1820, their numbers had become so reduced the fur trade began to decline.

Fortunately for Hawai'i, and for Kōloa, the third phase of foreign trade, for sandalwood, had already begun. Hawaiians knew the sandalwood tree as *'iliahi* and for centuries had ground its heartwood into powder to scent their *tapa* cloth. American fur traders were aware the Chinese coveted this aromatic wood even more than they did furs. They used it to make boxes and chests, as a perfume, as an ingredient in herbal medicines, in cosmetics, and they burned it on religious and other ceremonial occasions. During their stopovers in the Islands the Americans learned that sandalwood trees grew in Hawai'i.

The first cargos of Hawaiian sandalwood shipped to China met with puzzling indifference. It turned out the wood had been poorly selected, and the Chinese concluded Hawaiian sandalwood was inferior. It was not long before the traders understood which parts of the tree contained the aromatic oil the Chinese wanted, and insisted the Hawaiians gather them. After 1811, as the sandalwood trade intensified, the Chinese referred to Hawai'i as *Tan Heung Shan*, or The Sandalwood Mountains. The sandalwood trade was interrupted briefly by the War of 1812 but resumed with even greater intensity in 1815. When it did, Kōloa Landing shipped out most of the sandalwood gathered on Kaua'i.

The war had caused a breach between the Americans and British that lingered for many years. Great Britain continued to enjoy an influence with Kamehameha, who believed he was under British protection as a consequence of the treaty with Vancouver. The American traders wanted only sandalwood and supplies, not influence. On Kaua'i they tended to side discreetly with Kaumuali'i while at the same time maintaining friendly relations with Kamehameha.

Kamehameha did not indulge himself in the expensive trinkets of the outside world, as would the chiefs who came after him. He proclaimed all of the sandalwood in the Islands to be his property, controlled the harvesting, and directed the young saplings be spared in order to conserve the supply. The tree grows slowly, reaching maturity in about forty years. The perfume comes from oil in the heartwood, most of which is near the roots. Thus trees were harvested by chopping them down as near to the roots as possible or by ripping the young trees out of the ground. Sandalwood was not an immediately renewable resource and Kamehameha knew it. He also knew his chiefs, who received a share of the profits, were urging the people to leave their taro fields to gather sandalwood, and he asserted his authority to control this. Kamakau wrote that Kamehameha, aware of the imminence of famine, "ordered the chiefs and people under them to farm."

After the death of Kamehameha in 1819, his successor Liholiho, as Kamehameha II, allowed his chiefs to share in the sandalwood monopoly. Released from restraint, the chiefs worked the commoners unmercifully, forcing them to abandon their crops to gather the precious wood. As a result, famine was widespread during the 1820s. Since most of the Kaua'i chiefs resided on other islands and were unaware of the plight of the commoners, the famine was especially severe on Kaua'i.

A contemporaneous comment portrayed Governor Kaikio'ewa and the chiefs of Kaua'i in these words: "He is remarkably fond of purchasing novelties, and almost whatever is offered by foreigners, with little regard either to the cost or the utility of the article. This propensity to buy, seems indeed, to be deeply rooted in most of the chiefs . . ."

Reverend Peter Gulick, who was stationed in Waimea and frequently visited Kōloa, recorded in his journal in 1830:

> Felt distressed and grieved for the people who collect sandalwood. They are often driven by hunger to eat wild and bitter herbs, moss, &c. And though the weather is so cold on the hills that my winter clothes will scarcely keep me comfortable, I frequently see men with no clothing except the maro [loincloth].

Malnutrition of the weary workers, compounded by exposure to the cold mists of the mountains, was a significant factor in the decline of the Hawaiian population on Kaua'i and the other islands during the 1820s. By 1830, the forests were nearly exhausted of sandalwood, but commoners were forced to search out the last trees high up in the mountains to pay for the merchandise the chiefs had received on credit. When there were no more trees to be found, the trade came to a halt in 1835.

While the sandalwood trade was at its height, the most bizarre episode ever to disturb the pre-missionary torpor of Kauaʻi occurred. It had three roots: Russia's need to supply its posts in Alaska and along the northwest coast of the American continent; the continuing apprehension of Kaumualiʻi over Kamehameha's intentions; and the friction between the Americans and British that continued after the War of 1812. Men from both countries were among Kamehameha's advisors, although the British predominated, and the advice he received from these two sources was, more often than not, conflicting. Russia was to exploit these differences and the fears of Kaumualiʻi. What occurred was so strange it is told here in detail.

Russia's interest in the Hawaiian Islands dated back many years before these events took place. In 1741, Captain Vitius Bering (after whom both the Strait and Sea were named) had claimed Alaska for Russia, under whose control it remained until Russia sold it to the United States in 1867. During the decades after Bering's claim, Russian interests in the fur and fisheries of the Aleutian Islands and Alaska gradually extended down the coast of North America. Their pursuit of furs intensified after the discovery of fur-bearing marine mammals in large numbers.

In 1790, the Russian-American Company was formed as an agency of the Imperial Russian government. Alexander Baranoff became the first manager of the company and governor of Russian America in 1799. His most difficult problem proved to be supplying his posts and personnel. He sent some supply ships from the Baltic, purchased supplies from American and other traders, and tried growing crops in northern California. But his outposts still suffered, especially during the winters.

In 1804, Baranoff sent the first Russian ships to Hawaiʻi in search of provisions. It was apparent to him the Hawaiian Islands could supply sufficient food for all of the Russian settlements in Alaska and North America, as well as a good part of Asiatic Russia. He made plans either to establish a settlement in the Islands, or to conquer them.

In 1808, he dispatched the *Neva* under Captain Hagemeister to the Islands, ostensibly for a cargo of salt, but in reality to look into the possibility of realizing either of his plans. At the same time, he sent two ships south along the coast of California to look for sites where he could establish agricultural colonies, despite the fact Spain claimed this coast.

Hagemeister learned a great deal about the political situation in Hawaiʻi. He perceived the rivalry between the British and Americans and the threat that Kamehameha posed to Kaumuali'i, at least in the latter's mind. When the *Neva* called at Kaua'i, Kaumuali'i sought Russia's aid against Kamehameha. His pleas presumably were referred to the Russian government through the Russian-American Company but went unanswered.

During the War of 1812, Baranoff bought several American vessels whose captains feared British warships and privateers. In 1814, he sent the recently purchased *Bering*, still under her American Captain Bennett, to Hawai'i for supplies. On the way back to Alaska the ship stopped at Kaua'i, was caught by an onshore *kona* gale at Waimea, and wrecked. Captain Bennett requested help from Kaumuali'i, but despite the efforts of some 2,000 Kauaians the *Bering* could not be refloated. An agreement was struck whereby the wreck would belong to Kaumuali'i for its iron, but the cargo of furs would remain the property of Russia. Most of the cargo was salvaged and taken ashore to be stored by Kaumuali'i at Makaweli, near Waimea. Kaumuali'i dictated a letter to Captain Bennett, addressed to Baranoff, dated 27 December 1814, in which he asked for muskets and cannon with powder and shot for them, as well as other supplies for battle. Bennett and his crew eventually secured passage aboard a passing ship to Sitka. When he reported to Baranoff, the latter decided the situation on Kaua'i presented an ideal opportunity to establish a settlement there.

It was at this time that Georg Anton Scheffer strode onto the scene. Born and raised in Munnerstadt, Germany, he had been expelled from medical school in Germany because of his contentious personality, but became a physician in 1805 by examination. His personality was to create most of the drama that was to follow. Scheffer was educated, cultured, and could be charming, which about exhausts the list of his virtues. Joesting describes him as "cross-grained, quarrelsome, sententious, opinionated, and full of petty conceits, systematically falling out with almost everyone he met."

Scheffer served in the Russian Army for a time as a staff physician, and then as a physician on the Russian-American Company ship *Suvarov*. When the ship arrived in 1813 at Sitka, he left it and took a position there as a physician with the Russian-American Company.

Baranoff now wanted to get the *Bering's* cargo back, in addition to establishing a settlement on Kaua'i. His shrewd scheme was to send Scheffer, and if he were successful, fine. If not, then he was merely a German without portfolio and would not bring discredit to the Russian-American Company. In

October of 1815, Scheffer sailed for the island of Hawai'i under instructions to pose as a naturalist. He was to obtain trading privileges for the Russian-American Company, which was to include a monopoly of the Hawaiian sandalwood trade, and to secure Kamehameha's help in reclaiming the *Bering's* cargo or payment for it in sandalwood. If neither assignment in regard to the cargo could be obtained peacefully, he assured Scheffer armed ships with troops would arrive, and Kaua'i was to be conquered.

On arrival at Kailua, Scheffer found both Kamehameha and Ka'ahumanu ill with a fever. He treated them and they recovered. Kamehameha's American and British advisors suspected that Scheffer was more than he appeared to be but counseled conflicting courses of action. The king ignored all of them and showed his gratitude to Scheffer by building him a house and granting him land. As time went on, Scheffer's duplicity began to emerge in various affairs. Kamehameha's rival advisors were becoming more unified in their advice in regard to the danger he posed. Scheffer's stay on the island consequently became untenable. He obtained permission from Kamehameha to move to O'ahu, where on his own initiative he promptly laid out a fort near Honolulu Harbor. Work on the fort was begun by a few of the Russians living there, some Aleuts who had arrived on a Russian ship, and a handful of Hawaiians. Personality problems that had plagued Scheffer at Kailua did so on O'ahu as well. One incident, ordering the Russian flag to be flown over the unfinished fort, infuriated Kamehameha. Scheffer learned of this, and one of his few rational acts was to leave Honolulu in 1816.

He had learned of the tensions between Kamehameha and Kaumuali'i as well as the different aims of the Americans and British in the Islands. Hoping their conflicting advice would inhibit any action Kamehameha might take in response to his next plot, he sailed to Kaua'i. There he exploited Kaumuali'i's fears by offering him the protection of Russia against Kamehameha. He hoped not only to obtain the *Bering's* cargo but to persuade Kaumuali'i to turn over Kaua'i to Russia. He promised Russian protection against Kamehameha if Kaumuali'i would swear allegiance to Emperor Alexander I of Russia. It was a reflection of Kaumuali'i's mental state that he believed Scheffer. He acceded to giving up the *Bering's* cargo and agreed to trade exclusively with the Russian-American Company, in addition to granting a monopoly on sandalwood from Kaua'i. Schaeffer, without any authority to do so, made Kaumuali'i an officer in the Russian navy. Kaumuali'i, in turn, bestowed gifts upon Scheffer and gave him the entire valley of Hanalei and other land as well.

Scheffer established a trading post at Waimea and built a house for himself there. At Hanalei he had two earthen redoubts constructed using local labor supplied by Kaumuali'i: Fort Barclay at the river mouth, named for a famous Russian General; and Fort Alexander on the bluffs above, named after the Emperor. Kaumuali'i had told him his lineage entitled him to rule over all the Islands, so Scheffer preyed upon Kaumuali'i's ego and concluded a secret treaty with him to conquer the other islands, promising Russian assistance in the endeavor.

Scheffer's activities by then had aroused Kamehameha's anger to the point he took action. He sent a force to seize the partially constructed fort at Honolulu Harbor, then built a larger fort of coral blocks on the site and stationed soldiers there to forestall any further such acts by Scheffer in Honolulu. The location of the fort was *makai,* or seaward, of the junction of what is now Queen Street and Fort Street Mall. Fort Street was named after the fort. At that time Queen Street was a only a path along the shore and Fort Street a trail to a nearby canoe landing.

Cut off from O'ahu, Scheffer continued his activities on Kaua'i. Kōloa Landing had not yet replaced Waimea as the most important port on the island. Waimea's recent history apparently convinced Scheffer it was, and always would be, the major port. He never seemed to look very far ahead when conceiving plans, not to Kōloa Landing a decade or so hence, and certainly not as far as Nāwiliwili and Port Allen less than a century in the future. So Scheffer drew up plans for a large lava-rock fort overlooking the mouth of Waimea River. Construction began on September 12, 1816, with labor assigned by Kaumuali'i and directed by Scheffer. There were no Russians or Aleuts at Waimea to assist him as there had been at Honolulu.

Scheffer designed the structure in the star-shape style of European forts at the time, which permitted enfilade fire of small arms and cannon to protect the walls against siege. The five points of the fort where cannons were mounted faced the ocean and river mouth. The base of the walls was 17 feet thick and constructed in the dry-stack method of the Hawaiians, using rubble fill without mortar. The walls tapered upward to an average height of twelve feet. Because the ground was uneven, the walls at places were 20 feet high. Within the enclosure, the barracks were located surprisingly close to the magazine, but the officers' quarters were at a more comfortable distance. The southern portion of the walls and some interior structures were finished late that year. The northern and eastern walls were not finished until the following year.

Scheffer named Fort Elizabeth in honor of Elizabeth, the consort of Tsar Alexander I, but spelled Elizabeth with an "s." Possibly the difficulty of passing Cyrillic letters through to English in his German mind caused him to make the mistake.

Tsar Alexander's consort was named Elizabeth after Tsarina Elizabeth Petrovna, who in turn had been named in honor of England's first Queen Elizabeth. There is no "s" anywhere along this line.

Scheffer also made a more serious mistake, but this act may have been intentional. He called the fort "Russian" despite the fact that no Russians were ever involved. Long before then, Baranoff had resorted to his alternate plan of referring to Scheffer as a German without any authorization from him or the Russian-American Company. All of the Russian ship captains calling at Hawai'i during those years, including officers of the Russian Navy, deplored and disavowed his actions that he claimed were on behalf of Russia. Scheffer appealed to the Tsar for verification of his imagined role representing Russia, although he must have known it would take months for his appeal to reach St. Petersburg. It was not until well after the fort had been completed that the official repudiation of his actions by the Tsar arrived.

Undeterred by his lack of support from Russia, Scheffer hoisted the Russian flag over the fort with his own hands. He was a German citizen when he did so. It was never at any time a Russian fort, nor was it built on behalf of that nation or the Russian-American Company. Yet the sign "Russian Fort Elisabeth" at the fort today perpetuates Scheffer's errors. When queried by the author, The State Department of Land and Natural Resources, which has custody of the fort, acknowledged the sign is incorrect but is concerned a change might confuse tourists.

By now aware of the true nature of Scheffer's activities, Kaumuali'i, in addition to the Americans at Waimea, wanted Scheffer out of there. Oblivious to the rising resentment around him, Scheffer claimed the entire island of Kaua'i in the name of the Emperor of Russia and raised the Russian flag over Fort Alexander at Hanalei. At this, Kamehameha ordered Kaumuali'i to evict Scheffer, who fled to O'ahu. By this time Scheffer was beginning to catch on and feared Kamehameha might have him taken from the ship while it was in Honolulu Harbor, so he hid out on it until it departed. He left Hawai'i to become a "Count," or something of the sort, in Brazil, leaving his remarkable story behind him.

Following Kōloa Landing's growing importance in supplying whatever ships called, its ascendancy during the fur trade, and service as the main port for shipping Kaua'i sandalwood, by 1830 it became widely recognized as the major port of the island. It was not officially designated as such by the Hawaiian government until

1855, however, when the only customs officer on Kaua'i was transferred there from Waimea.

Kōloa Landing's foremost role on Kaua'i carried into the heyday of the next phase of foreign trade, the Pacific whaling industry. This began before the passing of the sandalwood era and continued well into the period of sugar production by Kōloa Plantation.

The impact of Pacific whaling on Hawai'i started almost by chance. In 1819, two whaling ships, the *Balena* and *Equator*, while searching for new whaling grounds, took a whale off the island of Hawai'i. They anchored in Kealakekua Bay and were able to obtain water, wood, and provisions there. At the time the most popular whaling grounds were near Japan in the North Pacific, thirty days' sail from Hawai'i. Once again, as in the fur trade, the location of the Islands proved to be ideal. Most of the whaling ships were out of New England ports, especially New Bedford. In the Islands the ships could stop for provisions, repairs, and rest, allowing them to remain on the whaling grounds longer. Their number increased rapidly. In 1824, over 100 ships came to Hawaiian ports for this purpose.

By the 1830s, the best whaling grounds were in the Arctic seas of the North Pacific, and Hawai'i was almost directly en route from Cape Horn to and from this destination. Because of its superior facilities, Honolulu was the most frequented port, followed by Lahaina on Maui. But the former became crowded and provisions there were often in short supply. At Lahaina, ships had to anchor offshore in the open Lahaina roadstead.

As recounted above, Waimea had fallen into disfavor by then as a port of call on Kaua'i because of the unpredictable onshore winds. Kōloa Landing became the third busiest island port in Hawai'i during the whaling period, behind Honolulu and Lahaina, hosting 40 to 60 whaling ships each year. Concerning its role during this era, Joesting wrote that "prices were lower than in Honolulu, and Kōloa became known for the quality and variety of goods sold." The whaling ships either anchored or lay off-and-on, while the whalers rowed to Kōloa Landing for recreation and supplies. This is why it is still called by many "Whaler's Cove."

Once again, the produce available in the Kōloa area flowed out of Kōloa Landing. Crops in demand by the fur traders and whalers had been added, and Kōloa Plantation was beginning to produce unrefined sugar and molasses. Massive quantities of wood, required for heating the try-pots to render blubber into whale oil, were still available in the forests above Kōloa. Other areas of the island had also increased production of commodities, and these were brought overland to Kōloa Landing. From Wailua Valley came barrels of salt beef and kegs of butter; from Hanalei, oranges and coffee; from Hanapēpē, salt in quantities Kōloa no longer made; and rice from several nearby valleys.

For Kōloa, the busiest years of the whaling industry lasted from the early 1830s to 1861, peaking in 1840. With sandalwood depleted and sugar production still somewhat uncertain, this source of income was a godsend. During the period from 1840 to 1870, Kōloa and its small port was the most thriving center on the island. Residents twitted the town of Līhu'e and its harbor of Nāwiliwili as being "suburbs of Kōloa."

Recreation was important to the crews of whaling ships because their life was hard. The men lived in the dark, dank forecastle where there was little ventilation. It reeked of sweat, tobacco, mildew, and rancid whale oil. Food was mainly salt beef or pork and hardtack. After months at sea the meat was spoiled and the hardtack crawled with weevils. The crews were worked to the point of exhaustion. Even though flogging was outlawed on American ships in 1850, the men still suffered curses, kicks, and worse. Little wonder when the sailors got ashore at Honolulu and Lahaina they let it all out in drunkenness, brawls, and even riots when they gathered in large numbers. Kōloa was spared most of these indignities because relatively fewer whaling ships called there, and because their captains preferred to tack back and forth in the bay rather than anchor, which kept much of the crew aboard. Moreover, the missionaries had more influence in Kōloa than in the larger ports. With the residents on their side, their presence helped to quell the violence so frequent at the other ports of call.

About 1850, ship owners learned they could hire or purchase merchant ships to bring goods to Honolulu and other Hawaiian ports at a profit, then transship the accumulated barrels of whale oil to them each winter. This way, whaling ships not only could prolong their annual stay in the whaling grounds but also extend their trips away from home port to three or four years, increasing profits immensely. The transshipment, and the refitting of ships required because of their longer absence from home, took place by necessity in the quieter waters of Honolulu Harbor. This was an indirect boon to Kōloa Landing, nevertheless, because under this system the whalers visited there more often and purchased more supplies.

The decline in whaling began in 1859 when petroleum was discovered in Pennsylvania and kerosene was found to be superior to whale oil for lighting and other purposes. The sale of baleen alone could not sustain the industry. At the outbreak of the Civil War, the North had sunk ships loaded with boulders in the entrances of many Southern ports to augment their blockade. Since some whalers had home ports in the South, the combination hindered the whaling industry. Nearly forty whalers were bottled up in Charleston alone. Close to the end of the war, the Southern raider *Shenandoah* entered the Pacific and sank or captured many whalers. In one week of action in 1865, the privateer sank or captured 24 whaling ships in the Bering Straits and Bering Sea.

Although for Kaua'i the whaling industry had all but come to an end as the Civil War began, the final blow came in 1871, when 33 whaling ships—most of the whaling fleet by then—were caught in the ice of the Bering Sea. As their crews abandoned ship to escape across the ice, the vessels were left behind to be crushed by the ice pack.

Chapter Seven

Puritans in Paradise

The day was Saturday, October 23, 1819. A small group of missionaries stood on the Long Wharf in Boston Harbor and wept as they bade their farewells. This first company of missionaries to the Sandwich Islands consisted of six newly married couples, another couple with their five children, and four Hawaiian youths who were returning home.

They set out on the long voyage aboard the brig *Thaddeus*. The members of the company called itself a "family" and each other "brother" and "sister," but this was in a religious sense because most were in fact almost strangers. They would not be by the time they arrived in Hawai'i. The first company, and the eleven companies to follow, would bring about profound and permanent changes in the Islands, including Kaua'i and the small settlement of Kōloa.

The background of this missionary movement up to the date the *Thaddeus* sailed is a short one. Inspired by the London Missionary Society, an association of New England churches formed the American Board of Commissioners for Foreign Missions (ABCFM) at Boston in 1810 for the purpose of carrying Christianity to the heathen. In 1817 A Foreign Mission School was founded in Cornwall, Connecticut, to educate young natives from faraway places who would return to their homelands as missionaries. Ships in the Hawaiian trade had brought several young Hawaiians back to New England, and among the first students taken into the Foreign Mission School were Hawaiians. Although the Board was first active in Africa and India, the presence of these young men from Hawai'i, and the stories of the crews that had called there, prompted the Board to consider sending missionaries to the Sandwich Islands.

In September of 1819, volunteers were sought as missionaries to "save the souls of the Sandwich Islanders and to convert them from their idolatries and superstitions and vices." Among the first to come forward were Hiram Bingham and Asa Thurston, students of theology at Andover Seminary. The Board promptly accepted and ordained both of them. It also ensured the six single men who volunteered were married before sailing. The Board was not only concerned about the unseemly intimacy of such a long trip, but also feared the temptations male missionaries would face in a land where the women were known to be free with their favors.

The following members, whose names loom large in the history of Hawai'i, comprised the first company: Rev. and Mrs. Hiram Bingham, Rev. and Mrs. Asa Thurston, Dr. and Mrs. Thomas Holman, Mr. and Mrs. Samuel Ruggles, Mr. and Mrs. Samuel Whitney, Mr. and Mrs. Elisha Loomis, and Mr. and Mrs. Daniel Chamberlain with their five children. The three Hawaiians who had been students at the Foreign Mission School were Thomas Hopu, William Kanui, and John Honoli'i. The fourth Hawaiian was Prince Humehume of Kaua'i, the son of King Kaumuali'i, who had sent him to America at the age of seven for an education. Now, fifteen years later, he wished to return to his native island. A rather reluctant Christian, he had squandered his patrimony on pursuits other than education and favored "ardent spirits" to excess. These, and other character flaws, proved to be his undoing.

One couple in the company was to play a large role on Kaua'i, and in Kōloa: Samuel Whitney, a struggling student of 26 at Yale; and his bride Mercy Partridge Whitney, age 24. Samuel was a tall, handsome man with a high forehead and prominent chin. His portrait, at the Hawaiian Mission Children's Society in Honolulu, caught a determined expression on his face. Mercy had large, soft eyes but a firm set to her lips. Her letters, also at HMCS, were written in an exceptionally fine, even hand. The Ruggleses, Samuel and Nancy, also were to have a part to play in Waimea and Kōloa, but a lesser one than the Whitneys.

Dr. Thomas Holman joined the first company because the Board had realized a doctor in the group was essential. The ABCFM was concerned about the health of the missionaries they were sending to a strange land. The Board was also aware Cook and others had introduced diseases that were ravaging the Islands and hoped to help. Nearly half the population had died as a result, some thought. Dr. Holman agreed to go and married Lucia Ruggles, whose brother, Samuel, had already volunteered.

The two-masted brig *Thaddeus* was 85 feet long, with a 24-foot beam, and fully loaded with furniture and provisions. The staterooms were six feet square, with two bunks, upper and lower, on each side. There was scarcely room for one person to stand amid the luggage. Once at sea the passengers had to rig straps in order to stay in their bunks. All members of the group were seasick the first days or weeks out. Bathing and washing clothes was possible only in salt water. When the ship rounded Cape Horn in early February of the new year, the missionaries were wretchedly cold; near the equator they suffered as much or more from the heat.

Hiram Bingham had begun to assume leadership of the group even before departure, and the Board had tacitly allowed this. He was a gaunt man of 30 with a severe expression and piercing eyes. Bingham was eager to do the Lord's work among the "pagans, heathens, idolaters, savages, lewd and loathsome beings," as he described the Hawaiians. His contentious personality emerged as soon as the *Thaddeus* got underway. He declared that no personal property existed—what belonged to one belonged to all—and demanded a basket of fruit that had been given to Lucia Holman by her family. She refused graciously, but Bingham thereafter held a grudge against her. The conflict inevitably involved Lucia's husband and was to have unfortunate consequences.

The long voyage of 18,000 miles was finally rewarded when the peak of Mauna Kea on "Owhyhee" came into view on March 30, 1820. The *Thaddeus* approached the Hāmākua coast of Hawai'i Island and sailed along the north shore. A landing party went ashore at Kawaihae and learned of Kamehameha's death ten months before. He had been succeeded by his eldest son Liholiho, age 23, but political power resided in the hands of Ka'ahumanu, who had been Kamehameha's favorite wife. Officially, she was acting as regent, but her strong personality and shrewd intelligence made her the real ruler. Soon after the death of Kamehameha, and four months before the arrival of the missionaries, she had persuaded Liholiho to abolish the *kapu* system, in which women were subservient. She insisted that the legal structure Kamehameha had promulgated be the law of the land instead.

Their voyage of 164 days ended when the missionaries went ashore at Kailua on the west coast of Hawai'i on April 14, 1820. Liholiho, who lived there, met them and requested that some missionaries remain at Kailua. Bingham, apparently because of conflicts with the Thurstons and Holmans, chose these two couples to remain at Kailua to establish a missionary station. Kailua, then as now, was almost without water and covered by bleak, black lava which the sun baked during the day and on which almost nothing grew. Fresh water had to be brought from miles away in gourd calabashes. There was not enough water for the missionaries to bathe or wash their clothes. Liholiho himself intended to leave Kailua and reside permanently in Honolulu.

Thurston began to preach in English, which baffled the Hawaiians. Dr. Holman treated the sick but encountered opposition by the *kāhuna lapaʻau* (medical practitioners) whose influence was strong while Liholiho remained in Kailua.

The rest of the company went to Honolulu on the *Thaddeus* to set up mission headquarters there. Honolulu was a rowdy and rough waterfront town, consisting of about a hundred grass houses in two clusters; one at the harbor and the other near Nuʻuanu Stream. Along this stream were a few better homes belonging to ship captains and merchants. At first, the new arrivals stayed in some of these homes because Governor Boki of Oʻahu, at Liholiho's direction, would not let them build houses of their own. After considerable delay, Liholiho decided they could remain for one year and permitted them to build a row of grass houses where Kawaiahaʻo Church is located today. At the time the site was nearly a mile from Honolulu along the footpath to Waikīkī. The one-year limitation was either forgotten or ignored by Liholiho when the time expired.

In Honolulu, the missionaries were grateful for the opportunity to bathe and to wash their accumulated laundry in the fresh water of Nuʻuanu Stream. Though the climate was healthy, the missionaries did not adapt to native customs. Continuing to wear clothes suitable for New England, they suffered from the heat and humidity. Nor would they eat the nutritious local fare, but subsisted on the stale food they had brought with them and on what was given to them by passing ships. When Hawaiians first saw the missionary ladies in their bonnets, it seemed to them the bonnets were extensions of their necks, which thus appeared to be very long. The ladies were called "long necks," and after a time all missionaries were referred to this way.

While their wives remained in Honolulu, Samuel Ruggles and Samuel Whitney sailed for Kauaʻi on the *Thaddeus* to return Prince Humehume to his home. Ruggles wrote in his journal, "beautiful plains and fruitful valleys present themselves to view . . ."

When the party landed at Waimea, King Kaumualiʻi, overjoyed at seeing his son, welcomed the two missionaries warmly and pressed noses with them in the Hawaiian custom of greeting. He urged them to establish a missionary station at Waimea. Ruggles and Whitney were impressed with the rich land and their cordial welcome by both Kaumuali'i and his chiefess Kapule. They returned, laden with lavish gifts, to Honolulu, where the brethren contrasted the warmth of Kaumuali'i with the coolness of Liholiho and Boki. Samuel Ruggles and his wife Nancy, with Samuel and Mercy Whitney, returned to establish the first missionary station on Kaua'i at Waimea. They settled in a grass house near Fort Elizabeth, close to Kaumuali'i's residence. The two couples shared the house assigned them by hanging a mat between them. They started a day school and held religious services outdoors.

Meanwhile, Lucia Holman's health began to fail under the trying conditions at Kailua. In 1821, Dr. Holman took her to Lahaina, Maui, where the climate and conditions were better, in hopes of improving her health. He continued to care for the missionaries and the Hawaiians, sailing to other islands. When Bingham heard the Holmans had left Kailua, he was furious they had not obeyed his orders. When Holman was called to Honolulu to treat the master of a ship, incidentally saving his life, Bingham threatened to exclude Holman from the mission and to take his medical supplies and instruments if the couple did not return to Kailua. Thus continued the conflict that had begun months before over a basket of fruit.

Saddened at this, the Holmans sailed to Kaua'i because both Mercy Whitney and Nancy Ruggles were expecting and Dr. Holman wanted to deliver them. Also, Lucia Holman had not seen her brother Samuel Ruggles in some time. In due course, Dr. Holman delivered the babies of both ladies. The Holmans were entranced by the beauty of the island and found Kaumuali'i to be so hospitable they decided to stay while pondering what to do about the problem with Bingham. Thus Holman became the first missionary doctor to serve on Kaua'i. Kaumuali'i supplied most of the Holmans' needs, so the prospect of being cut off by Bingham was of less concern. The Holmans remained on Kaua'i for four months without resolving the situation with Bingham.

Meanwhile, Bingham had called a meeting of the missionaries in Honolulu and read a list of his grievances against Dr. Holman. He demanded a unanimous vote on Holman's excommunication. To a devout believer such as Holman, this meant exclusion from the Kingdom of Heaven. The missionaries had no choice: a divided vote would have split the mission from that day on. Holman was excommunicated and his wife was suspended. The Holmans lost heart and sailed for Boston on October 10, 1821.

This left no doctor in the Islands for the missionaries or the Hawaiians, which did not appear to concern Bingham.

Samuel Ruggles was in poor health, and Nancy only a little less so, so the couple did not accomplish much in Waimea. In December of 1822, they moved six miles east to Hanapēpē, where they started a small school. The following summer they left Kaua'i for Hilo, where a mission station had just been established. After a few years there, they returned to the United States.

The Whitneys, however, stayed on at Waimea. Kaumuali'i had given them two fishponds and tracts of land in Waimea Valley and Hanapēpē, including the services of about 50 workers. Together, they produced more than enough food for themselves, the workers, and the workers' families. In 1820, Whitney experimented with grinding cane to produce sugar and molasses. He employed skilled Chinese immigrants living in the area, and the small mill yielded enough for the Whitney family table. This was the first sugar production on Kaua'i. By the end of April 1821, the Whitneys had built a large wooden house with glass windows and a wooden floor near Waimea River. In their new house the Whitneys continued both a school and church services. Then they built a "great thatched church" on the west bank of Waimea River.

The instructions from the American Board of Commissioners for Foreign Missions to the first company of missionaries included the phrase, "You are to obtain an adequate knowledge of the language of the people . . ." This admonition was given for a good reason. The missionaries knew little of the language when they were appointed, despite the presence of Hawaiian students at Cornwall. At that time in the Boston area there were a dozen lists of Hawaiian words and their English equivalents, which had been assembled between 1778 and 1819 by voyagers from many nations, but there is not a hint in the records the missionaries had availed themselves of these. William Anderson, who had landed at Waimea with Cook, spoke Tahitian and had prepared the best list, incorporating 229 words and phrases plus a group he labeled "as at Otahiete." Hiram Bingham did familiarize himself with a few Hawaiian words and phrases, and Samuel Ruggles had worked out a tentative alphabet with one of the Hawaiian students at Cornwall, but that was it.

On the long voyage to Hawai'i the only mention of language study is in Sybil Bingham's journal. She recorded the ladies would gather on deck from time to time to do so. This almost total lack of interest seems surreal in retrospect. Their intention, apparently, had been to rely upon the three Hawaiian youths, whose English was poor, as interpreters. One indication of their thinking is that they had brought *English* schoolbooks to teach the Hawaiians how to read and write their own language.

At that time the London Missionary Society (LMS) had been active in the Society Islands for 23 years, and their missionaries had become accomplished in the Tahitian language. They had learned that teaching materials had to be in the local language. Soon after arriving in the Societies the LMS missionaries had set about putting a language that had been oral for millennia into print, a feat that posed great difficulties. Nevertheless, they succeeded, were sensitive to the nuances expressed in the spoken language, and created workable printed equivalents for use in the schools they had established and for other purposes. These works, refined by use over twenty years, were printed in London and used throughout the Society Islands. They also served reasonably well in the LMS mission stations and schools among the Maori in New Zealand. That this material existed was widely known years before the *Thaddeus* set sail, yet the ABCFM had made no effort to obtain it. For two years after the missionaries' arrival in Hawai'i the small printing press they had brought with them remained idle.

Perhaps Bingham's reluctance to encourage the missionaries to pursue language studies was because he feared a challenge to his authority, in that his own facility with the Hawaiian language was poor and had been arduously acquired. There is one clue this may have been the case. A long-time resident of Honolulu, Don Francisco de Paula Martin, spoke Hawaiian fluently, and his services as an interpreter were employed regularly by ships arriving at Honolulu. Bingham wrote in his journal, "Calling on the interpreter, Mr. Martin . . ." and referred to him numerous times; but he wrote nothing about utilizing Martin's expertise, nor is there evidence that he did.

The printer Elisha Loomis had recognized the importance of diacritical marks in rendering the Hawaiian language into print and asked the ABCFM for special type that included them. When it arrived after a delay of several months, it was the wrong size and could not be used.

In 1822, a ship carrying two London Missionary Society missionaries from Tahiti was blown off course and arrived in Honolulu. It happened that Bingham was on Kaua'i at the time, and the LMS missionaries were received courteously by the rest of the brethren. One of the visitors was Reverend William Ellis, who preached to Hawaiians the following day in the Tahitian language. He was understood by them without an interpreter. The

Hawaiians had listened to the preaching of the American missionaries for two years, but Ellis' sermon was the first they had understood. Ellis agreed to remain for a time and quickly adapted to the Hawaiian language through his knowledge of Tahitian. With his facility in speaking the language he accomplished more in four months than all of the American missionaries together had achieved to that date. At their urging, he returned from the Societies to Honolulu in 1823 and stayed for 18 months. He caused Bingham considerable concern because he advised changing the orthography Bingham had all but decided upon to a more workable one based upon LMS experience in the Societies and elsewhere in Polynesia. Meanwhile, Loomis produced the first speller in Hawaiian without diacriticals. It was an eight-page booklet containing the alphabet, numbers, and simple phrases.

In 1825, Bingham appointed a committee to decide upon the orthography of the Hawaiian language. The committee consisted of himself and two other missionaries, who polled the members of the mission. Based upon their responses the committee decided in 1826 how the Hawaiian language was to be put into print. Thus, seven missionaries, whose own knowledge was far from perfect, decided how Hawaiians were to read and write their own language.

By "vote of the Mission," the alphabet was to consist of twelve letters. The five vowels (a, e, i, o, u) were to be pronounced as in the Latin languages on the European continent because of the wide variation in pronunciation of vowels in English. Perhaps by chance, this had been the direction taken by the LMS and others who had translated Polynesian languages.

The consonants presented a problem. The Tahitian sound similar to "t" made with the tongue at the dental ridge had become more of a "k" in most parts of Hawai'i. The Hawaiians, as well as other Polynesians, were comfortable with the entire range of sounds between the two. As long as the sound started with the tongue somewhere on the palate they understood. The committee voted for "k" because Bingham believed a decision had to be made on either of the two extremes in the English alphabet. A similar situation pertained with "l" and "r." The Hawaiian sound was neither one, but somewhere between the two. Also contributing to the consonantal chaos were "v" and "w." The Hawaiian sound was softer than an English "v," but not so aspirant as "w," and pronunciation varied with its place in a word. Again, a continuum was made into a dichotomy in order to conform with English. The missionaries were actually changing the Hawaiian language. The votes were counted, and seven consonants (h, k, l, m, n, p, w) survived.

These and other decisions did not seem that important to the American missionaries at the time but caused serious difficulties later. One example is that spoken Hawaiian incorporates a glottal stop similar to the catch in the voice saying "oh-oh." Today this is represented in print by a reversed apostrophe termed a hamzah, a word taken from Arabic orthography. In Hawai'i, it is more often referred to by its Hawaiian name *'okina*, which means "severance" or "separation." In the evolution of the Hawaiian language from ancestral Polynesian, it represents a missing consonant in the "t-k" spectrum. It is a letter that must be represented in print but had been disregarded by the missionaries. They also ignored the lengthening of certain vowels in the spoken language which required a second diacritical. The importance of these can be illustrated by an example using both. The word *pau* without a glottal stop means "finished"; but pā'u with the "a" stressed or held slightly longer in pronunciation and a glottal stop as indicated, is the word for soot obtained from burning kukui nuts for use in tattooing. The word *pā'ū* with both vowels stressed and a glottal stop means "a woman's skirt."

Stressed or lengthened (not accented) vowels are frequent in Hawaiian and, as shown, change the meaning of the word. Today the stress in pronunciation is indicated in print by a macron over the vowel, a term taken from Greek orthography. In Hawaiian it is called *kahakō*. An example of the importance of the *kahakō* alone is the word mana. Without either "a" stressed it means "spiritual power," while māna with the first "a" stressed is a chewed mass of food; mānā with both vowels stressed means "arid" or "dry."

The missionaries were in a strange land working with a strange language, and they lacked linguistic training, so some forbearance is called for. Still, their errors and omissions have worked their way back from the printed word to the spoken one and have profoundly affected the Hawaiian language for more than a century and a half. The first dictionary of the Hawaiian language to attempt the consistent use of diacritical marks was published in 1945. There has been a sincere and continuing effort since then to undo the harm that was done. At the present time, hyphenation is being introduced to separate the components of important proper names so that their derivation may be better understood.

The second company of missionaries had arrived in Honolulu aboard the *Thames* on April 27, 1823. With them was Abraham Blatchely, M.D., and his wife Jemima. Hiram Bingham, perhaps chastened by more than a year without a physician, treated Blatchely more mildly than he had Holman and allowed him to pursue his duties without interference. Dr. Blatchely, the only physician in the Islands, was perhaps too conscientious for his own good in responding to the need for his services. He visited all the Islands frequently caring for missionaries and treating Hawaiians. Horses were scarce then, so he walked everywhere. He slept and ate where he could. His wife Jemima often accompanied him and shared his hardships. When she remained in Honolulu during his absences, she devoted long hours, day and night, to caring for the ill herself. This hard life wearied both of them; they became ill and left the Islands in 1827.

Ka'ahumanu honored Kaua'i with a visit in 1822 and toured the island with Samuel Whitney. She enthusiastically approved of the schools Whitney had established and requested more spelling books from the "long necks" in Honolulu, saying, "Many are the people, few are the books." Her interest and influence stimulated education on Kaua'i, so that by 1831 there were 200 schools with 9,000 students on the island. For three years Samuel Whitney's role on Kaua'i was limited to that of a teacher because he had not completed studies for the ministry before embarking on the *Thaddeus*. He was alone at Waimea and acutely felt the call to bring religion to the Hawaiians. In 1823, Bingham, Ellis, and Thurston visited him and gave him license to preach. That year was a landmark for Kōloa. Hawaiians gathered there in a thatched structure, and Whitney came from Waimea to conduct the first Christian services ever held in Kōloa. Whitney was ordained in 1825.

The Whitneys left Waimea in 1837 and moved to the Wailua River, where they built a stone house and continued their work. They lived in Wailua until Whitney was taken ill in 1845 and went to Lahaina Luna, Maui to recuperate. He died there that year. Mercy returned to Waimea to serve the Hawaiians in whatever way she could until her death in 1872. Both of the Whitney graves are in the cemetery behind the Waimea Foreign Church.

Reverend Peter Gulick and his wife Fanny had arrived with the third company in 1828 to assist Whitney at Waimea. In 1834, they were transferred to Kōloa, where they established the second missionary station on Kaua'i. They left their comfortable sandstone home with a thatched roof they had built in Waimea, and with their five small sons settled in a *hale pili*, or thatched house, with a dirt floor, near Maulili Pond at Kōloa. Gulick built a small school nearby and held services there on Sundays. In 1835, Gulick organized the first Christian church in Kōloa in the schoolhouse. By this time "Toloa" was favored as a port of call by ship captains over "Waima-ah." At Kōloa Landing the missionaries and their families on Kaua'i received letters, supplies, gifts from friends, and occasional articles of furniture that arrived by ship.

An elderly Hawaiian lady helped the Gulicks in the kitchen of their home in Kōloa. The Gulicks disapproved of the use of tobacco, so she puffed her pipe secretly. One day, in danger of being discovered, she hurriedly hid her pipe in the thatch siding. The Gulicks' house burned to the ground. From then on the missionaries on Kaua'i used adobe and rock for the walls of their structures, but the roofs were still thatched. Gulick and his Hawaiian congregation built a chapel in 1837 where Kōloa Church stands today; the next year the parishioners built an adobe home for the Gulicks where the parsonage is located now. Gulick made certain the kitchen of this house was separate from the main structure, which was the Hawaiian custom for just that reason. Their residence was used both as a home and school. It stood for over fifty years, and was later occupied by Dr. James W. Smith and others. The Gulick home became a landmark in Kōloa.

The small thatch school near Maulili had deteriorated by 1841, so Hawaiians in Kōloa helped Gulick build a second school immediately *makai* of the present site of Kōloa School. The Hawaiian language was used as the basis of instruction as in all schools in Hawai'i at the time. After eight years at Kōloa, the Gulicks were transferred to Moloka'i, and later to Honolulu.

The first physician to serve on a permanent basis in Kōloa was Rev. Thomas Lafon, M.D. He and his wife, Sophia, had arrived in Honolulu with the eighth company in 1836 and were assigned to Kōloa in 1837. In addition to caring for the missionaries and Hawaiians on Kaua'i, Dr. Lafon helped in Gulick's Kōloa school and conducted religious services there. He also organized a church and school at Nāwiliwili. Gulick arranged for him to treat the workers at the sugar plantation of Ladd & Company in Kōloa, and so he became the first of a long line of plantation doctors in the Hawaiian Islands. Dr. Lafon resigned in 1841 to protest the acceptance of money from slaveholders in the United States by the American Board of Commissioners for Foreign Missions. The couple left the Islands for New England in 1842.

In 1841, Hiram Bingham had to leave Honolulu for the United States because of the illness of his wife, Sybil, who died on the mainland two years later. After that, Bingham applied to the Board several times to return to Hawai'i but his offers were declined. He spent the next several years writing an account of the early missionary efforts in Hawai'i from his own particular point of view.

Dr. James W. Smith and his wife, Melicent Knapp, with Reverend George Rowell and his wife Malvina, were the only members of the tenth company, which arrived in 1842 in Honolulu. Dr. Smith was assigned to Kōloa to replace Dr. Lafon, and the couple settled in Lafon's former house. Rowell was assigned to the station at Wai'oli on the north shore of Kaua'i. When the Gulicks left Kōloa, Dr. Smith and Melicent moved into the Gulicks' adobe house.

Rev. John F. Pogue had a short but adventurous interlude in Kōloa. He was a single man who had arrived in Honolulu with the eleventh company on July 15, 1844 after an arduous journey of 224 days during which the ship nearly was nearly lost in a storm. Maria Kapule Whitney, the daughter of Reverend and Mrs. Samuel Whitney, was also aboard, returning from her education in the United States. She had been the first missionary daughter born in the Hawaiian Islands, at Waimea in 1820. Pogue was assigned to Kōloa to assist Dr. Smith and moved into Lafon's thatched house. Three years later the house was completely destroyed by a flash flood that almost drowned Pogue and left him clinging to the branches of a large tree. Referred to for years as "the Pogue flood," it severely damaged Smith's new house, swept away most of the Hawaiian houses in Kōloa, ruined taro patches and fishponds, and even damaged the sugar mill. After recuperating under the care of Dr. Smith, Pogue married Maria Whitney, who had been living with her parents in Waimea. The couple then left Kaua'i for the island of Hawai'i.

Reverend Daniel Dole and his wife Charlotte came to Kōloa in 1855. He had been ordained in 1840 before both he and his first wife Emily became members of the ninth company, which had arrived in Honolulu in 1841. There he served as the first principal of Punahou School for missionary children. Emily died in 1844, and Dole married Charlotte Knapp in 1846. After nearly 15 years at Punahou, Dole decided his services were needed more on Kaua'i, where there was no English-language school. He resigned from Punahou and settled in Kōloa with his wife and two sons by his first wife, Emily. Dr. Smith sold him ten acres of land for one dollar and Dole built their home that year on the east side of Po'ipū Road, a short distance *makai* of the present Kōloa School. He opened a school next to his home for missionary and other English-speaking students who boarded with his family. On Sundays, the school served as a chapel where Dole conducted English services. This was the first foreign church on Kaua'i, the word "foreign" being used then to mean services were in English. In 1860, Dole built an English day school across the road. When the Hawaiian government established English as the official language of instruction in

1884, the students at Gulick's school transferred to Dole's school, and Gulick's school closed. Dole continued his educational efforts in Kōloa until his death in 1878.

Dr. Smith was ordained in 1854 and took over the religious responsibilities in Kōloa from Dole, conducting services in Gulick's 1837 adobe chapel until it blew down in a gale in 1858. Dr. Smith and his congregation then built the wooden Kōloa Church in 1859 on the same site. In an 1860 letter he wrote, "We have been successful in building a house of worship sufficiently large, substantial & commodious, & suitable to the people & the place."

After three years at Waiʻoli, Rowell and his wife Malvina were transferred to Waimea. He was energetic and enthusiastic during his first years in the new assignment. Peter Gulick had built a house there in 1829, and the sandstone foundation and walls remained. Rowell repaired and expanded the house with imported lumber and moved in. The Gulick-Rowell House still stands, under a large monkeypod tree. It is the best example of unrestored missionary architecture in Hawaiʻi and is listed on the National Register of Historic Places. Under Rowell's supervision, his parishioners commenced construction of a large sandstone church on a rise above Waimea in 1846. The Waimea Foreign Church was completed in 1854. Rowell conducted Sunday services there in English and later in the day a Hawaiian pastor did the same in Hawaiian. Although religious affiliations have changed from time to time, giving new names to the church, it stands today a magnificent monument, the last of the great missionary stone churches to be built in the Hawaiian Islands.

Unfortunately, after such a zealous start the skies seemed to darken over Rowell. Although his problems apparently had begun sometime around 1860, discretion was observed and pen not set to paper for the first few years. The earliest written record of his difficulties appears in Dr. Smith's journal of 1864 in which he laments the *hihia*, or troubles, in Waimea caused by Rowell. A letter he wrote the next year in a labored and barely legible hand to mission headquarters expresses deep concern over Rowell's "heterodox notions" on ecclesiastical matters and inattention to pastoral duties, but there was more. Later, in a letter to Gulick, he wrote that Rowell had admitted to *"kolohe me kekaki mau wahine,"* or having sinned with Hawaiian women. Mrs. Rowell was aware of this, he added, but said she had married him "for better or worse" and hoped God would forgive him.

Gulick, then in charge of mission headquarters in Honolulu, came to Waimea and patiently gathered information. A formal hearing by the Ecclesiastical Committee was held on

March 29, 1865, and Rowell was discharged from the mission and as pastor of the Waimea Foreign Church. The following Sunday, Rowell confessed his transgressions before the congregation, but in a bizarre twist, he and some followers tried to take over the church by force later that week. Failing that, he started conducting services for Hawaiians in his home. He also openly resumed his affair with a Hawaiian woman named Emele Kamawili, who had played the melodeon in the Foreign Church, and by whom he already had a child. Some Hawaiians stood by Rowell and built the small wooden Hawaiian Church near the shore in 1858. Rowell continued as their pastor until his death in 1884. Dr. Smith cared for him during his last days.

The Waimea Hawaiian Church today is an inconspicuous wooden building opposite the police station. Although destroyed by Hurricane 'Iniki in 1992, the structure has been restored. To this day, services are conducted in the Hawaiian language for the congregation, whose members are mostly from Ni'ihau. Their older Hawaiian language and hymns are a delight to hear.

After Rowell was discharged, Smith's parish extended from Waimea to Wailua. Smith continued as pastor of Kōloa Church until resigning in 1869. This was in accordance with the decision of the Board in 1863 that all mission stations should become financially independent, and that churches have Hawaiian pastors as soon as these goals could be achieved. Although Smith was the only physician on Kaua'i, he charged little or nothing and supported himself, his family, and the church in Kōloa by raising cattle and growing sugar cane with the help of the congregation.

Smith would have had his hands full with just his medical duties. In October 1848, measles was brought to Hawai'i on the American frigate *Independence* and was soon ravaging Kaua'i. Burning with fever, Hawaiians rushed into the ocean to cool off, and hundreds died. Then in 1853, smallpox came to Kaua'i. Smith vaccinated most of the residents of Kaua'i and Ni'ihau and quarantined active cases, so only a handful died on the two islands. However, it spread like wildfire elsewhere in Hawai'i, especially the larger settlements such as Honolulu. In those days, leprosy was difficult to diagnose, but it was probably brought to Hawai'i in 1854 or earlier on at least one of five ships arriving from China crowded with laborers. In any event, Hawaiians called leprosy *ma'i Pākē*, or Chinese disease. For this disease and endemic tuberculosis there were no cures, and all Smith could offer was his compassion. The venereal diseases that so concerned Cook continued to run rampant, joined by diseases of more recent introduction, such as whooping cough and influenza.

In 1860, Smith commented in his journal about developments at Kōloa:

Here is a seaport, not a harbor, but a good anchorage in an open roadstead; and 2 or 3 vessels ply regularly between this place and Honolulu. It is a 'port of entry' and during spring and fall whale ships—20 or 30 in number—touch here for supplies. About two miles from the landing is Doctor Wood's plantation, formerly Ladd & Co.'s. It gives employment to 6 to 8 foreigners and to from 100 to 150 natives. There are in the place about 25 foreigners including 4 females [in the margin he wrote 'Mrs. Wood, Mrs. Burbank, Mrs. Dole & Mrs. Smith'] besides about a dozen children. There are three retail stores and a post office in the place. Here is our new church standing on high ground and seen far at sea forming a landmark for ships approaching the port. In Kōloa also is Mr. Dole's school for the children of missionaries and others—here also is an English school for native children with 23 pupils taught by my two daughters; and in the district are 6 government schools with about 110 scholars.

Dr. Smith died in 1887, and Melicent in 1891. They are buried in Kōloa in the private Smith-Waterhouse graveyard. When the Kōloa Church was rebuilt in 1929, a small wooden box was found beneath the pulpit with a note dated Sept 9, 1859 and signed "Rev. J. W. Smith, Pastor." The box contained newspapers of the time, a list of church trustees, and the names of the carpenters who had rebuilt the church.

The contributions of the American missionaries in Hawai'i and to the small town of Kōloa are far too great to be summarized here. It is often said of them that they came to do good and did very well indeed, but it was their offspring who entered business and became wealthy. An overlooked result of missionary activities is that Hawai'i eventually became an American state. From the time of Cook's arrival, the Hawaiian Islands had been under the influence of Great Britain more than any other outside power. Largely because of the missionaries, the Hawaiian government began to come under increasing American influence by the middle of the nineteenth century, and this was not to change thereafter. The culmination was statehood for Hawai'i in 1959. Other factors also led to statehood, but they are so many, and their interactions so complex, that the subject is beyond a book on Kōloa.

James William Smith

The Smith-Waterhouse family collection

In all, 153 missionaries were sent by the American Board of Commissioners for Foreign Missions, the last ones in 1848. Another 28 Protestant missionaries came independently, as well as priests and clergy of the Catholic Church and representatives of other denominations from the western world. To this day, these missionary names redound in the life of the Islands: Alexander, Andrews, Baldwin, Bingham, Bishop, Castle, Cooke, Dole, Gulick, Judd, Lyman, Lyons, Rice, Spalding, Thurston, and Wilcox, among others.

Tall Cane

Kōloa, "Tall Cane," is an appropriate name for the place where the sugar industry in Hawai'i started. In ancient times, Kōloa Marsh was famous for its large size and the sugar cane growing abundantly around the edge without attendance. For this reason, Hawaiians called the marsh Kōloa. As it was also the major landmark in the area, they named the ahupua'a for the marsh. After contact, the small settlement that was to become the town was called Kōloa, its landing Kōloa Landing, and the sugar mill Kōloa Mill. When Kōloa District was separated from Puna District early in this century, the town of Kōloa was the largest in the district, so the name was given to the district. But some ambiguities about the derivation of the name Kōloa exist and should be cleared up.

The most credible reference, *Place Names of Hawai'i* by Pukui, Elbert, and Mo'okini, describes the above locations with the name capitalized and with a kahakō, or macron, over the first "o" as Kōloa, but gives no meaning for the name. Throughout the reference this indicates either no meaning is known or the authors disagree among themselves. In these cases, two or more differing accounts might be given, or none, with an interesting anecdote instead. For Kōloa, a legend is mentioned about a large black rock called Pali-o-kō-loa that was broken off on one side to form a *pali*, or cliff. This legend is vague and laden with *kaona*, or hidden meanings, not interpretable today. It gives no clue as to the supposed location of the rock, nor has anybody ever seen such a rock on Kaua'i. Hawaiian legends which concern nonexistent places and events that never took place are not uncommon

The Smiths' English Boarding School for Hawaiian girls, about 1867. Dr. Smith himself can be seen at the far right.

Kaua'i Museum

and according to scholars and Hawaiians alike were never intended to be taken literally.

Pukui and Elbert's *Hawaiian Dictionary*, the most authoritative of its kind, defines the word "koloa," without capitalization or a macron over the first "o," as "Hawaiian duck." The indigenous Hawaiian species of non-migratory duck, *koloa maoli* (now endangered), did inhabit the Kōloa Marsh, but was widespread throughout the Islands. Hawaiians traveled from island to island and would have been well aware of this. Also, they were very careful about putting the proper stress on vowels. For these reasons the origin of the name could not be this duck.

In the same dictionary the word "kōloa," without capitalization but with a macron over the first vowel, is defined as a long cane with a crook. Such canes were used by elderly Hawaiians on all the Islands much as shorter canes are used today, so this origin of the place name Kōloa has not been advanced by anyone.

Reducing the word to its two components, *kō*, with the "o" sound stressed or held slightly longer, and correctly written with a macron over it as "ō," is defined in the same dictionary simply as sugar cane. The word *loa* can mean "distance," "length," "height," "distant," "long," "tall," "far," or "permanent," depending upon the context in which it is used. Because "long" is listed just before "tall," careless reading of the definition by those not familiar with the Hawaiian language may be the reason Kōloa is sometimes erroneously translated as "long cane." English-language dictionaries point out in their explanatory notes that glosses are listed in the order they came into use historically. This lexicographic term is derived from the Latin word for "tongue" and may be more familiar to us as the root of the word "glossary." The term is roughly equivalent to "alternate meaning." Lexicographers preparing Hawaiian-English dictionaries are denied the luxury of tracing back the date a Hawaiian word entered into that language because of the lack of documentary sources. Instead, they have adopted the custom of listing glosses according to their frequency of usage, and the appropriateness of a particular gloss is determined entirely by its context. Hawaiians observed sugar cane growing vertically for two years to maturity; then, with the swish of an adze, it was horizontal only for as long as it took to be cut into pieces and chewed. Following the Hawaiian language rules of relevancy and context, the choice of definition for *loa* as applied to sugar cane is "tall."

When *loa*, in this context meaning "tall," is recombined with *kō*, and capitalized as a name, the result is Kōloa or Tall Cane. The name of the marsh, the *ahupua'a* around it, the town,

Although Rev. Whitney produced a small amount of sugar by grinding came in 1820, the first significant production on Kaua'i was in 1825-6 at Māhā'ulepū near Kōloa by Chinese who brought these granite grinders and "receiver" with them from China.

Hawai'i State Archives

the district, and the landing are all pronounced with a lengthened first "ō."

The author was fortunate in having the ambiguities mentioned above cleared up in 1976. After purchasing property in the Kōloa area, and while doing research for another book, he happened to encounter Mary Kawena Pukui at the Bishop Museum in Honolulu. She had been his teacher of the language at the University of Hawai'i many years before, so he felt no hesitancy in asking her about the derivation of the name. She graciously offered the explanation given in the first paragraph of this chapter. It hardly need be mentioned she stressed or lengthened the first "ō" every time she pronounced "Kōloa."

Both groups of Polynesian settlers had brought sugar cane with them to Hawai'i. They chewed it as a sweet, and for energy, but did not extract sugar from it. Grinding the cane and making sugar from the extracted juice began in China. Marco Polo reported tasting sugar there in 1270. The first Chinese to come to Hawai'i arrived independently beginning in 1789. They had been hired in China as carpenters, cooks, and crew on trading vessels that stopped over in the Hawaiian Islands to provision and winter.

Among the Chinese who stayed, a few knew the process of making sugar. One, Wang Tze-Chin, using granite grinders and boilers from China, produced the first sugar in Hawai'i on Lāna'i in 1802. After processing one crop he abandoned the effort. From 1820 to 1832, Chinese were involved in sugar production on Kaua'i in small mills at Waimea, Kōloa, Māhā'ulepū, and Lāwa'i. The raw sugar and molasses from these operations were consumed locally. None of these endeavors was commercial and none lasted for more than a few months. What had hindered these early ventures had nothing to do with the skill or dedication of the entrepreneurs. Rather, they had encountered insurmountable difficulties with local chiefs who controlled access to both labor and land.

On July 27, 1833, three young men arrived in Honolulu from New England aboard the ship *Hellespont*: William Ladd, Peter Alan Brinsmade, and William Hooper. They formed a mercantile company known as Ladd & Company that supplied provisions to whaling ships. Successful in this enterprise, they began looking for other opportunities. Owning a branch store at Kōloa, they were familiar with the area and knew that sugar cane grew well there.

Early in 1835, William Hooper came to Kōloa to look into the possibilities of growing cane commercially. He took note of the fertile soil, a water supply adequate for irrigation and to power a mill, and the presence of a suitable landing nearby. Hooper returned to Honolulu to recommend the growing of sugar cane at Kōloa, and the company decided to do so. The changes this decision would bring about in the ensuing years may be put into perspective by a traveler's description of Kōloa in 1834 as "a mere hamlet, seldom visited by even a missionary."

On July 29, 1835, Ladd & Company obtained a 50-year lease on a 980-acre tract of land in the Kōloa area east of Waihohonu Stream, and a mill site at Maulili waterfall. Signed by Kamehameha III and Governor Kaikio'ewa of Kaua'i, this lease was the first of its kind in the history of Hawai'i. It was also the first formal recognition of the right of someone other than a chief to control land. This profoundly affected traditional notions of land tenure dominated by the chiefly hierarchy throughout the Islands.

The lease specified that " . . . the said Brinsmade, Ladd and Hooper, shall be allowed at their wish to hire native laborers to work on said land . . ." provided they compensate Kamehameha III and Kaikio'ewa for the use of native workers, who were to be exempt from taxation by the chiefs. Taxation of Hawaiian commoners traditionally consisted of labor and products rendered to the chiefs upon demand and at the time of the *Makahiki.*

In addition, plantation workers were to receive wages and other benefits themselves. These changes in land and labor use would have more far-reaching effects than anyone, including the signatories, could have foreseen. The idea that workers would receive wages to spend as they wished gave them an independence they could not comprehend at first. As Joesting wrote, "There was nothing in their history, no precedent, no legend, that could bridge this gap."

William Hooper, the youngest partner, was chosen to run Kōloa Plantation. Neither a farmer nor an engineer, he had unbelievable tenacity as compensation, which he would need. Hooper put twelve acres into cane in 1835. Other than a few stalks planted by Hawaiian farmers on the banks of their taro ponds, this was the first stand of sugar cane planted and cultivated in the Islands. Hooper built the first sugar mill at Maulili in 1836 using koa-wood rollers and whaling try-pots to boil the juice. The mill produced 100 barrels of molasses from the first crop, but very little sugar. The wooden rollers wore out rapidly and the try-pots proved unsatisfactory. The following year Hooper built a new dam and mill just downstream, using iron rollers and copper boiling pans. He hired 25 Hawaiians to tend the fields and two Chinese to boil sugar in the mill. In its first year the new mill produced 30 tons of sugar and 170 barrels of molasses. The raw sugar was dried in the sun on *lau hala* mats, then put into woven bags with rawhide handles. A fascinating description of the oper-

This grass house is similar to those built by Kōloa Plantation near Maulili Pond for Hawaiian plantation workers starting in 1835. William Hooper himself lived in one like this.

⌒ Bishop Museum

ation of the plantation in these first difficult years is found in Alexander's *Koloa Plantation 1835-1935.*

Labor was Hooper's most serious problem. Only Hawaiians were available, and the chiefs interfered constantly because they saw their authority over the *maka'āinana* being undermined. Hooper railed most bitterly in his letters about the inability to get the *kanakas* (native Hawaiians) to work as he desired.

James Jarves, a frequent early visitor to Kaua'i, commented on the difficulties facing Ladd & Company in the *Hawaiian Spectator:*

> All the difficulties incidental to a new country and a total want of agricultural implements, and an ignorant, indolent people, unavoidably retarded the immediate execution of their [Ladd & Co.] plans. The jealousy of the petty chiefs, in seeing their lands thus alienated, proved, for some time, a great obstacle to their success. They carried their opposition so far as to forbid all sale of provisions . . .

In truth, Hawaiian workers were not the most suitable for Hooper's purpose. The Western entrepreneurial spirit emphasized individual initiative, investment of capital, enterprise, hard work, and ownership. In the Hawaiian tradition, chiefs controlled the use of the land and all resources, with complete authority over their people to the point of death. Whatever the *maka'āinana* produced was subject to the demands of the chiefly hierarchy at any time. In addition, the Hawaiian ethos placed high value on communal customs of sharing whatever one possessed with members of their *'ohana* (extended family) as well as with others. Ownership of anything by the ordinary man or woman was a nebulous concept at best. Hawaiians garnered an adequate living from the ocean and their taro fields with much less effort than working in the cane fields. Following traditional ways, they did not produce much excess for the chiefs to claim, or which they would have to share with others.

By 1838, workers and their families lived near the Maulili mill in grass houses, as did Hooper himself. His report for that year referred to "vassals, including men, women and children and self—101, which look to me for their daily poe [poi]."

James Jarves' description of Kōloa during this period is illustrative.

> The surf breaks heavily along the shore, but a safe landing is effected at the mouth of a small stream.

Clusters of native dwellings are scattered on the plain, but the principal village is situated a mile from the beach, at a short distance from the missionary buildings. These buildings, which are encircled by a pretty garden, are neat and substantial. A new church, capable of holding nearly two thousand persons, surrounded by a thatched veranda, supported by neat wooden columns, shows prettily in the distance.

Fields of sugar cane, taro, yams, and other vegetables, bespeak a more than usual attention to agriculture. The population of Kōloa, which is about three thousand, is increasing rapidly by emigrations from other districts.

They at present have eighty acres [of sugar cane] under cultivation, and intend the ensuing year to cultivate two hundred more . . . With the leases orders were given for thirty-six men, as laborers on the two estates; as the common people are held rigidly by the chiefs, it was with difficulty that they could be obtained; and when procured proved to be the offscourings of the Islands.

By 1838, a local Saturday market had been established, which Jarves depicts as follows:

At sunrise the little shops on the plantations are open, to redeem the paper money, and purchase such articles as the natives bring for sale. Crowds of them in the rudest attire, or no attire at all, early throng the house . . . One brings vegetables, another fish, fine tapas, mats . . . Women leading fat pigs, which ever and anon they press to their bosoms to still their deafening lamentations, join the throng; while dog and fowl add their voices to the dulcet strain.

In contrast to this Saturday scene, Jarves was struck by the New England Sabbath at Kōloa. Hundreds of well-dressed Hawaiians, responding to the call of a sonorous conch shell, "are seen quietly wending their way to the house of God." The missionaries at Kōloa and Waimea were supportive of the sugar industry. Some hoped the profits would be "devoted to the support of schools or churches, charitable institutions or internal improvements in the nation."

Hooper made many innovations on Kōloa Plantation in the first years. Because of the shortage of coins, he instituted the use of scrip for purchases at the plantation's store. This scrip was the first paper money in Hawai'i. Initially, Hooper wrote denominations on pieces of cardboard, but he soon discovered his workers were counterfeiting these. The Chinese were especially adept. Even after Hooper started signing the scrip, Chinese forgers duplicated his signature so well Hooper himself could hardly distinguish genuine scrip from counterfeit. In 1839, he asked the Honolulu headquarters of Ladd & Company to print scrip from engraved copper plates and, to foil the counterfeiters, incorporate a background of "fine waved lines, or a delicate net work, and the border highly wrought." Not only was this scrip redeemed at the plantation store for goods, it also became widely accepted by all merchants on Kaua'i. With its use, the traditional barter system of Hawai'i began to change.

Despite Hooper's innovations and indefatigable efforts, the enterprise operated at a continual loss. After three years Hooper was so discouraged he left. The plantation continued under other managers employed by Ladd & Company, each of whom tried to make it profitable. They encountered similar problems, among them the first labor dispute ever to occur in Hawai'i. In July of 1841, the workers demanded a higher wage and cash in payment instead of scrip. The strike was not organized; while one group refused to work, others did. Edward Beecher, in *Working in Hawai'i: A Labor History*, quotes a contemporary letter writer who put it succinctly: "the workers failed to carry their point."

An illustrative account of a venture similar to that of Ladd & Company appears in *The Sandwich Island Mirror* of April 15, 1840. After witnessing the start of Hooper's operation, William French, a Honolulu merchant, brought equipment and skilled laborers from China to Waimea in the fall of 1835, with the understanding he would process Governor Kaikio'ewa's cane from the area. Under the governor's direction Hawaiian workers were to cut and haul the cane to French's mill. In return, Kaikio'ewa would lease land to French to grow his own cane. Not only was Kaikio'ewa's cane slow and irregular in coming to the mill, but the lease for the land French wanted was not forthcoming. After three years of frustrating effort, during which he had been able to process only a small amount of cane, French abandoned the project and shipped his equipment to Honolulu, where he sold it.

The managers of Kōloa Plantation persevered. The plantation provided housing for the workers as well as plots of land for them to plant taro and keep animals. In addition, they were supplied with fish and *poi* on the days they worked. At Kōloa Landing, near the mouth of Waikomo Stream, supplies and equipment were brought in and sugar and molasses shipped out. Ships anchored offshore in the bay or tacked to-and-fro while passengers and cargo were rowed to and from the rocky beach. In 1840, a stone house for the plantation manager was built east of the mill, as was more substantial housing for the workers and several other buildings.

The king, local chiefs, and even missionaries put land into cane which the mill processed on half shares, soon exceeding its capacity. In 1841, a third mill was built on Waikomo Stream just below the confluence of Waihohonu and 'Ōma'o streams. In Louisiana, during this period, the sugar industry was flourishing, so modern equipment available in the United States was brought over for the new mill.

Financial problems continued, in no small part engendered by the chiefs, who constantly tried to reassert their influence over the workers. Their interference finally caused Ladd & Company to withdraw from the undertaking in 1845. That they had held on this long was due to Hooper's efforts at the start, and the fact that Kamehameha III had signed the lease, providing some leverage with the local chiefs. Although the endeavor ultimately failed, in its first ten years of operation Kōloa Plantation had initiated many changes in the traditional way of life on the island. Perhaps most important, the endeavor established the pattern followed by all subsequent plantations in the Hawaiian Islands.

One far-reaching consequence of Ladd & Company's experience was commented upon by a writer for the *Polynesian* of June 19, 1841:

> When the workers found that their time and labor was worth something more to them than hard words and little food, they were not slow in letting their rulers know it. The result has been that they have enjoyed more personal freedom ever since, and their condition has been gradually improving.

Kōloa Plantation itself survived under new owners. Dr. Robert Wood, a physician and Hooper's brother-in-law, was the first of them. In 1847, he obtained a new lease for approximately 2,200 acres of land and began to purchase other parcels. Wood bought a ship to transport supplies and sugar. He also improved Kōloa Landing, which he described in 1848:

> A stone wharf and slip or dock; a boat or lighter of ten tons burden with a cradle for hauling up; two buoys, one near the wharf for convenience, at which smaller vessels can ride in four and a half fathoms of water, the outer buoy for safety is in seven and a half fathoms of water, at which vessels of two or three thousand tons can ride securely, say, ten months in the year.

During the early decades of Kōloa Plantation, other sugar plantations had started up on the island. One was to result in the ascendancy of Līhu'e to the principal town and seat of government on Kaua'i, replacing Wailua. When Kaikio'ewa was appointed governor, he located his home in what is now the Līhu'e District. He planned to grow sugar cane but died in 1839 before his plans could be realized. Kaikio'ewa was responsible for the name, however, which means "cold chill," the name of his previous home at a higher and chillier altitude on O'ahu. When James Jarves passed through the Līhu'e area in 1838, he found only a church built by Kaikio'ewa and a few grass houses. He commented the governor had selected Hanamā'ulu Bay as the harbor, "entirely overlooking the fact that it opened directly to the windward."

In 1849, Līhu'e Plantation was established on the site Kaikio'ewa had chosen, and the cluster of homes and stores around it was the start of the town of Līhu'e. When the first crop produced sugar two years later, the hazards of using Hanamā'ulu Bay became apparent. Starting in 1898 a series of improvements to the bay and breakwater were made, and in 1921 a dock was built at Ahukini where ships could tie up. Strong trade winds and ocean swells made the dock dangerous much of the time, especially in the winter months. In 1923, a storm tore out 78 feet of the breakwater, and the port was unusable until repairs were made. In 1950, Ahukini was abandoned in favor of Nāwiliwili. Ahukini Landing is now a quiet fishing spot frequented by local residents.

By the 1850s, the buildings around the Kōloa Plantation mill consisted of a stone barracks, mill house, storehouse, two trash houses, dwellings with outhouses, a blacksmith shop, tool house, cart house, dozens of grass houses, and a warehouse at the wharf. The town of Kōloa had been born. That decade also saw a marked increase in other crops grown around the town, elevating Kōloa to a major agricultural region. Regular interisland steamship service was established in 1853 with the coal-burning *Akamai*, ushering in more reliable shipping.

Fowler steam plows were introduced on Kōloa Plantation in 1893. These were used in pairs and pulled a device with multiple shares from one end of a field to the other by cable.

⌐ Bishop Museum

Oxcart hauling cane to Kōloa Mill about 1904.

During the 1860s, improvements to the mill and additions to the acreage under cultivation continued. When rainfall proved inadequate to water the increased acreage, the first of several irrigation systems bringing water from mountain streams was constructed. During drought conditions the mill race in Waikomo Stream was insufficient to power the mill, so a steam engine was installed in 1869. Dried bagasse, called "trash," the dried fibrous remains of the cane after it has been ground, was burned to make the steam.

In the 1870s, the most significant event was the signing of the Reciprocity Treaty of 1876 between the United States and Hawai'i. The treaty removed the tariff of approximately 30 percent on unrefined sugar entering the United States, and certain other products from both signatories were given special status. Although the United States desired closer ties with Hawai'i, the loss of import duties made Congress reluctant to embrace the treaty in the first place, then to renew it when it expired. Only when the Kingdom offered the United States exclusive use of Pearl Harbor in 1887 was the treaty formally renewed. Anticipating hefty earnings as a result of the treaty, Kōloa Plantation put more land into cane, leasing and cultivating Māhā'ulepū Valley in 1887. Kōloa sugar production more than tripled during the 1870s as a consequence. Production remained high through the 1880s, until the McKinley Tariff of 1890 eliminated most of the benefit of the Reciprocity Treaty.

In the 1880s, the coming of the railroad was the most important event on Kōloa Plantation. Starting in 1882, the first narrow-gauge 30-inch permanent tracks were laid for cars drawn by steam locomotives. Bagged sugar, equipment, and supplies were more efficiently transported to and from Kōloa Landing, but the most important benefit was realized during harvesting. Oxcarts, which had previously carried the cut cane to the mill, were slow and frequently mired down in the mud. Cane often spoiled before it could reach the mill. When a cane field was to be harvested, the permanent tracks were temporarily extended by lighter sections of rail. About 12 to 15 feet long and weighing 170 to 180 pounds, the sections could be moved from one area to another. Locomotives did not venture on the portable track because it was not sturdy enough. Mules or oxen hauled individual cane cars on the temporary track to and from the main line. The railroad meant that cane land could be extended far beyond the limits imposed by the slow oxcarts.

In the 1890s, several important events took place, one of which had a profound effect throughout the Islands, though little direct impact on Kōloa and the plantation. The overthrow of the Hawaiian monarchy in 1893 is a highly complex issue and, today, it has become an emotional one. Since this and subsequent political events only indirectly affected Kōloa Plantation, no more need be said about the overthrow of the Kingdom, or about the Republic that followed.

The introduction of Fowler steam plows that same year was a great innovation for sugar plantations throughout the Islands. The roots of sugar cane grow downward and do not spread widely. Furrows up to two feet deep had to be plowed prior to planting or the cane growth would be stunted and the yield poor. With as many as 20 oxen pulling a single plowshare, this was laborious. Fowler plows, operating in stationary pairs, were actually steam engines that pulled an ingenious device with multiple shares from one end of a field to the other by cable. The shares were arranged on a V-shaped frame, those on one arm facing one way and those on the other in the opposite direction. One arm would plow while the other was canted up so the device did not have to be turned around at each end.

The first "water lead" fed by mountain streams was constructed in 1869, extended in 1885, and greatly enlarged in 1893 to include tunnels and a 3,000-foot siphon traversing a wide canyon. In 1897, Kōloa Plantation dug wells to irrigate the relatively dry *ahupua‘a* of *Māhā‘ulepū*, but encountered an ineluctable law of physics: pumps could not bring water up from the water table 50 feet below the surface. This problem was solved by digging a large pit, lining it with concrete, and placing a coal-powered steam pump at the bottom of the pit. Wells and irrigation systems, including reservoirs, were necessary because sugar cane is a thirsty crop. The production of one pound of unrefined sugar requires 500 gallons of water.

The Hawaiian Sugar Planters' Association, headquartered on O‘ahu, was formed in 1895 to lend support to the industry. Its purpose was to explore the advantages of different varieties of cane, the best use of fertilizers, the most efficient irrigation techniques, and similar matters of interest to all planters. Starting in 1901 the HSPA also helped planters speak with a united voice on matters involving wages and other labor issues.

The most momentous event in the history of Kōloa Plantation up to then took place at the close of the century. In 1898 the United States annexed Hawai‘i, and the Organic Act passed by Congress in 1900 structuring the new territory nullified laws of the Hawaiian Republic not in accord with the Constitution. The Organic Act specifically prohibited labor contracts like those that had provided most of the workers on Hawaiian plantations. The work force dropped to half within a year, and increasingly strenuous efforts had to be made to obtain and retain workers. One innovation was the institution of cultivation contracts in 1902 by Kōloa Plantation. Walter McBryde had conceived of the idea through an experimental project the year before in nearby Lāwa'i with employees of McBryde Sugar Company. Kōloa Plantation took up the idea and became the first sugar plantation to demonstrate the success of cultivation contracts in an incontrovertible way. The Hawaiian Sugar Planters' Association recommended the idea be adopted by all planters in Hawai'i, but the scheme was not widely accepted until after the 1929 strike.

The purpose of the cultivation contracts was to give workers a personal interest in sugar cultivation and thus stabilize the work force. The terms of the contracts required the plantation to furnish from 50 to 200 acres of land, water, fertilizer, tools, and all services that required heavy machinery such as plowing, furrowing, and hauling cane to the mill. A house, garden, and fuel were provided for each worker and his family. On the larger tracts, several workers joined together. Payment for the cane was an agreed amount based on the weight produced.

By 1904, obtaining sufficient water to irrigate Kōloa Plantation's 1,614 acres in sugar cane had become a critical problem. Seeking a solution, the company undertook a massive engineering project to convert Kōloa Marsh into a reservoir. Completed in 1906, Kōloa Reservoir was the largest in the Islands for many decades. It soon came to be called Waitā Reservoir by the workers, an odd combination of wai, the Hawaiian word for water, and ta, the Japanese word for rice paddy.

Two adjacent plantations began to play important roles in the history of Kōloa Plantation in the opening years of the new century. Grove Farm Plantation, to the east, was the first to be established in 1870, followed by McBryde Sugar Company, to the west. The latter was the first to become involved with Kōloa Plantation, so will be described here.

Duncan McBryde, originally from Argyleshire in Scotland, settled on Kaua'i in 1856 and had two sons who would form McBryde Sugar Company. The elder McBryde raised cattle on land purchased in Wahiawa, eventually expanding the operation to include the entire *ahupua'a* of Wahiawa and a crown lease of Kalāheo. He married Elizabeth Moxley in 1860 and built a home, "Brydeswood," in the upper Wahiawa District. The couple had six children before Duncan died in 1878, at age 52. In 1886, his widow acquired the *ahupua'a* of Lāwa'i from the estate of Queen

Emma. Elizabeth McBryde moved to California a few years later but two of their sons, Alexander and Walter, remained on Kaua'i. In 1899, with financial assistance from B. F. Dillingham of Honolulu, they formed the McBryde Sugar Company. It was comprised initially of their cattle ranch, small Ele'ele Plantation with its old mill, and some cane land in Kōloa.

McBryde Sugar Company built a new mill in Wahiawa east of Ele'ele in 1902. The Hawaiians called the mill "Numila," their pronunciation of "new mill," and the name was eventually adopted by everyone. Within a few years McBryde Sugar Company was growing cane on all of the *makai* land from Hanapēpē River to Kōloa. Because the local streams were inadequate for irrigation, McBryde dug several wells and installed coal-powered pumps. The pumps proved expensive, so in 1906 the plantation constructed a hydroelectric plant on the opposite side of the island in Wainiha Valley. They brought in power 34 miles overland to operate the well pumps and run the new mill. This plant generated the first electricity on the island. McBryde also built a railroad parallel to the coast and about half a mile inland, which ran from Ele'ele Landing to Numila, and beyond to the edge of Kōloa Plantation at Waikomo Stream. In the early 1930s a spur was extended north to the town to connect with the Kōloa Plantation line behind the hospital/dispensary.

The "McBryde-Kōloa War," a locally famous dispute over water rights, took place in 1908. The management of Kōloa Plantation firmly believed it possessed rights to water from 'Ōma'o Stream, one of two sources of Waikomo Stream that powered the mill. The company built a dam on 'Ōma'o Stream and one of its tributaries to divert water through an old ditch to its fields. The McBryde brothers just as firmly believed they possessed water rights farther up 'Ōma'o Stream, and use of the water by Kōloa Mill was only permissive. What followed was a furious frenzy of building and removing a series of dams. Guards were posted with firearms by whichever side had built the dams, "to scare off the other side," but no shots were ever fired. Kōloa and McBryde finally reached a compromise: Kōloa Plantation obtained water from a tributary of 'Ōma'o Stream, and McBryde got Kōloa's land west of Waikomo Stream in exchange for McBryde's land east of it.

At this point Grove Farm Plantation near Līhu'e, established by George Norton Wilcox in 1870, entered the picture. The son of Lucy and Abner Wilcox, missionaries assigned in 1846 to Wai'oli near the shore of Hanalei Valley, George N. Wilcox first leased, then purchased, 1,000 acres of land about a mile from the Līhu'e Plantation mill, where he had his cane processed. He named the plantation for a nearby grove of *kukui* trees that has long since disappeared. In 1881, he doubled the acreage by purchasing nearly all of Ha'ikū, an *ahupua'a* that occupied most of the area between Līhu'e and the Hā'upu Range. This addition of land made Grove Farm the nearest plantation to Kōloa on the east.

Hulē'ia River in Ha'ikū, large and dependable, provided more than sufficient water for Grove Farm's use. Kōloa Plantation, with nearly 2,000 acres in cane by 1910, had a need for water that surpassed what the watershed of Waitā Reservoir could supply. In 1914, Kōloa Plantation reached an agreement with Grove Farm to dam Ku'ia Stream, which flowed into Hulē'ia River, and to construct a tunnel through the Hā'upu Range to Waitā Reservoir. At the same time, Kōloa Plantation allowed Grove Farm to build a ditch across Kōloa land to convey water to McBryde Plantation.

In the meantime, McBryde had begun to improve the facilities at Ele'ele Landing, which until then had consisted of a small wharf used by rowboats from ships anchored offshore. McBryde built a substantial breakwater, dredged the harbor, and constructed a wharf suitable for large ships to come alongside. In 1909, McBryde changed the name from Ele'ele Landing to Port Allen. In 1912, Kōloa Plantation began using Port Allen because it could accommodate ships going directly to and from the United States without transshipments of sugar in Honolulu. Port Allen was further improved by the federal government in 1923 and subsequently.

By 1912 the need for a larger and more efficient mill at Kōloa had become evident. The 1841 mill was on land leased from the Knudsen family, and a large investment in a new mill on leased land was not considered wise. Kōloa Plantation had previously purchased the *ahupua'a* of Pā'ā southeast of the town, and a large parcel of it was unproductive. A new and much larger mill was built there in 1913 about a mile from Kōloa, and the 1841 mill was closed.

Plantation records do not indicate officials were prescient in predicting the First World War, but despite this lack of foresight, construction of the new mill proved to be immensely profitable. During World War I, demand for sugar soared and no price controls were imposed. By the end of the war Kōloa Plantation was producing 9,000 tons of sugar a year with annual profits of nearly $300,000. This was the financial high point for Kōloa Plantation; unfortunately, neither the demand nor the high prices lasted past the war.

In the 1920s, tractors were introduced for plowing. They were more mobile and efficient than Fowler plows and were able to operate on irregular ground where Fowler plows could not. Within a few years all the Fowler plows had been replaced. The tractors were also used for many other tasks.

In the opening years of the 1930s, the decade of the great depression, the financial status of Kōloa plantation looked promising. John T. Moir, who took over in 1922, had instituted many measures to make the operation more remunerative. As a result, production reached a new high of 18,833 tons in 1933, but lower sugar prices translated into a net profit of only $196,295. He resigned in July of that year. His brother Hector Moir replaced him as the last manager of Kōloa Plantation, and planted a new variety of cane that eventually would have turned a substantial profit. However, the new variety required two years to mature. As production fell off in 1934 and 1935, profits for both years were low.

The chronicle of Kōloa and the plantation is momentarily suspended here in order to introduce in the next chapter the many immigrants who came to work the fields and the mill, setting the scene for the chapter following that describes the plantation way of life in Kōloa during the thirties. The year 1935 is a particularly appropriate time to review the history of labor migration to Hawaiian plantations.

The recruitment of Japanese laborers had slowed after the Gentlemen's Agreement of 1908. It stopped almost completely when a 1924 law prohibited Japanese immigration to both Hawai'i and the continental United States. As a consequence, almost complete reliance had to be placed on importing Filipino labor to sustain the industry. In 1934, however, Congress passed the Tydings-McDuffie Act establishing the mechanism for the independence of the Philippines. An unforeseen consequence was a sharp drop in the influx of Filipino workers. The inflow of laborers from other parts of the world had almost ceased by 1935.

Before ending this chapter, a closer look at the workings of the Kōloa Plantation railroad will help us understand the context of events to follow. From its start in 1882, the railroad was extended as new land was planted. The route therefore reveals much about how the plantation operated and grew. An excellent map in the back of *Alexander's Koloa Plantation 1835-1935* shows the extent of the railroad in 1935. Interested readers are advised that this map is relatively unknown. This is because it was glued into the book after printing and is just enough smaller than the pages to stay hidden. A brief verbal description follows.

The plantation was then leasing its best land on both sides of the part of "Old Government Road" that is now Maluhia Road leading into Kōloa. Beginning at the end of the railroad near Kōloa

In 1882 Kōloa Plantation began using cane trains which gradually replaced the slow oxcarts.

☞ Hawai'i State Archives

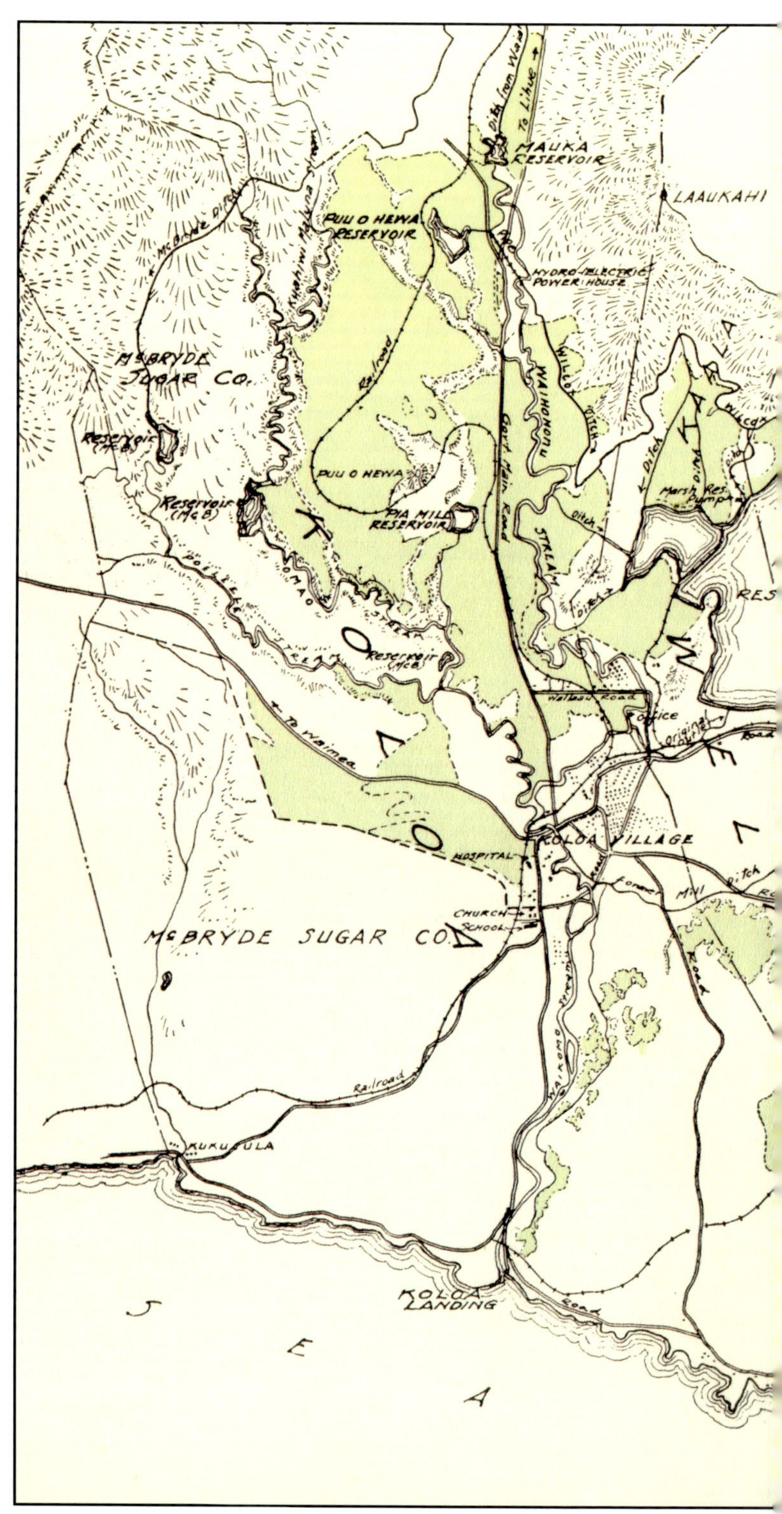
MAUKA RESERVOIR
Ditch from Wai
To Līhue
LAAUKAHI
McBryde Ditch
PUU O HEWA RESERVOIR
HYDRO-ELECTRIC POWER HOUSE
McBRYDE SUGAR CO.
RESERVOIR (McB)
Reservoir (McB)
PUU O HEWA
PIA MILL RESERVOIR
WAIHOHONU STREAM
Wilcox Ditch
Waihohonu Ditch
Marsh Res. Pump
Ditch
RES
Reservoir (McB)
Wailua Road
Office
original
Road
KOLOA VILLAGE
HOSPITAL
To Waimea
CHURCH SCHOOL
McBRYDE SUGAR CO.
Mill Ditch
Waihohu
Railroad
KUKUIULA
KOLOA LANDING
Road
S E A

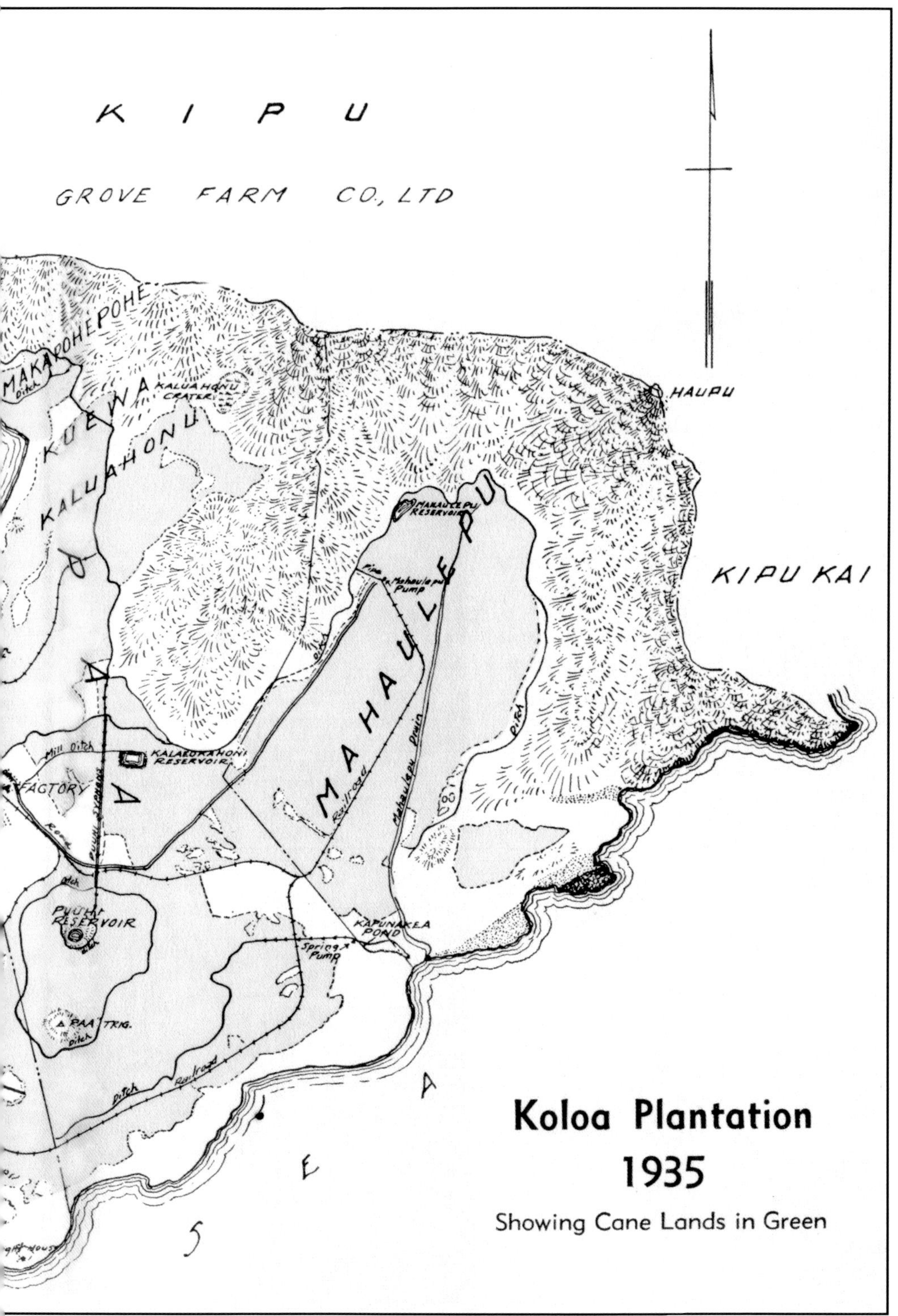

Koloa Plantation
1935

Showing Cane Lands in Green

Gap, the track wound south toward Kōloa in what appears to be a haphazard way. But it was not haphazard at all. The route was calculated for minimum grade, and to be as equidistant as possible from the east and west boundaries of the cane land to minimize the labor of harvesting.

The railroad bed is still visible where it crossed Waila'au Road between the row of supervisors' homes and Spanish Camp. From there the track led west of town to the site of the old 1841 mill and then continued behind the hospital/dispensary to join the McBryde railroad. A junction of the two railroads, as with others on the island, was mandated by the federal government in the 1930s as a condition for funding improvements to Nāwiliwili Harbor near Līhu'e. In those days it was possible for trains to run from Mānā, at the western tip of the island, through Līhu'e to Kīlauea Plantation.

Just before the tracks entered Kōloa, a long branch headed east to cross Wailana Road at the edge of Japanese Camp. That spot was called the "crossing," where workers gathered in the morning to be taken to work and were let off after work. This branch ran along the southern edge of Waitā Reservoir and then split in two. One branch led to the rich cane fields in the Kaluahonu area east of the reservoir, and another went south to the 1913 mill. Past the mill, the line continued toward the shore then divided into two branches. One went to Kōloa Landing, and the other to the Māhā'ulepū fields.

The branch to Kōloa Landing was especially important in the operation of Kōloa Plantation. In ancient times the small shelving beach was used by Hawaiians as a place to store and launch outrigger canoes. After contact, it was dignified with the name Kōloa Landing, and, as discussed previously, by 1830 had become the principal place on the south shore where Hawaiians exchanged supplies for pieces of iron and other items. It served in supplying vessels engaged in the fur trade, then as the main port from which sandalwood was shipped. Its role in the whaling industry has been described. Improvements were made by Kōloa Plantation, especially after the railroad reached the landing in the 1880s. When that branch was renovated in 1895, a short spur ran along the eastern side at the landing so trains could back cars onto it for easy unloading of bag sugar and loading of supplies. A derrick, resembling an upside-down "U," straddled the narrow landing area. On the east side a shed contained a winch and gasoline motor, called a "donkey." Bagged sugar was stored in a warehouse on the west side. The winch lifted a dozen or so bags of sugar at a time from either the warehouse or train

Shipping sugar out of Kōloa Landing, 1910. This shows a cane car on the tracks filled with bagged sugar, and the derrick powered by a gasoline motor called a "donkey."

"Boat Day" at Kōloa Landing about 1917. The people are gathered to meet a ship of the Inter-island Steamship Company from Honolulu.

☜ Bishop Museum

cars, and the load was carried laterally to boats rowed in from ships moored at buoys in the bay. Incoming supplies were handled in a reverse fashion.

One part of the old rail bed to Kōloa Landing can still be seen alongside the road to Kiahuna Golf Course. It appears to be a stone wall but is actually a 10-foot wide berm constructed of fitted rock.

The Kōloa Plantation railroad continued to be the main mode of transportation in the operation of the plantation until World War II. Although suitable trucks were available as early as the 1920s, and would have been more efficient to operate, plantation management viewed the transition as potentially difficult. A heavy investment had been made in locomotives, cane cars, repair facilities, and tracks. A changeover would involve removing the tracks and constructing roads, purchasing dozens of heavy trucks, setting up maintenance facilities for them, and retraining personnel in their use. One Kōloa Plantation official, when asked in the 1930s why it was not done, replied simply "the trains work." It took the labor shortage of World War II to trigger the transition, which was complete by 1948.

An old locomotive, affectionately named "Paulo" for Paul Isenberg, is stored today in a Grove Farm warehouse in Puhi, where it keeps company with one from Līhu'e Plantation and another from McBryde Sugar Company. In 1935, Paulo was put in working order for the centennial celebration of the start of the sugar industry in Hawai'i. A section of track was laid just *mauka* of the mill site in Kōloa, and Paulo chugged along sounding its once familiar whistle. Anyone who wanted to could hop on for a ride.

As part of the celebration, the granite grinders used by Chinese settlers at Māhā'ulepū in the 1820s were assembled and exhibited in the yard of the plantation office. Over a thousand people dressed in period costume attended a *lū'au* that must have been one of the largest, if not the grandest, ever. In 1985, Paulo was again repaired for the sesquicentennial and puffed along a section of track laid in the same place, and once again rides were offered to everyone. Every year since, a weeklong festivity called Kōloa Plantation Days celebrates the event. Paulo is ailing now, and the little locomotive has had to take part in the annual parades on a flatbed truck, but toots its whistle as lustily as ever.

The next chapter recounts the fascinating story of the immigrants who came to Hawai'i and Kōloa. They arrived from many parts of the world for more than a century and a half. This gathering of so many diverse peoples and cultures may have been, without intention, the greatest social experiment of its kind ever carried out. While it is true the tired and the poor arrived at New York and other East Coast ports in much greater numbers, most were European and able to form their own communities and remain within them until they chose to leave. In Hawaiʻi, the immigrants were far more diverse and interacted with each other daily, often in dynamic and dramatic ways. In their interaction is a lesson we can all learn and profit from today, and in so doing perhaps make race relations in our country far less rancorous.

Chapter Nine

Sojourners and Settlers

It is doubtful that there has ever been such an intriguing interweaving of races and cultures as in Kōloa during its later plantation days; it is less than certain such an interweaving will occur anywhere again. Although Kōloa was similar in many respects to other plantation towns in Hawai'i during that era, life in this one had a unique quality.

Some day, perhaps, sociologists will explore the culture of each group that came to Kōloa, and the melange that was the result in the 1930s. This will not be attempted here. Instead, a few characteristics of each group will be noted and one emphasized, their traditional musics. The importance of music in the assimilation of the diverse groups and individuals in Kōloa cannot be stressed enough. The music of any people embodies their uniqueness, expresses their values and beliefs, and gives an idea of their views on universal themes such as love, loneliness, sorrow, and beauty. No culture is without music, and because much of its expression is nonverbal, people of other cultures respond even though the words and the music are unfamiliar. Through music and its associated art forms, cultural barriers are crossed, and this leads to better understanding and closer human relationships among people of disparate origins.

Of course, the foundation of the way of life in Kōloa was Hawaiian culture. Many elements of it have been described and will not be repeated. The legacy of the Hawaiians was surprisingly strong in the 1930s. To this day, the influence of Hawaiian traditions upon life in Kōloa and all of Hawai'i continues, constituting the "host culture" of the Islands.

The *mele* or chants of the Hawaiians were one of their most important cultural expressions. The words themselves were and are believed to have *mana*, or spiritual power. An ancient Hawaiian proverb illustrates this: *"I ka ʻōlelo nō ke ola; i ka ʻōlelo nō ka make."* This means, "In the word is life; in the word is death."

In pre-contact times there were two principal categories of chants, *mele oli* and *mele hula*. *Mele oli* were performed by a solo chanter without accompanying instruments. Celebrating ancestral names, places and events, some were dirges chanted at the death of a loved one, and others were prayers. They were performed solemnly within a narrow range of tones, and included *ʻiʻi* or breaks similar to the glottal stops of the Hawaiian language. In *mele oli*, the message was more important than the method of its delivery.

The most moving example of one type of *mele oli*, the *mele pule*, or prayer chant, is one that originated on Kauaʻi. In *"Ka Wai a Kāne,"* "The Water of Kāne," words and tones flow like water in a clear stream. As noted before, the god Kāne is the source of sunshine, water, and other life substances of nature. Pacific folklorist Katherine Luomala, author of *Voices on the Wind*, wrote that in this chant Hawaiians "poured into the concept of Kāne their most beautiful thoughts and poetry . . . it is the most beautiful chant in Polynesia." The complete translation can be found in Emerson's *Unwritten Literature of Hawaiʻi*.

The second major category of mele is the *mele hula*. These are performed with a wider range of tones and variations such as vibrato, and are accompanied by percussion instruments in intricate rhythmic patterns to which hula is performed. Among the instruments are the *pahu*, a drum made from a partly hollowed coconut log with ray or sharkskin stretched across the top; the *ipu*, two joined gourds thumped on a pad of *tapa* while being slapped on the side with the fingers; the *ʻohe*, or bamboo nose flute, played in the pitches of the chanter; the *ʻulīʻulī*, a feathered gourd rattle; the *ʻūkēkē*, a plucked string instrument played as a mouth harp; and the *kālāʻau*, a pair of resonant sticks.

A beautiful example of the *mele hula* is *"Māpu ka Hanu ō ka Lauaʻe,"* or "Fragrant the Windblown Scent of the Lauaʻe." This tells of the beauty of a forest setting where the delicate lauaʻe fern grows, but the text has veiled meanings as it ruminates about destiny. The site is a misty and mystical place near a beautiful waterfall on Mauna Hina, a mountain in the very heart of Kauaʻi. The first two lines give a sense of this chant,

Māpu ka hanu ō ka laua'e
Māpu noe ka poli ō ka wai aloha

Wafted is the breath of the laua'e fern
The essence of the beloved waters alights like mist

The movements of hula interpret the poetry of the chants. Hula *kahiko*, or ancient hula, is danced in the traditional way. Hula *'auana*, literally "the hula gone astray" or contemporary hula, incorporates elements introduced since contact and is the type most often seen today.

A distinctly Hawaiian musical form that developed after contact was *hīmeni* or hymn singing. These are a glorious merging of ancient chants with Christian hymns learned from the first missionaries. These hymns can be heard every Sunday at the Hawaiian Church in Waimea, the Wai'oli Hui'ia Church in Hanalei, and many others throughout the Islands.

A unique Hawaiian innovation is *kī hō'alu*, or slack-key guitar. This is another variant on the ancient chants, as the lower three strings are loosened in a major triad to approximate the pitch of the chanter's tones. There are many tunings, but this one, called "taro patch," is most often used. The *kīkā kila*, or steel guitar, is another Hawaiian invention and characteristic of Hawaiian music. At first, Hawaiian musicians played a six-stringed Spanish guitar on the lap and used the back of a pocket comb to produce the desired notes. Over the years many other implements were tried, but all caused distracting noise as they were slid into the proper positions. Joseph Kekuku, a student at Kamehameha School in 1894, turned out the first steel bar in the school machine shop, and the steel-guitar style was born. Electric amplification was added in another time and place—1935, in Texas.

These traditional musical forms were heard and appreciated by all immigrants who brought their own music and often their own instruments. Hawaiians readily accepted the new influences and blended many of them with their own. In turn, the immigrants adopted elements of Hawaiian music. The same was true of the people themselves and their cultures. Hawaiians lived in a land of plenty and were generous with all they had. Tomorrow *did* take care of itself in Hawai'i, so why not enjoy today? Their heritage of a warm welcome to everyone, love of family, sense of humor, and pleasure in living—all these and more were transmitted to those around them.

Most important was the "aloha spirit" Hawaiians offered so freely. This flavored life in Kōloa during the thirties, which poses a paradox: how could this be if they were so few by then?

For the answer one has to look back to the earliest decades following contact. The rule by *kapu* had been abolished, chiefly authority was diminishing, and the missionaries were disparaging their religion. However, the lives of the *maka'āinana*, or ordinary people, who lived away from the urban areas continued to embody many of the traditional elements. The foreigners who first settled in Hawai'i did so mostly in Honolulu and other port towns. Away from these population centers, the number of Hawaiians was large in proportion so they maintained many of their customs. This was the major reason Hawaiian influence was as pervasive as their customs were persuasive.

In 1778, Captain Cook estimated the population of *"Atoui"* (Kaua'i) and wrote "there might be, upon the whole island, sixty such villages, as that before we anchored; and that, allowing five persons to each house, there would be, in every village, five hundred; or thirty thousand upon the island." Estimates of the total population of the "Sandwich Islands" made by his officers varied from 242,000 by William Bligh to 400,000 by James King. Figures from explorers who came afterwards varied widely for different reasons. One important reason was that few understood enough of the language to obtain reliable information from the inhabitants, most of whom were not accustomed to large numbers in any event. Another failure is that none made an effort to count the population in a systematic way. After analyzing all of the estimates of the Hawaiian population at the time of contact, Eleanor Nordyke concluded in *The Peopling of Hawai'i* that the total was between 250,000 and 300,000, and that of Kaua'i about 30,000. In recent years archeologists have quantified the artifacts that have been unearthed and produced the most accurate assessments. These are roughly comparable to the figures arrived at by Nordyke for the total and for the individual islands. They also provide the best estimate for Kōloa, about 4,000.

Soon after contact, the population began to decline on all the Islands. The major reason was that Hawaiians had lost their resistance to diseases of the outside world due to their isolation for so many centuries. Even childhood diseases of the West took a deadly toll. It was inevitable that first contact, in whatever form and from whatever source, would be catastrophic. The same fate befell Native Americans and many others in similar situations. Other factors also contributed to the decline. Warfare began to be waged with the more deadly weapons obtained from foreigners. Young men left the Islands as crew members aboard ships that called at Hawaiian ports. The birth rate declined, and disruption of the traditional social structure after the *kapu* had been abolished was an important factor in the increased infant mortality.

The missionaries were the first outsiders to be distressed over the rapid decline. Their initial estimate, by LMS missionary William Ellis, who toured the Islands in 1823, assessed the total at about 140,000, and Kaua'i, 10,000. After a few unsuccessful attempts, the first reasonably reliable census, conducted by the missionaries in 1836, numbered the total population of Hawai'i at 107,954; Kaua'i, 8,934; and Kōloa, 2,166. To some degree, the sugar planters shared this compassion but looked at the decline through a different lens. The resulting labor shortage was their main concern.

The Hawaiian government was greatly concerned. Kamehameha IV, in addressing the legislature, stated: "The decrease in our population is a subject in comparison with which all others sink into insignificance." Laws were subsequently enacted to protect the health of Hawaiians, but not effectively enforced. Kamehameha V was also deeply concerned. His major action was to bring in ten Rarotongans "to reinforce and reinvigorate the Polynesian stock," but little was done to help them adapt so most of them returned.

The Hawaiian government joined the sugar planters in 1850 to form the Royal Hawaiian Agricultural Society. Its purpose was to promote agriculture in various ways, such as addressing the labor shortage and thus the population decline. The Society discussed the importation of laborers from abroad for several years, but little action was taken. The discussions did bring into focus the dual purposes that would later come into conflict. The Hawaiian Kingdom sought to counteract the decline of the Hawaiian population by supporting the immigration of a "cognate race," or one kindred to Hawaiians, while the sugar planters wanted hard-working laborers of any race. Hawaiians were certainly capable of performing this hard work. Despite complaints of the planters to the contrary, and their own reluctance, those who worked on the plantations did it well. Sadly, their numbers were declining so rapidly that others had to be brought in. By 1886, Hawaiians would become a minority in their own land.

Also in 1850, the Hawaiian legislature passed "An Act for the Governance of Masters and Servants," a section of which provided the legal basis for the contract-labor system. In 1864 the government formed the Bureau of Immigration to regulate the importation of laborers, supervise their contracts, and encourage free immigrants. The Bureau brought in small groups from various Pacific islands between 1869 and 1884, but most returned to their home islands. The "cognate race" policy was futile if Pacific Islanders from the equatorial belt were to be employed in the sugar industry. They had adapted to their hot and humid environments over centuries by starting to work before daylight, and when the day grew warm they did lighter chores in the shade until late afternoon. The end of the day and into the evening was occupied with family activities and the preparation and consumption of the main meal of the day. Obviously, this routine did not suit the schedule of the plantations.

In due course, immigrant workers from three large ethnic groups and many smaller ones came to Hawai'i and almost all adapted well. The major groups were Chinese, Japanese, and Filipinos, while others came from a variety of origins and for that reason will be described first. As the immigration story unfolds, at least two factors should be borne in mind. One is that in 1900 Congress passed the Organic Act, which nullified all labor contracts that had been made under the laws of the Hawaiian Republic and forbade any further contracts. Another affecting individual plantations, including Kōloa Plantation, was their lack of say about the ethnic composition of the workers assigned them. Nor, in most cases, did they keep accurate records regarding ethnicity. Edward Beechert, in *Working in Hawai'i: A Labor History*, puts it this way: "The plantations seldom had the luxury of deciding the racial composition of their work force, although managers frequently expressed themselves [to the factors or agents making assignments] on the advantages of one or another racial mix."

The first outsiders to come to Hawai'i as explorers, traders, and seafarers were Americans and North Europeans. Many stopped, but few remained. Hawaiians referred to them as *haole* (without breath) because they spoke strangely. As Caucasians settled in Hawai'i and learned to speak Hawaiian, they were no longer "without breath," but by then the word *haole* had acquired the meaning "white" and has not changed since. The first Caucasian settlers brought Western concepts too numerous to mention, but which included land ownership, freedom and equality under law, commercial knowledge, enterprise, foresight, and persistence in undertakings. Later, they brought managerial and other skills useful in the sugar industry. Thus their influence tended to be out of proportion to their numbers. The impact of non-Caucasians depended more upon their numbers. Other circumstances were important, among them being the length of time they remained, and whether they came singly or with their families. White or non-white, each group that came to Hawai'i brought its culture with music in the matrix of each.

The Portuguese immigrants had a large influence in Kōloa because most came with their families and remained. About 12,000 Portuguese from the Islands of Madeira and the Azores came to Hawai'i from 1878 to 1888, followed by a second wave of approximately 13,000 between 1909 and 1913. They were honest, hard workers, and many became *luna*, or foremen. In proportion to its size, Kōloa received more Portuguese than other plantations, so their cultural contributions will be described more fully.

When the Portuguese arrived in Kōloa, the congregation of Saint Raphael Church was diminishing. The conversion of Hawaiians had been tapering as their numbers dwindled. The Portuguese, devout Catholics, reinvigorated the church, as the many headstones in the church cemetery bearing Portuguese names, and the dates, attest.

The Portuguese had a subtle influence on the Pidgin spoken by the workers on Kōloa Plantation because so many were *luna* who gave orders. The author noticed this more than 50 years ago, but it is almost impossible to detect today. The Portuguese language is characterized by nasal vowels, indicated in print by an *m* or *n* following the vowel (e.g., *sim* "yes," *bem* "well"), or by a tilde over the vowel as in *mão* for "hand."

Dancing and singing played a prominent role in the lives of the Portuguese. In Portugal at the time, almost every village had its own *terreiro*, a dance floor of beaten earth. In Kōloa, their best known dance was one that originated in the Azores and Madeira, a round dance called *chamarrita*. Other traditional dances were the *vira*, *chula*, *corridinho*, and *tirana*, which reflected Portuguese courting and matrimonial customs. The Portuguese workers especially loved the *desafio*, extemporaneous songs on any subject that came to mind. Singers often vied with each other in contests. All were fond of the *desgarrada*, or composed folk songs, which evoked memories of home.

The most distinctive Portuguese songs were in the *fado* style, which had Moorish roots and epitomized *saudade*. This word means more than "sadness" and takes in the yearning and romantic aspect of the Portuguese character. *Fado* means "fate" or "destiny," and the themes were often of unfulfilled love and betrayal. In this new land, many fado songs told of loneliness and longing for home. In Kōloa, two or three families would gather in a plantation home to listen, while those of other cultures sat outside where they could hear. The woman singer, or *fadista*, at first stood silently in the corner with a black shawl draped over her bent head, hands clasped before her. A chord would be strummed on the guitar, and she would start the song with a low moan, then sing with such emotion all could not help but respond. Two of the most popular *fado* songs in Kōloa were *"Uma Casa Portugesa"* and *"Solidão"*. Although the immigrants were not from Lisbon, they also loved the beautiful and nostalgic *"Lisboa Antiga."*

The first guitars were brought to Hawai'i in 1832 by Mexican cowboys (whom Hawaiians called *paniolo* for the language they spoke, Español). Kamehameha had recruited them from California to teach Hawaiians how to handle his cattle. The cowboys returned to California when their task was done. Later, the Portuguese popularized the guitar throughout the Islands.

The *'ukulele* came to Hawai'i on the first ship bringing Portuguese immigrants in 1878 in the hands of João de Freitas, who did not know how to play it. In Portugal the instrument was called *braguinha* because it had originated in the province of Braga. The second ship bringing Portuguese in 1879 brought more instruments, musicians who could play them, and craftsmen who could make them. It is uncertain how the instrument got its Hawaiian name *'ukulele*, which means "leaping flea." The leading theory is that Edward Purvis, who played it in Kalākaua's court, bore that nickname because he was small and had quick movements. Another theory, which better reflects the Hawaiian sense of humor, is that it is played with a motion not unlike a dog scratching fleas.

More than 3,000 Russians came to Hawai'i in 1879, worked well in the fields, but left the plantations when their contracts had been worked out. Some settled in larger metropolitan centers where their influence continues to this day, but none stayed in Kōloa so few elements of their culture lingered there. A similar pattern occurred when 600 Scandinavians arrived shortly thereafter.

German workers had come individually to the Islands from the start of the sugar industry and had done so well, both at work and in the communities, that they were actively sought. Most who came after 1882 were assigned to Kaua'i, another instance in which Kōloa received more than its share, so the story will be told. A firm in Honolulu, Hackfeld & Company, acted as the representative or "factor" for Kōloa Plantation and most of the other plantations on Kaua'i. Paul Isenberg (pronounced "eezenberg"), himself a German, had come to Līhu'e in 1862 from an influential position at Hackfeld to be the manager of Līhu'e Plantation. He bought stock in that plantation as well as Kōloa Plantation, maintained his ties with Hackfeld, and made certain, whenever possible, that German equipment was purchased by both plantations. According to "Iki" Moir, whose father later was manager, the first locomotive ordered for Kōloa Plantation under this policy arrived at Kōloa Landing unassembled; the accompanying directions for assembly were in German, which nobody on the Plantation was able to translate! Isenberg turned his attention to the labor shortage in 1881 and sponsored several groups of Germans to come to Hawai'i to work in the sugar industry. He ensured that all of the recruits were either agricultural workers or skilled in trades useful on the plantations. Under his guidance, 1,337 German workers had arrived in Hawai'i under contract between 1882 and 1897. The male-female ratio was nearly balanced; more were married than not, and those who had children brought them.

A total of 922 Germans went to plantations on Kaua'i. The largest number were sent to Līhu'e Plantation, and some to Grove Farm Plantation nearby, making a total of 595 in the Līhu'e area. They formed a close-knit community on a hill overlooking Līhu'e Plantation, which came to be called "German Hill." They built their own school and a beautifully crafted Lutheran church which is still there today. Kōloa Plantation received only 73 Germans, but this was a high proportion in relation to the number of workers on the plantation at the time. Because of the distance, they could not participate fully in the Līhu'e German community, but did maintain a linkage. All continued to speak German among themselves, retained their culture and married within their group, so their influence in the communities was not as great as it might have been.

In Kōloa as elsewhere, the German influence was most pronounced at work. In whatever tasks they were assigned, Germans set an example for others with their industry, attention to detail, high standards, and other aspects of their character. Many on Kōloa Plantation became managers or assumed highly skilled positions. Unfortunately, there was not one contract renewal on Kaua'i. Nearly all went to Honolulu or the United States after their contracts were completed. Thus, their influence in Kōloa by the 1930s, even on the Plantation, had become nebulous.

The effect of one German who was never on Kaua'i, let alone in Kōloa, deserves mention. Henry Berger arrived in Honolulu from Germany in 1872 at the request of King Kamehameha V to reorganize the Royal Hawaiian Band. He stayed on to compose, teach music at Kamehameha Schools, organize the Honolulu Symphony Orchestra, and make many other contributions that spread throughout the Islands. George Kanahele, in *Hawaiian Music and Musicians*, conveys some sense of his influence: "Henry Berger's impact upon Hawaiian music was greater and more lasting than that of any other single individual." He transformed the hymns sung by Hawaiians into the Hawaiian music we know today. Yet it is doubtful if workers in Kōloa who strummed their *'ukulele* and sang together in the evenings ever heard of him.

From 1907 through 1914, some 8,000 Spanish arrived in Hawai'i, and many of them came to Kōloa to live in "Spanish Camp." Almost all moved on to California after their contracts expired to join the Spanish population there. As a result, little of their culture was left behind in Kōloa, or anywhere else in the Islands.

Between 1879 and 1914, some 3,000 Greeks and Americans of Greek extraction arrived in Hawai'i. They also left the plantations after their contracts were fulfilled. Those who settled in larger towns and cities influenced culture there through their food, music, business acumen, and the Greek Orthodox religion. Their impact upon life in Kōloa by the 1930s was negligible.

After Puerto Ricans became U.S. nationals following the Spanish-American War, about 5,000 were recruited in 1900 and 1901. Most settled in the Islands, married members of other ethnic groups, and had large families. These Puerto Ricans were of pure Spanish origin and came from the mountainous regions where Spanish *jibaro* traditions prevailed; they were distinct from those of African descent who lived along the coasts. They were hard workers and thought well of by plantation managers and other workers. In their social life, music and dance were inseparable. In Kōloa as elsewhere, Saturday-night dances held in plantation homes were their major form of recreation. The *vals, guaracha,* and *seis* were the most popular dances. On Kaua'i, their dance music was, and still is, referred to as *kachi-kachi*, and this term has spread to other islands. It originated as an onomatopoeic term an unknown Japanese worker in Kōloa coined to describe the scratchy sound of the *guiro,* a serrated gourd. Apparently the Puerto Ricans thought it was appropriate, or perhaps somewhat humorous, or both, liked it and adopted it themselves. In addition to the *guiro*, a typical *conjunto* or ensemble included a Spanish guitar, a *cuatro* (a guitar-like instrument with five sets of double strings), a *sinfonia*, or button accordion, and often *maracas*. The Puerto Ricans left a Latin spice in Kōloa the Spanish themselves had not.

Other Caucasians whose immigration to Hawai'i was subsidized by the government or plantations included 372 Austrians, 84 Italians, a number of Scots, and about 100 assorted others, including Americans. These, and many who came of their own volition, brought skills of value and occupied positions relatively high in the plantation hierarchy.

There were other immigrants from a variety of sources who do not fit the category "white," or the three main groups mentioned above. After the American Civil War, many agricultural leaders had contacts with missionaries in "Freedmen's Aid," an organization assisting the newly freed slaves in the South. Lincoln's promise of "40 acres and a mule" had not materialized, so nearly 4,000,000 former slaves faced poverty. In 1867, these planters brought more than a hundred of them to Hawai'i, but they proved to be unsatisfactory both in the communities and on the plantations, so were returned within a few months at the planters' expense. The results of this effort stirred the Hawaiian government to extend and crystallize its "cognate race" policy. Instead of encouraging certain groups, for the first time it took the position of explicitly forbidding one. From then on it issued policy statements to that effect, such as this one in 1882: "The Legislature is decidedly averse to Negro immigrants, even opposing people from the Hebrides." In 1907, after the overthrow of the Hawaiian Kingdom, the mostly Caucasian Hawaiian Sugar Planters' Association decided to make another attempt. It brought 30 African-American families (again, about 100 total) from Tennessee and adjacent states, but the results once again were so unsatisfactory they were returned.

With the increasing racial strife in the United States involving African-Americans versus whites (especially Jews) and Asians from several countries, and with this antagonism extending to social institutions such as education and the law, qualified professionals should study these two attempts. On the mainland the canvas is large and the issues are more complex. Here in Hawai'i the situation was much simpler and some issues all but disappeared upon their arrival. Although the African-Americans had been slaves, they were able to live among those who had never known them as such. There was no segregation or discrimination. Hawai'i was fortunate in having

Chinese immigrant workers bound for Hawai'i about 1900.

one of the most tolerant societies in the world where many ethnic groups lived together harmoniously.

Neither movement affected Kōloa, or even Kaua'i, so no more will be said except for some bits of information that have come the author's way that might intrigue professional readers to undertake the task. Most documentation on the first effort is still in private hands and difficult to access. However, the author was allowed to read the diary of one who was involved in it and was dismayed by the change in his tone from buoyant idealism to pessimism. The diarist had hoped the experiment would evolve into a movement that would bring perhaps 100,000 African-Americans to Hawai'i, where they could live and work contentedly. Soon after their arrival, the diarist became discouraged. He lamented such qualities as the "loose morals," "laziness," and "dishonesty" of the immigrants, but part of this moral emphasis can be discounted as due to his missionary background. Documentation of the second attempt is public, but scant. In this, the emphasis is more upon work performance, but the observations are even more negative. Perhaps a study of these events would also shed some light on a question that has troubled the author for many years: why the percentage of blacks in the island population, leaving out those in the military, was nearly zero until WWII and since then has hovered around 1 percent.

As for the culture they brought with them, they had little to bring. Their primitive art did not come into vogue until much later in the U.S. and Europe. One form of musical expression that seemed to catch on among the young wherever blacks settled is the traditional "ring shout" of West Africa. This is characterized by a heavy repetitive beat with clapping, gyrations, and a shouting quality of the singing. This has been adopted in the U.S. by adolescents and the young who are chafing under the civilization they are acquiring, and is prominent in popular music there as elsewhere. No trace was left at that time in Hawai'i, however.

Another non-Caucasian group, about 8,000 Koreans, arrived between 1903 and 1905. The first ship brought 56 men, 21 women, and 25 children, approximately the same gender ratio maintained subsequently. The single men were allowed to send for picture brides and more than a thousand responded. Koreans were excellent workers but their immigration stopped in 1905 because of pressure by the Japanese government, which occupied Korea that year. Japanese occupation of their homeland also meant that most Koreans would remain in Hawai'i, although nearly all left the plantations when their contracts were completed. Only 16 percent returned to Korea; the rest settled in towns and started business enterprises, setting an example with their initiative, hard work, and orderly conduct.

Koreans also brought their culture, perhaps best understood as a combination of their indigenous customs with those of China and Japan, both having repeatedly invaded their country. *P'ansori* is the best known true Korean art form they have given Hawai'i, and it was brought to the plantations by traveling professionals. This is the presentation of a story in stylized speech by a solo vocalist accompanied only by a drum. The performer acts out the *aniri* (dialogue) of the characters, and sings the *sori* (songs) that enhance the story. Traditionally, the audience joins in by shouting approval or disapproval of the various characters.

The first of the three major immigrant groups to make Hawai'i their home were the Chinese. During the decades after 1790, when the trade in furs and sandalwood flourished, adventurers and seamen from China joined ships sailing from Canton. Some remained in Hawai'i, and on "Kow-Dai," as they pronounced Kaua'i. Their total number in the Islands did not exceed 100 until the middle of the nineteenth century. This was due to an imperial edict of the Ch'ing dynasty forbidding emigration from China. The rulers of this dynasty were Manchu, who had invaded China from Manchuria in the seventeenth century. The first break in China's isolation occurred in 1842 when Great Britain, in the Treaty of Nanking, forced China to cede Hong Kong and open four other ports to the West. The Ch'ing rulers soon became distracted by the Taiping Rebellion (1850—1864), while at the same time a series of floods, famines, and other disasters occurred. This combination resulted in a diaspora of more than a million Chinese to such places as Hong Kong, Taiwan, Manila, and Singapore. It also opened the way for migration to Hawai'i.

In 1852, the sugar planters brought two groups of contract laborers to Hawai'i from Canton Province through agents in China. The immigrants were of two different cultural and ethnic origins, which was to cause difficulties in their adaptation. The Hakka, people who had migrated south into Canton Province in several waves from the fourth century to the thirteenth century, predominated. "Hakka" is the Cantonese version of the Mandarin *k'o-chia*, which the northerners were called to distinguish them from the *pen-ti*, or natives of the region. After settling in South China the Hakka never assimilated into the host population. An industrious people, they were clannish and spoke their own Fukienese dialect. The *pen-ti*, more commonly called Punti after their arrival in Hawai'i, spoke a variety of dialects of Chung Shan Cantonese and would have little to do with the Hakka.

The Hawaiian Kingdom did not consider the Chinese to be a "cognate race" but raised no objection to their recruitment. They were virtually all male, and under contracts for five years. In the words of one widely quoted manager, they were "quiet, industrious, and thrifty."

The first adjective "quiet" was correct for good reason. As mentioned, there are many dialects of Cantonese and those who spoke one could converse with those who spoke another only with difficulty, if at all. The Hakka dialect was completely unintelligible to all who spoke Cantonese. The Chinese were resourceful in meeting this challenge, learned Hawaiian, and communicated with those who spoke other Cantonese dialects in the Hawaiian language. The description "industrious" was also apt, in part because they had been poor farmers in southern China, where hard work was required to survive. The last word "thrifty" also was valid because they saved all they could with the intention of returning home when their contracts were completed. The Chinese intended to be sojourners, not settlers, and referred to themselves as *wah kiu*, or "overseas Chinese." Some men arranged marriage by proxy to brides in China to establish an honorable link there, and at the same time married Hawaiian women. The rest remained single in anticipation of their return. Unknown to them, this was not to be for most.

Because of the permissive attitudes of both the Chinese and Hawaiian governments, brokers in China cooperated with entrepreneurial Chinese in Hawai'i to initiate recruitment from Kwantung Province and elsewhere in South China. The Bureau of Immigration was bypassed in the process, and none who were imported in this way were under contract when they were recruited, although their employers endeavored to work out various forms of commitment after their arrival. About half were employed by Chinese rice growers and the rest by sugar planters. The numbers entering Hawai'i averaged about 100 each year until 1876. That year the Reciprocity Treaty exempted both sugar and Hawaiian-grown rice from previously imposed tariffs on entry into the United States. The demand for labor increased sharply in anticipation of expanded production and future profits. Over a thousand Chinese were imported in 1876, and more than two thousand the following year.

The Bureau of Immigration, unable to recruit laborers from India and Malaya, then expanded its definition of "cognate race" to include Chinese, and over the next few years sponsored

13,500 immigrants. These Chinese were not as well selected as their predecessors. All were not "quiet, industrious, and thrifty." Some of them complained about working conditions to the Chinese government, which responded by prohibiting emigration to Hawai'i after 1881. This edict was easily circumvented by planters, brokers, and ship owners. In the first year prohibition was in effect, more than 4,000 laborers were smuggled in from China and California.

Resentment had risen in California over the influx of Chinese throughout the 1880s, reaching a peak in 1886. Reading the newspapers of the time, one is left with the impression this was mostly due to their willingness to work harder than others and for less. Much of the antipathy also had racial overtones, but without apparent reason. In contrast, Hawai'i was relatively tolerant for the first few years of that decade.

By 1884, there were 18,254 Chinese in the Islands, a surprising 22.6 percent of the population. This rising tide soon brought the first rumblings of discontent from many sources, augmented by the hostility present in California. That year, a re-evaluation by both the Hawaiian government and the sugar planters was undertaken. The government was convinced, since about 98 percent of the Chinese were single males, they constituted a "corrupting influence" on Hawaiian women that caused social instability. The government also was disturbed because the Chinese had held onto their penchant for gambling and use of opium. The planters were more pragmatic. As long as gambling and opium did not interfere with their work, such behavior was overlooked. What most troubled the planters was that the Chinese, on completion of their five-year contracts, did not renew them. A few stayed on the plantations as "free" (meaning free of contract) laborers. About 40 percent returned to China and the rest took up rice farming or moved to population centers to enter retail trades. To finance their larger enterprises, they formed traditional *wui* or groups of families who pooled their resources and could withdraw an agreed amount in turn. The word wui was later incorporated into the Hawaiian language as *hui*.

After leaving the sugar plantations, the Chinese were successful in almost every enterprise they entered. By 1890, they had over 8,000 acres in rice production and were exporting rice to the Chinese market on the West Coast. They raised vegetables for the local markets, which also was lucrative. They had little competition in their agrarian pursuits, but in urban centers they found themselves in conflict with merchants and artisans of all races. In Honolulu, Hilo, and even in small towns such as Kōloa, those who were already established found it diffi-cult to compete with the Chinese who, it was said, "could live on a ball of rice a day." This comment, obviously grim hyperbole, was also being heard in California.

The sugar planters were troubled by the move off the plan-tations because they needed to rely upon a steady labor force, but it was agitation due to competition in population centers that precipitated a crisis. The Hawaiian government in 1888 imposed restrictions on Chinese immigration that remained in effect until the monarchy was overthrown in 1893. Agitation on the West Coast for similar reasons resulted in Congress passing the Chinese Exclusion Act of 1882, which applied to Hawai'i in 1898 on annexation. Still, for many years after that about a thousand annually were smuggled into Hawai'i by Chinese organizations.

One cultural consequence of the Chinese presence in Kōloa when their numbers were still high came through touring musical groups. All who lived in Kōloa enjoyed the performances, which may have had more to do with the scarcity of entertain-ment than an appreciation of Chinese music. Ensembles from Honolulu gave open-air concerts of Cantonese folk music, or *siu kook*. The musicians played bamboo flutes called *er hu*, a two-stringed fiddle, *jung hu low*, and a hammered zither known as *yong kum*. Perhaps one reason others could appreciate Chinese music is because the teachings of Confucius (K'ung-fu-tzu) are expressed by it. He taught that music is to put man and his world in tune with the universe, which added another element beyond the Hawaiian tradition of reverence for nature in chant and song that pervaded the Islands.

Chinese opera, *tue kook*, was especially popular in Kōloa because it was a striking combination of performing arts: song, instrumental, stylized speech, dance, and acrobatics. The elabo-rate costumes, headgear, and colorful makeup combined to create a spectacular scene. In addition to the instruments above, percus-sion in Chinese opera was provided by bells, drums, cymbals, and wood blocks. Little wonder the plantation workers were entranced, even though they did not understand it.

An interesting evolution was underway among Chinese immigrants by the 1880s. Most had arrived as illiterate peas-ants, but they valued education and were intent upon provid-ing it for their children. By that time, Chinese-language schools had been established in most cities and towns. The Chinese who could afford it returned periodically to their native land, where they eagerly embraced Chinese culture and returned with art and ceramics for their homes. A flowering of

Chinese culture in the Islands had begun. Historian Clarence Glick commented:

> Chinese who entered from the mid-1880's onward in one or another exempt category played a disproportionate role in this process. They included merchants, bankers, newspaper editors, Chinese-language-school teachers, physicians, Christian ministers and priests, priests of Buddhist and Tao sects, professors, artists. . . there were probably no more than a few hundred in all the other categories combined.

The overthrow of the Manchu Ch'ing Dynasty by the rebellion of 1911-1912, led by Sun Yat-sen, affected the Chinese in Hawai'i in many ways. One was obvious to all. The Manchu had forced the conquered Chinese to braid their hair into a long queue or "pigtail" as a sign of loyalty. When the dynasty fell, the Chinese in Hawai'i, who had been afraid to do so before, cut off their queues.

By the 1930s, the effects of Chinese culture were manifested mostly in the population centers to which they had migrated, especially Honolulu and Hilo. In a small town such as Kōloa the Chinese legacy was less apparent because most had left many years before. By then no Chinese were working in the field for Kōloa Plantation, and only one or two sugar masters, or *tong see*, worked in the mill. A scant 1,000 Chinese remained on the entire island of Kaua'i, according to the 1930 census. Most were growing rice in the valleys where Hawaiians once had grown taro.

Nonetheless, the Chinese left some strong traditions behind in Kōloa. Their cheerful disposition while performing the hardest work was commented upon repeatedly in plantation records and became something of a gold standard for other workers. As long as they were available in sufficient numbers, Chinese had been used almost exclusively for such dangerous tasks as digging irrigation tunnels. Their custom of honoring their elders had reinforced a similar tradition of the Hawaiians. Although other Asians to follow had cooperative enterprises similar to the Chinese *wui*, the concept was novel in Hawai'i at the time, considered peculiarly Chinese, and emulated by others.

The Chinese who had married Hawaiian and other local women, and settled in Kōloa, had set up businesses such as stores, tailor shops, laundries, bakeries, and restaurants. In the 1930s these enterprises continued to prosper in the hands of their descendants. The older Chinese and their part-Chinese offspring in Kōloa maintained ties with friends and relatives in the Chinatowns of Honolulu and Hilo, resulting in a lot of visiting back and forth. When enough gathered in Kōloa, Chinese New Year was a big celebration with a lion dance, or *sing see*, performed to the delight of all Kōloa residents. If visitors were few, festivals were celebrated in a more muted way. The Chinese gathered to share their common bonds; the only evidence to others in Kōloa was the sound of the strings of firecrackers they set off.

It is believed by many, tourists and residents alike, that the first Chinese who came to Hawai'i originated "Pidgin" which, modified by succeeding waves of immigrants, is spoken by locals today. Some of the lilt of Hawaiian Pidgin did come from the Cantonese tones of Chinese immigrants. But the origin of Pidgin is complicated and the literature on the subject extensive; for the inquisitive, a good treatment is found in the *Encyclopedia Britannica*. Because it is such a common controversy, a brief summary is inserted here. First, some terms need to be defined.

"Lingua franca," originally meaning "Frankish language," was the limited language developed during the Middle Ages by traders from southern France and Italy who plied the Levant and Barbary coasts. A similar language was employed during the Crusades. Now generic, the term "lingua franca" applies to any third language created for use between two peoples who have no other language in common. The designation is Western in origin, however, and in a strict sense is limited in application to those based upon a European language.

The second term is "makeshift language." It has come into use in preference to "lingua franca" because it designates any third language defined as above, whether or not it is based upon a European language. The need for a more precise term becomes apparent when one realizes no makeshift languages used today are Frankish in origin. Some makeshift languages have evolved to become complex with large vocabularies, and have remained in use for many years.

The third term requiring closer analysis is "Pidgin." During the period of European exploration and colonization, rudimentary languages developed in many places around the world, each based upon the language of the exploring power. When Great Britain established a trading post in Canton in 1664, the British found Chinese a difficult language to learn, and the Chinese disdained to learn English. The British traders developed a form of makeshift language that had a rudimentary grammar and a limited vocabulary. Because it was used in business, it was called "Pidgin," a Cantonese corruption of the English word "business."

Pidgins based upon English and other languages have developed elsewhere. During World War II, American troops both encountered and created Pidgins on Pacific islands. The term "pidgin" is applied to these as long as the grammar remains rudimentary and the vocabulary limited. In general, Pidgins reflect the ethnocentric European view of indigenous peoples as intellectually and culturally inferior. Usually, they are created by necessity and disappear when the necessity for them disappears. Examples still spoken are Melanesian Pidgin in the South Pacific, and Bazaar Malay in the East Indian archipelago. No one speaks a true Pidgin as his or her native language.

The fourth term is "creole language." If an entire community gives up its former language and adopts a Pidgin as its tongue, it evolves to become more sophisticated and is then called a creole language. This term first arose in Haiti, where the indigenous people created a new language, Haitian Creole, made up of French spoken by the settlers and African languages of former slaves. It is used by more than 90 percent of the population of Haiti, and has replaced both the original Native American tongue and the languages of the West African slaves. There are many creole languages around the world; all by definition have displaced native languages. Typically, a creole language arises when the speakers of one language are economically or politically dominant over speakers of another language, particularly if the latter are illiterate. English creoles are still spoken in the Islands off the South Carolina coast; French creoles remain in Louisiana and Haiti; and the creole in Curaçao is based on Spanish and Portuguese.

The last term is "dialect." This is a variety of a language used by one group that has features of vocabulary, grammar, and pronunciation distinguishing it from other varieties of the same language used by other groups. Dialects develop as a result of barriers between groups of people who speak the same language. These barriers can be geographic, economic, political, or social. Examples are Yankee English of Cape Cod, Australian English, and Tuscan Italian. Dialects are especially clear-cut when geographic isolation has played the major role.

With these terms in mind, we can look closer at the origin of the Pidgin spoken in Hawai'i. When the British began stopping by the Hawaiian Islands during the fur-trade era, they attempted to use their Cantonese form of Pidgin to communicate with Hawaiians, but met with little success. Americans observed this, learned more Hawaiian, and interspersed Hawaiian words. More successful, they began to create an essentially new Pidgin with only this tenuous relationship to Cantonese Pidgin. As mentioned before, the first Chinese immigrants had learned enough Hawaiian to converse with Hawaiians and with fellow Chinese who spoke different Cantonese dialects, so they contributed little to the Pidgin developing in Hawai'i. Each wave of immigrants that followed added new elements. Although the Pidgin spoken by each group today has its own characteristics, a commonality in the Pidgin evolved so that all groups were, and are, understood by each other.

Here is where the confusion comes in. In the 1920s and 1930s the Hawaiian language seemed to be dying out. It was spoken on Ni'ihau, by some on Kaua'i because of the influence of those who came from Ni'ihau, and by only a few thousand Hawaiians elsewhere in remote areas. At that time, the Pidgin spoken by locals could be described correctly as *becoming creolized*, because it was replacing Hawaiian. Some went too far, however, and called it a creole language. Since the 1950's, a resurgence in the use of the Hawaiian language has taken place. It is now taught to varying degrees at all levels of the public-education system, and several Hawaiian-language immersion programs are now flourishing. At the University of Hawai'i more students major in Hawaiian than any other language, including English. A new pride is emerging in the ability to speak Hawaiian and pronounce it properly. Diacritical marks are now used when Hawaiian is written or printed. In this chapter, "Sojourners and Settlers," music was chosen as being representative of various cultures. It holds true here as well, for more Hawaiian music is being composed and sung in the Hawaiian language than ever before.

On the other hand, Standard American English also has been emphasized in the public-school system since the 1950s. Students have greater motivation to acquire facility in English for its economic and social advantages. With these emphases on Hawaiian and English, Pidgin is used less today, mostly by those born in the Islands as an expression of their common bond. It is not replacing either Hawaiian or English, nor does it appear that it ever will; therefore, it cannot be called a creole language as some were starting to do in the 1930s. The literature has not used this term in reference to Pidgin since about 1960.

Hawaiian Pidgin is based upon English but has a unique grammar, pronunciation, vocabulary, and intonation. It is used in just this one region and differs from all other regional varieties of English. These criteria fit the definition of an English dialect. It seems to this author that Hawaiian Pidgin is not a true pidgin, but a dialect. Yet this is Hawai'i, after all, where life is relaxed and such distinctions do not matter much. It is called

Pidgin by everyone, the custom is not likely to go away, and that term is satisfactory for practical purposes.

Returning to Kōloa in the 1930s, mechanized methods of growing and husking rice had become more efficient in California than in Hawai'i. As a result, competition during the decade drove the Chinese in Hawai'i out of rice farming. Some switched to taro, but most left to join their fellow Chinese in urban areas. This exodus decreased their numbers on Kaua'i further. By 1940, only about 200 Chinese remained on the island, and a mere handful in Kōloa.

In summary, between 1852 and 1899, approximately 56,000 Chinese came to Hawai'i. This figure is tentative because the number brought in illegally from California and China is not known. Estimates range from 5 percent to 15 percent of the number cited but are not customarily added to it. Reentrants are included in that figure, however, and about 10,000 returned permanently to China. Thus the most widely accepted figure for the Chinese who remained in Hawai'i is 46,000. A *caveat* by Hawai'i State Statistician Robert Schmitt is appropriate here: "Most statistics on migration are in fact subject to incomplete coverage, misreporting, and other deficiencies . . . estimates of net migration are at best rough approximations, and data on out-migration are extremely limited."

Overlapping the Chinese, the Japanese were the next major wave of immigrants to Hawai'i. The isolation of Japan for more than two centuries had begun to loosen after Commodore Matthew Perry called there with his warships in 1853. The Tokugawa Shōgunate was overthrown in 1868, and during the confusion of the transition, the Hawaiian consul in Japan hastily recruited a group of 148 Japanese from among the unemployed in Yokohama and sent them aboard a British ship to Hawai'i. He took this action because he foresaw a possible delay of years under the new regime before the emigration of Japanese workers would be approved. The recruits proved to be unsuited to the work and complained to the Japanese government, which returned most of them and suspended further emigration.

In 1881, during a world tour, King Kalākaua met with the Emperor of Japan. One of the subjects discussed was the possibility of Japanese workers coming to Hawai'i. For the first time, the term "cognate race" was used in regard to the Japanese in these conversations. As a result, an agreement was reached that specified, among other things, that only Japanese with farming experience would be recruited, and an emphasis would be placed on admitting a high proportion of women and children. In 1885, the first two groups of nearly a thousand each arrived. They were farmers from the hard-pressed rural areas of southwest Japan. The government-sponsored program ended in 1894, and thereafter Japanese emigration companies contracted to meet the demands of the planters for labor.

By 1900, the total number of Japanese immigrants in Hawai'i had reached 68,777. During what was called the "free period" of immigration from 1900 to 1907, the Japanese became the largest ethnic group in the Islands as 71,281 more arrived. Most Japanese recruits planned to return home. They called themselves *dekase-ginin*, or people working away from home.

The Japanese were hard workers, much like the Chinese, but both the Hawaiian government and the sugar planters soon became aware of certain differences. The Chinese had difficulty communicating with one another because of their variety of dialects, while the Japanese had a common language. The Chinese had come with little national consciousness; their loyalties were to family, clan, and village. The Japanese had a strong national spirit and more cultural homogeneity. They were in close touch with their homeland, which had become a world power under Meiji rule.

The Japanese knew that refusal to work would not be punishable by the courts after Annexation. They waited patiently until the formal date of annexation on June 14, 1900 and then began to assert themselves. Some organized, and during the remainder of the year Japanese workers went on 20 strikes throughout the Islands. The next year, strikes of a thousand or more Japanese at a time were taking place, alarming both the sugar planters and the government. Adding to the concern, during the so-called "free period" a surge of 35,000 Japanese left for California to seek better pay because they no longer were legally bound to the plantations.

In California, the Japanese were willing to work for lower wages than Americans and work harder. This stirred animosity against them, as it had against the Chinese. Thus, in 1907, Theodore Roosevelt by executive order stopped those with visas for Hawai'i from continuing to the West Coast. Under the Gentlemen's Agreement of 1908, the U.S. and Japanese governments agreed to reduce the number of Japanese migrating to both Hawai'i and the continental United States. The agreement allowed parents, wives, and children of the issei, or first generation, to enter, as well as "picture brides." The latter's presence had a beneficial effect on the workers, and many of them became workers in the cane fields themselves.

The idea of brides chosen by photograph may seem strange, but it was a natural outgrowth of the Japanese custom by which marriages were arranged by heads of families, and photographs were frequently exchanged in the process. A total of nearly 10,000 brides chosen by their photographs came to Hawai'i.

Even during the "restricted period" from 1908 to 1924, more than 61,000 Japanese entered Hawai'i and a larger number went to the West Coast. Because of the distress Japanese competition caused on the mainland, Congress passed the 1924 immigration law prohibiting Japanese immigration both to Hawai'i and the continental United States. This came to be called the Japanese Exclusion Act, although it did not refer specifically to the Japanese. It excluded all "aliens ineligible for citizenship," but the intent was clear since other Asians, also ineligible for citizenship, had been excluded earlier. As it had with the Chinese, however, smuggling of workers continued to both destinations. Precise figures of those smuggled are unavailable.

The vast majority of Japanese immigrants were simple peasants. Starting in 1900, more educated Japanese began to arrive and to exert the most effect upon others in Kōloa. The Meiji Period had ushered in mandatory elementary education and the rapid spread of literacy in Japan. This established a common language derived from the Tokyo dialect. In writing, Chinese characters adopted by the Japanese in the seventh century had become more cursive and were called *kanji*. They usually had uniquely Japanese meanings, but the Chinese and Japanese were able to recognize each other's ideographs and occasionally understand their meaning. The Japanese had developed two different systems of phonetic representation, both based on *kanji*. One system, *hiragana*, simplified and stylized the cursive *kanji*. The other system, *katakana*, or partial kana, was and still is used for foreign loan words. Neither form was interpretable by the Chinese.

Many traditional Japanese customs, such as the daily *furo* (hot bath), the *chanoyu* (tea ceremony), and *ikebana* (flower arranging), remained within their group, but some of their art, music, and drama spread to others in Kōloa. The effect of Japanese art on the community was mixed. Calligraphy, ink-monochrome painting, polychrome *ukiyo-e* style, and narrative *emaki*, or picture scrolls, were not picked up significantly by others. But Japanese abstraction from nature in screen and panel paintings was appreciated by the more sophisticated. Japanese laquer work, ceramics, and cloisonne also appeared in the wealthier Kōloa homes.

Japanese music played by workers in their camp intrigued other groups. The bamboo end-blown flute (*shakuhachi*) and drum (*taiko*) were inexpensive and relatively easy to learn. The workers' sometimes amateurish skill was supplemented by the traveling professional musicians who came to Kōloa Japanese Camp. They brought the *samisen*, a three-stringed instrument played with a plectrum, and the *koto*, a long thirteen-stringed instrument played similarly. Both were enjoyed by other plantation workers. The hauntingly beautiful *koto* solo *"Sakura"* entranced all, although most had no way of knowing the title means "Cherry Blossom," which is a symbol of spring and rebirth to the Japanese.

Traveling groups of performers brought songs that were not understood, and the notes sounded strange, but there were many who liked to listen to songs of traditional tales or variants of ancient geisha songs. These songs were accompanied by percussion instruments, *samisen*, and *koto*. Japanese plays (*shibai*) and puppet theater (*bunraku*) were often performed in Kōloa by traveling troupes, but because neither the words nor plot were understood, other ethnic groups rarely attended. This was not true when a *kabuki* troupe appeared. This form of drama, with stylized singing, dancing, and acting by performers in spectacular costuming, and the rich blend of music, caught the interest of all. Performances went on for hours, but attendance for a single play or scene was common. The interplay between actors and spectators delighted others almost as much as it did the Japanese themselves.

A few Japanese immigrants to Kōloa were Christian, but most were Buddhist, predominantly of the Hongwanji sect prevalent in the prefectures from which they came. But what puzzled many was that most Buddhists were at the same time Shinto. This was to have a significant effect upon the Kōloa community as World War II approached. The word Shinto literally means "the way of *kami*," or divine power. An ancient religion in Japan, it had been resurrected by the Meiji government and transformed into a national ethic. The Emperor came to be revered as the descendant of Amaterasu, the Sun Goddess, and the *kami* of the imperial household became the *kami* of the nation and its people. One consequence was that the emperor's birthday, *Tencho-setsu*, became a national holiday in Japan. In Kōloa it was celebrated with sumo wrestling, music, and a feast, which others enjoyed without understanding its full significance.

The Japanese festival that most other Kōloa plantation workers participated in was the annual *bon* ceremony. This was often referred to with an honorific prefix as *"o-bon,"* or in English, the Festival of Souls. The rites, like those of China, consist of commemorative services at the temple and graves in honor of the spirits of the dead, who were believed to return at the time. Reverence for, rather than worship of, ancestors is a more accurate description of the beliefs and practices. These were carried out quietly in the Buddhist temples without participation by others. Afterwards, outside each temple, the stately and colorful *bon-odori* dances to the measured beat of *ondo* music and *taiko* drum were enjoyed by all. Crowds came to watch the dance, and for small sums purchased the exotic foods that had been prepared and joined in the games and fun. The last part of the ceremony, *toro nagashi*, was held at the Kukui'ula shore. Floating lanterns were placed on the water and set adrift seaward as a way of bidding farewell to the spirits of departed ancestors. This was a moving ceremony and was quietly observed by throngs.

These are some of the cultural contributions of the Japanese who came to work on Kōloa Plantation. Those who traveled back to Japan then returned to Hawai'i brought accounts of the continuing hard life there and the lack of social mobility. As Eileen Tamura stated in *Americanization, Acculturation, and Ethnic Identity: The Nisei Generation in Hawaii,* "Those Issei who decided consciously to remain did so because Hawaii afforded them a better life than they could hope for in Japan."

When their contracts were fulfilled, many Japanese entered retail enterprises only to find the better ones had already been taken by Chinese. This did not deter them; they merely worked harder and catered to Japanese clientele. Although some remained on the plantation as day laborers, many Japanese pursued other activities, such as fishing, or became small farmers growing coffee or rice. For their larger enterprises they formed *tanomoshi*, or loan groups, similar to the *wui* of the Chinese, in order to finance them. By 1930, the Japanese in Hawai'i operated almost half of the retail enterprises and 70 percent of the small farms. Although Japanese immigration officially stopped in 1924, those who had arrived in Hawai'i and remained would undergo an interesting evolution, about which more will be said in the next chapter.

The total number of Japanese who came to Hawai'i was about 223,000. This figure includes recruited groups, those who came independently, and picture brides, but not reentrants, those who were smuggled into Hawai'i, or those smuggled from there to the West Coast. Okinawans are grouped with Japanese in these data.

Assuming that 5,000 returned to Japan and 35,000 went to the West Coast, but making no assumption on the number smuggled, then 180,000 remained in Hawai'i. This differs from census data that report the Japanese population of Hawai'i in 1920 as 109,274, and in 1930 as 139,631. These numbers are much lower than estimates made on other grounds and undoubtedly reflect undercounting. If the continuing outflow to the West Coast is factored into the 180,000 figure, then approximately 160,000 Japanese were in Hawai'i in 1924 at the time of the Japanese Exclusion Act.

The third and last major group of immigrant workers to come to Hawai'i were the Filipinos. The first wave began in 1906 and overlapped the Japanese. It was noted before that during the years leading up to annexation, the sugar planters had become increasingly concerned over their dependency upon the large number of Japanese workers on the plantations who had indicated their dissatisfaction with wages and other conditions of employment. In 1900, upon annexation, the Japanese, who comprised nearly 70 percent of the work force, had immediately gone out on a series of strikes. Another concern of the planters after annexation was the constant stream of Japanese workers leaving the Islands for California and higher wages. In the background of both concerns was the rising antipathy, both in the Islands and on the West Coast, to the large numbers of Japanese in their midst. It was time to look for another source of labor.

The Philippines had been ceded to the United States as a result of the Spanish-American War, and both the Philippines and Hawai'i became territories of the United States in the same year, 1898. The Filipinos were then American nationals so there were no immigration restrictions. The Hawaiian Sugar Planters' Association decided the Philippines would be an ideal labor source. The HSPA sent recruiters who went from village to village in rural areas extolling the merits of employment in Hawai'i. The recruiters were prohibited by the Organic Act from offering labor contracts of the type used previously, with periods of indenture and other provisions enforceable by the courts. Instead, they drew up contracts somewhat similar but with generous provisions. Filipinos were offered a salary several times what they were earning in the Philippines, free transportation to and from Hawai'i, a free home, fuel, water, and health care. This was in exchange for three years of agricultural work. The hours they were to work each day were specified, as were the number of work days each month.

The Filipinos were an ideal labor pool for the Hawaiian Islands in one respect. The Philippine economy at the time was largely agricultural, and this sector employed about half of the work force, mostly as tenant farmers. The climate resembled that of Hawai'i, and many of the crops were similar. Rice was the leading staple, but the Philippines also produced coconuts, sugar cane, bananas, pineapples, and abaca (Manila hemp). Most farmers lived in abject poverty, a compelling motivation to seek a better life elsewhere.

Young males with farming experience were recruited preferentially. Although women were encouraged to sign up as workers in order to achieve a gender balance, both their Catholic religion and ethnic customs opposed women going abroad. As a result, almost all of those recruited in the first years were single males. The first group of 15 came in 1906, followed by 150 the next year. This trickle grew to a stream. Tagalogs were the first; then Visayans, Ilocanos, and others. All proved to be good plantation workers.

To understand their diversity, something should be said about the Islands from which they came. The Philippine archipelago consists of about 7,100 islands and islets. It helps to visualize the geography as consisting of two principal islands, Luzon in the north and Mindanao in the south, with Visayan or the central group of islands more or less between them. The people were primarily of Malay stock from the southeastern Asian mainland, as well as from Indonesia, but several sub-groups had developed because of the rugged topography and isolation of the many islands. About 70 languages and dialects were spoken by eight major linguistic groups: Tagalog, concentrated in Manila, central and south central Luzon; Cebuano; Ilocano, dominant in parts of northern Luzon; Hiligaynon (Ilongo); Bicol; Waray-Waray, in Samar and Leyte; Pampango, spoken in parts of central Luzon; and Pangasinan, in central Luzon. Tagalog was spoken by nearly 25 percent of the population. Pilipino, based upon Tagalog, has since become the official language. Spanish was the second language for most at the start of their immigration to Hawai'i, but English became the official second language soon after the United States took control of the Philippines.

Under Spanish hegemony dating back to the late sixteenth century, the central government in Manila had dominated the Islands. The government consisted of elite Spanish-descended large landowners allied with an oppressive ecclesiastical organization. The Spanish had converted 80 percent of the population to Catholicism, at least nominally. The Moros, as the Spanish referred to the Muslims of Mindanao and the Sulu Archipelago, were never completely subdued.

The typical rural settlements in the Philippines were made up of Malay-style houses (bamboo, pile-supported, thatch-roofed) with surrounding rice fields, gardens, and groves of coconut and bamboo. Domesticated animals included chickens, pigs, and water buffalo. Most of the male immigrants to Hawai'i remained single because they hoped to return, the major reason they were content to live in the barracks provided for them.

One unusual aspect of the Filipino immigration was that it occurred in three separate waves. The Tydings-McDuffie Act of Congress in 1934 set up the structure for Philippine independence ten years from that date, and at the same time imposed immigration restrictions. This, and the effects of the Great Depression in Hawai'i, brought the inflow almost to a halt. Immigration and independence were both suspended by World War II. Although the waves that followed are beyond the time frame of this chapter, they will be mentioned. After World War II, and before Philippine independence on July 4, 1946, the Secretary of the Interior made an exception, as allowed by the Tydings-McDuffie Act, and let 6,000 men, 446 women, and 915 children come to Hawai'i with the understanding the men would work on the plantations, as would many women and older children. When the Philippines achieved independence, quotas were imposed by U. S. immigration law as on all other nations. This translated into 100 annually from the Philippines. The Immigration and Nationality Act of 1965 abolished national-origin quotas and allowed 20,000 immigrants each year, plus close relatives of U.S. citizens, from the Philippines. An average of about 5,000 took advantage of this every year. This number included many women, so that a near gender balance was reached in Hawai'i within a few years. It was only then that Filipino culture began to flower and make an impact in the Islands.

It has been pointed out before that culture is carried best to other lands by family units. Once there, traditional ways continue to be followed and are often transmitted to others. Because most Filipinos who had come to the Islands by the 1930s were single, not many elements of their culture or social structure survived in Kōloa, or anywhere else in Hawai'i. This was a loss because the Philippine culture from which the workers had come was an interesting if incongruous blend of diversity and homogeneity. Geographically their country was part of the East, but culturally it was largely Western. The Philippines had been strongly influenced by nearly four centuries of rule by Spain, but traditionally strong family ties and other Southeast Asian moorings remained.

Filipinos have a rich folklore tradition. Their myths and legends deal with such subjects as the origin of the world and of mankind and explain the essence of nature. Other tales are associated with the Spanish conquest. Muslim Filipinos tell a dramatic epic called *Darangen*, and the Ilocanos of northern Luzon tell another entitled *Biag ni Lamang.* In their homeland Filipinos played a variety of musical instruments and performed traditional songs and colorful dances to celebrate courtship, marriage, the harvest, and other occasions. All this would have to wait more than half a century until Filipino families formed a significant part of the population in Hawai'i.

One thing the first immigrants did bring with them was a willingness to work hard. As with preceding groups, the Filipinos on their arrival were assigned the most menial tasks. They followed instructions well, were persistent in accomplishing the tasks assigned, and endured the heat and dust with a smile. They did not share the emphasis on education and upward mobility characteristic of both the Chinese and Japanese, nor did organization and leadership develop in their communities in the same way. More than a third of the first immigrants were illiterate when recruited, and as late as 1930 some 60 percent remained illiterate. Having been under Spanish domination, they were unaccustomed and untrained to enter occupations requiring enterprise when their contracts expired, as the Chinese and Japanese had done. In the 1930s, more than 90 percent were still unskilled agricultural workers.

The Filipinos who came in the two succeeding waves have demonstrated more enterprise and interest in education. They have purchased land and entered into various businesses by forming rotating credit associations called *hulugan*, similar to the *tanomoshi* of the Japanese who had preceded them, and to the *wui* of the Chinese, who had preceded both. As this is being written, the governor of the State of Hawai'i is a Filipino.

A total of 125,917 Filipino men, women, and children arrived in Hawai'i up to 1934. About 88 percent were male adults, and nearly two-thirds of the total remained in the Islands.

A final summary of immigration to Hawai'i from all sources can be stated simply. The numbers peaked from 1885 to 1910; the total was approximately 450,000; and more than half of these remained in the Islands.

Chapter Ten

Plantation Life

The last chapter told of the waves of immigrants who came, like breakers upon the shore, to Hawai'i and when they came. It also told something of the culture each group brought. Together, that gave a sense of the *process* that produced the plantation way of life in Kōloa in the 1930s. This chapter will describe the result of that process.

Imagine you are walking along a dusty road in the town of Kōloa in the mid-1930s. It is afternoon, *pau hana*, following a long and hard day plantation laborers have spent in the cane fields. The people passing you are Japanese, Portuguese, Chinese, Hawaiian, Filipino, and others who have come from many lands. All are friendly in the *aloha* tradition. One remarks to another in marvelous and melodious Pidgin, "Hey, da kine tako 'ono, eh?" You may not understand he thinks the octopus he had for lunch was delicious, but the words have an exotic sound. A Portuguese lady passes you with a bag of *malasadas* (round doughnuts) and some *pão doce* (sweet bread) to give her friends. The aroma almost overwhelms you. You hear the clatter of *mah-jongg* tiles drifting from a window in the upper story of a Chinese home. Colorful *koi* kites fly from a bamboo pole nailed to the side of an unpainted wooden house. They had been put up for Japanese Boy's Day but looked so beautiful they are still there. Plantation workers sit on a porch and "talk story" while sipping homemade beer bottled in soy-sauce bottles picked out of the trash. Now and then an intriguing scent wafts from one of the small ethnic restaurants along the road. A grizzled old Filipino sits on a stoop stroking his rooster, which he plans to enter in a fight somewhere secret next weekend. A pair of Japanese men walk by in *yukata* robes. Their faces are red and their bodies steam from a hot bath in a *furo*, even though the afternoon is warm. You pass the only Chinese store still in town and see shark fins, herbs, and hundreds of unidentifiable things. Two or three *keiki*, or children, plod by on a horse, heading to the beach or a favorite swimming hole where they will romp in nature's bathing suits. Some girls laugh as they play hopscotch with stones tossed into squares they've drawn in the dust with their fingers. In an empty lot, boys are playing baseball with a ball made of wound string, using a *hau* branch for a bat. In the distance, multicolored homemade kites soar high overhead.

This gives a glimpse of what life in Kōloa was like then for the multicultural mosaic of people who had come, and for their children. But this is only a glimpse of *pau hana* life, when the workers were not working. It is just enough to make us want to know more about their leisure activities as well as their working day. The place to start is the ethnic makeup of the people living in Kōloa and those working on the plantation.

The last chapter concluded with the fact that some 450,000 immigrants had arrived in Hawai'i from the middle of the last century to the 1930s, and approximately 250,000 remained. This means little unless we know more about the ones who remained and the population into which they merged, as we proceed through the Islands to Kaua'i and finally to Kōloa and its plantation in the 1930s.

First, we turn to census figures. The immigrants who remained, and their descendants, were part of the total population of Hawai'i in 1930 of 368,336. The population of Kaua'i numbered 35,942, of which 13,905 were Japanese, 12,562 Filipino, 2,554 Portuguese, 1,758 part-Hawaiian, 1,363 Hawaiian, 1,201 Chinese, 1,171 Caucasian, 841 Puerto Rican, 362 Korean, 204 Spanish, and 21 others.

Census figures available for Kōloa in 1930 and 1940 record the ethnic makeup in those two years but not the middle of the decade, our primary interest. Nor do they distinguish between those working on the plantation and those who were not. Kōloa was a plantation town in every sense. The hierarchical organization of the plantation and its demands upon the lives of its workers made the plantation a dominant factor in community life.

Rather than cluttering the page with census figures and ethnic makeup, these statistics can be used in a more informative way. The most detailed ethnic breakdown available for Kōloa Plantation employees in any one year during that decade happens to be for 1935. The data were gathered carefully for this and other aspects of Kōloa Plantation for its centennial-year history, *Koloa Plantation 1835-1935*. If one can be forgiven for averaging census figures of Kōloa for 1930 and 1940 in order to compare them with those working on the plantation in 1935, more is gained than lost.

Even with both sets of figures, there is a caveat to observe. The use of any set of numbers for a single year gives only a pale reflection of the prevailing culture, because the people who had lived in Kōloa in the past, those who had died or departed, left their ethnic influences behind.

With this caveat, the comparison in 1935 is:

	Estimate from censuses	On Kōloa Plantation
Filipinos	487	434
Japanese	475	181
Caucasians	108	33
Portuguese	92	37
Hawaiians and Part-Hawaiians	71	9
Chinese	29	0
Puerto Ricans	28	13
Koreans	4	3
Others	35	11
Total	**1329**	**721**

The plantation figures were for adults while census figures included everyone (although under-counting was common), making the comparison even more interesting. Filipinos were the most numerous, a majority of them were in the labor force, and few had families; more than half of the Japanese had left the plantation and had families; a third of the Caucasians were employed by the plantation; either half of the Portuguese had left the plantation, or they had much larger families, or both; a number of Hawaiians and part-Hawaiians lived in the area but few worked for Kōloa Plantation; there were no Chinese in the plantation labor force but a number remained in the community; Puerto Ricans had followed the same patterns as the Portuguese by leaving the plantation, or having larger families, or both; and Koreans had all but vanished from both Kōloa and the plantation.

These figures provide a basis for understanding life both in the town and on the plantation. By 1900, as described in a previous chapter, Kōloa had become a community with schools, churches, stores, and recreational facilities. It slowly grew from then to 1930 but still retained its rural character. The main street, Kōloa Road,

Kōloa Landing Road, 1920, as viewed from its intersection with Government Road. These are now Po'ipū Road and Kōloa Road, respectively.

as yet unnamed, was surfaced with crushed gravel but still turned to mud in heavy rains. A drainage ditch ran along the southern side. Stores also lined that side, as they do now, and in order to enter one had to "walk the plank" each store placed across the ditch. Government Road, then also referred to as "the belt road" running through Kōloa, was completed with many laterals in 1917. Kōloa Landing Road had been asphalted in 1912 and was the first in the Kōloa area to be improved for a reason. Sand blew over the road as it neared the ocean; although a horse and buggy could get through, the cars that were appearing on the island got stuck. Old county records describing various roads as "paved" are rather humorous to read. Often this meant the road had been improved with compacted coral, or a thin layer of tar had been spread on the road. In the latter case, rocks soon emerged and gravel had to be spread over them. The records are more reliable starting in the 1930s when federal funds became available.

Automobiles were rare on Kaua'i until 1920 or so. George N. Wilcox bought the first one in 1908. New owners were listed every year in *The Garden Island*, the local newspaper. According to *The Garden Island* there were 367 on the island by 1916. After World War I, the number increased rapidly and that quaint news item was abandoned. Still, there was little automobile traffic in Kōloa. Perhaps one would see a parked car and a horse or two plodding along. Most everyone walked, so there would be several people here and there on the road. Some gathered on store porches to sit in the shade and socialize. Crime, except for gambling, cock-fighting, and an occasional drunken brawl, did not exist. Doors were left unlocked. In fact, most doors didn't have locks. A few chickens foraged about. Above all, Kōloa was quiet.

Two questions are frequently raised about relations among the various immigrant groups then living in Kōloa. The one most often asked is how the groups were ranked socially by plantation management and by each other, if at all. For the first few years after each group arrived, their skills and labor were so sorely needed they were ranked according to these. The *haole* managers held themselves above the largely uneducated groups and treated workers with the respect due their skills. Other groups tended to follow the *haole* lead in relation to one another. As more came, the tendency was to rank individuals of an ethnic group according to previous experiences with that group in respect to education, literacy, and skills. In the thirties, the Portuguese still occupied a unique position. Cultured and educated Portuguese would have been regarded as *haole* and accepted into that community. But those who came were poor farmers with swarthy skin who labored in the fields. A *haole* didn't do that sort of thing, so the Portuguese took a place in society between the workers and *haole* supervisors, not quite *haole* but not common laborers either.

This question about social ranking is almost always followed by another: how did the ethnic groups interact? In general, the Japanese regarded other groups in a somewhat stereotypical way, ranking them in a strict social order with themselves at the top of the hierarchy. This is part of the reason they rarely married outside their own group. They brought with them their prejudice against Koreans and Okinawans. When the Philippines were invaded at the start of World War II, the Filipinos of Kōloa felt hostility towards the Japanese but rarely demonstrated it. With these exceptions, the answer, then, is "surprisingly well."

Individuals of each ethnic group preferred to socialize within their own but worked and mingled easily with the others. Every group in Kōloa was a minority. There is no record or memory of any significant conflict between ethnic groups. Perhaps in our troubled times today, we can learn something from this. When there is no majority there can be no target at which a minority group can riot, or rail in paranoid posturing while demanding special rights. The makeup of society on the mainland is approaching one in which all groups will be minorities, so there may be hope in this.

Most of a worker's waking hours, six days a week, were spent in the fields. Thus, an ordinary day should be described before more is said about leisure life.

As sugar plantations go, Kōloa Plantation was medium-sized in the thirties, employing fewer than a thousand workers. The larger ones in the Islands at the time had 2,000 to 3,000. From the beginning, perhaps because of the missionary presence in Kōloa, it was considered one of the best plantations in Hawai'i on which to work. Only Grove Farm had a better reputation on Kaua'i and it employed free laborers almost exclusively. The managers and other officials of both plantations realized more work would be done when the workers were healthy and reasonably content, and the deserters fewer. During one period from 1882 to 1900 this did not apply to Kōloa Plantation. The manager was a reserve officer in the German army and operated the plantation along strict military lines. He sent his plantation police to arrest "runaways," for example, and at one point in 1889 had 63 workers in jail. A reliable contemporary account characterized him as "exacting, impetuous, and at times tactless and overbearing." Otherwise, employees of Kōloa Plantation were reasonably content, although the work was very hard.

Women field workers, Kōloa Plantation, about 1910.

☞ Bishop Museum

Cutting cane, or *kālai kō*. The Hawaiian word *kālai* means "to cut or carve" and *kō* means cane. The stalks were then cleaned of leaves, called *hole hole* or "strip strip" work. When mechanical harvesting began, the leaves were removed by burning the cane fields first.

Bishop Museum

In the 1930s, a typical working day began when the bell rang at the train "crossing," as it did six days a week, at 4 A.M. to waken the workers. The mill whistle did likewise for those at Mill Camp. The *luna* would go through the camps shouting *hana hana*, or "work work" to make sure everyone was awake. The men got up, washed, and dressed while the women fixed lunches and put them in pails. Workers assembled at the "crossing" before 5 A.M. when, with a toot of its whistle, the train pulled out promptly. It stopped near places where workers would be needed to let off the ones assigned there. They walked in the dark to where they were to work, then started as soon as it was light enough to see.

While the men were in the fields, the women left behind cleaned the houses, sewed, cared for children, fed the chickens, and tended vegetable gardens. Some women did work in the field, although few in the early years of the plantation. When large numbers of Japanese began to arrive, as many as 15 percent of the women worked in the fields for the first few years. If the women had babies, they worked with them slung on their backs or put them down in a shady place. Within ten years or so after their arrival, most women had learned other ways to supplement the family income. Some laundered bachelors' clothing or cooked supper for single workers. Two or three decades later, as more Filipino women arrived, some worked in the fields.

The luna called a breakfast break of 15 minutes at 8 A.M., and a half-hour break for lunch at 11 A.M. Workers sat together in the shade of the cane, which was 10 to 12 feet high, and often shared portions of their ethnic foods. They relieved themselves in the fields. If they were in tall cane, both men and women walked only a few feet away for privacy. If in a cleared field, workers walked a short distance; the men turned for modesty and women squatted, covering themselves with their skirts. Workers had to request permission from their *luna* to defecate but could take a *shishi* (urination) break when they needed to. In either case, the *luna* made sure a worker was not gone long.

The Kōloa area was rocky, so the land was constantly being cleared. The rocks were piled in places where cane growth was poor. Plowing had to be deep for the cane to grow well. By 1930, the Fowler steam plows had been replaced by tractors. Seed cane, consisting of sections of selected cane about 15 inches long, was placed in the furrows by hand. During the two years each crop took to mature, the necessary fertilizing, irrigating, and weed-hoeing also were done manually.

Although rainfall could be relied upon for about 20 percent of the water needed, a system of ditches from mountain sources

A Japanese "piler" woman about 1900 stacking the cane in bundles to be loaded on a cane car.

☞ Bishop Museum

A *hāpai kō* man loading cane. The word *hāpai* is Hawaiian for "carry".

Bishop Museum

and pumps at Māhā'ulepū provided the rest. Work on the irrigation system was referred to as *hanawai*, from the Hawaiian words *hana*, work, and *wai*, water.

Weeding was called *hō hana*, or hoe work. Early Hawaiian workers had coined the word *hō* to sound like "hoe," an implement unknown to them before the sugar industry. With that spelling it became part of their language.

When the cane was mature and ready for harvest, the stalks were cut close to the ground with long cane knives or machetes. This was called *kālai kō*, the Hawaiian word *kālai* meaning to cut or carve. The leaves were then stripped off using cane knives by those doing *hole hole* (strip strip) work. This was easier than cutting cane, so women and older children customarily did this. By 1937, when mechanical cane cutters began to appear, the fields were set afire to remove the leaves. *Hole hole* workers had only to strip those not burned off.

"Piler boys" (or women) arranged the cut cane into piles and tied them with a cane leaf. Then came the hardest work of all, loading the cut cane onto the cars. This was called *hāpai kō*, the Hawaiian word *hāpai* meaning to carry, lift, or bear. Each cane car held 2 to 3 tons of cut cane. A good *hāpai kō* man could fill 5 or 6 cars in one day, carrying bundles of 70 to 80 pounds on his shoulder each trip up the narrow loading board on which cleats had been nailed. Mules or oxen pulled the loaded cane car to the permanent track. From there a locomotive hauled a string of cane cars to the mill.

All during the day, a "water boy" passed among the workers with buckets filled from the nearest irrigation ditch. The buckets were slung from both ends of a pole carried on his shoulder.

A working day averaged ten hours. *Pau hana*, or quitting time, depended somewhat on the season and the time the sun rose so they could start. Usually it was about 4 P.M. and signaled by the mill whistle. When the *luna* gave the order, the workers stopped and made their way back to the permanent track the same way they had come. The train came puffing up and stopped; they boarded and were returned either to Mill Camp or to the "crossing" in Kōloa. Usually enough daylight remained for the workers to tend their vegetable gardens or do chores around the house.

Although the Hawaiian Sugar Planters' Association had attempted to standardize wages by making recommendations to the plantations, their advice was not widely followed. Wages on Kōloa Plantation in the 1930s were paid according to the aggregate utility of each ethnic group. The pay and perquisites also reflected

A Chinese food and tea vendor returning from the fields about 1900.

☛ Hawai'i State Archives

Numbered brass tags, later called bangō, the Japanese word for "number", were worn by early immigrant plantation workers for identification. The numbering system worked so well it was adopted by supervisory personnel, and remained in use on Kōloa Plantation into its latest years.

what the workers from a particular place, such as those from Europe, had demanded in order to be recruited, The law of supply and demand also affected wages. Filipino recruits were then abundantly available, as the Japanese had been before 1924, so their wages were correspondingly lower. There was no individual evaluation for laborers, only for the skilled employees. With few exceptions, the most recent groups to arrive received the lowest wages. Within a decade or so they were adept at their chores, hardened to them, more productive, and had learned to understand the *luna*. By then, those who were dissatisfied with the work had left and the remainder were "volunteers." Wages were increased to the range received by the others, but even within that range a differential according to aggregate utility persisted.

If possible, each team in the fields was composed of workers of the same race or similar ethnic origin and language. A *luna* was assigned to each group largely based on how well the workers could understand his orders.

The introduction of small brass identification tags called *bāngo* (bāngo is Japanese for number) had started early in the plantation experience. Workers either pinned them to their clothes or wore them on chains around the neck so as not to lose them. At the start *bāngo* were used because foreign names were difficult to remember and pronounce, but the workers and the *luna* learned and remembered numbers. Bāngo were shown at the Kōloa plantation store to put the items purchased on account. On payday, the amount owed the store was deducted on the spot. One of the disciplinary methods was docking a worker's pay, which also took place on payday. Insubordination or failure to report for work, for example, was worth half a day's pay. *Bāngo* numbers were found to be so useful in bookkeeping, their use persisted long after the *luna* and others had learned the workers' names. Even supervisory personnel were assigned numbers.

Most of the *luna* on Kōloa Plantation were Portuguese, who in turn had *haole* field supervisors as their superiors. The Hawaiian word *luna* means "above" or "over." Each *luna* supervised groups of 20 to 30 workers, usually from horseback, and occasionally snapped his whip to spur on the workers. The Hawaiian kingdom had outlawed whipping in 1853, as did regulations of the Bureau of Immigration since 1869. Federal labor laws in effect after 1900 also forbade such mistreatment. Yet, many *luna* still carried whips in the 1930s, partly as symbols of their authority, but mostly because the "snap" made the workers respond with greater alacrity. Perhaps the noise startled them, but more probably each thought, "you just never know."

Kōloa Mill and workers' camps about 1900. The base of the smokestack stands in the heart of Kōloa today. The railroad track in the foreground led to Kōloa Landing.

Hawai'i State Archives

The first plantation houses built were for Hawaiian laborers and made of grass thatch. They were either near the mill or dispersed in the cane fields near streams where Hawaiians could irrigate their taro. Workers walked or rode in oxcarts to the field locations where they labored. Apparently not much thought was put into the location of housing for the Chinese before they arrived. They did not grow taro but wanted to raise vegetables instead. It was much more efficient to locate their housing centrally, and wooden barracks were built in or near Kōloa. Most of the Chinese were male and content to live in the barracks, called "long houses." Each had 10 or 12 bunk beds and a kitchen, an outhouse in back, and plots of land assigned nearby to raise vegetables.

The immigrant groups that followed the Chinese saw the introduction of plantation camps consisting of individual houses. Far from their homelands, workers wanted to live near others who spoke their language and practiced the same customs and traditions. Separate camps were built for each new ethnic group as it arrived. They also were located near the town of Kōloa. Later, as workers adapted to their new lives, they were allowed to choose the camp in which they wanted to live. From then on, the composition of each camp was mixed but they retained their early names. When the railroads were laid out starting in 1882, camps were built within walking distance of the "crossing." In later years individual plantation houses were built in the town of Kōloa itself when the advantage of living close to stores, schools, and theaters became appreciated.

The main camps, now all but gone, were laid out according to the following:

"Haole Camp" was not really a camp but a row of supervisors' homes located along the *mauka* side of Waila'au Road. Although these houses look new today, only one is. The rest are all well-maintained originals.

Spanish Camp was just north of Haole Camp and reached by a path at the eastern end of Haole Camp. Built when the Spanish arrived between 1907 and 1914, it consisted of three rows of five houses each. After the Spanish left, Puerto Ricans, Portuguese, and others who had similar customs and languages lived there.

Stable Camp was a small camp for workers at the plantation dairy and stables, located on the east side of the curve where Waila'au Road turned south. The railroad ran through the area so manure could be taken to the fields for fertilizer. About 180 horses and mules were kept in the stables and fed ground-up cane tops and pineapple skins to supplement grazing in the pasture.

A typical Kōloa Plantation worker's camp house, built about 1910.

Photograph by author, 1999.

Portuguese Camp was just south of the stables and had 20 to 25 houses in three rows. Each row had an outdoor Portuguese oven, as did some individual houses.

Filipino Camp was the next camp south of Portuguese Camp. The influx of Filipino immigrants overflowed Filipino Camp into vacant housing in other camps.

Japanese Camp was a short walk east of the plantation store (now the First Hawaiian Bank). A path led to the camp along the left side of the smaller Kōloa Jodo Mission Temple, the only temple there then. The camp had about 40 homes and stretched east behind the mission.

Korean Camp was nearby to the southeast. Small, it was located just inland from the intersection of Waoke and Waikomo Roads. Filipinos occupied Korean Camp by 1930.

New Mill Camp, built just south of the 1913 mill, consisted of about 20 structures. Most were barracks, or "long houses," for single Japanese and Filipino men. These were an improvement over the barracks built for the Chinese. Each had from four to a dozen rooms and each worker had his own room. Homes for skilled mill workers and supervisory personnel were built nearer the mill. The barracks were demolished in 1952 when more cane land was needed, but most of the houses at the mill are there today and rented out by Grove Farm.

In the mid-1930s, Kōloa Plantation had a total of 24 houses for skilled employees or supervisors, and 310 houses and barracks for unskilled workers, most of them in the various camps. When Kōloa Plantation started selling houses to workers after the 1946 strike, the era of plantation camps came to an end. Many of the new owners rebuilt their homes, often in the camp-house style but enlarged. Some remained in the original houses that are still there.

The typical camp house in the thirties was a simple wooden frame structure with board and batten walls. The exterior was painted when the house was built, but from then on it could be painted by the occupants if they wished. The usual exterior colors were green or rust, with off-white trim. The interior walls were whitewashed yearly by the plantation. Floors were made of tongue-and-groove hardwood and left unpainted. The occupants scrubbed the floors with soap and water using coconut husks for brushes. The roofs of corrugated galvanized sheet iron had no inside ceilings. Most houses were one or two bedroom with a dining room and a kitchen. Usually a married couple shared a two-bedroom house with another couple. In a three-bedroom house each couple had a bedroom and all three shared the kitchen. Exceptions to this general rule were made when the families had children.

A cold shower and laundry shed was at the back door of each house, and an outhouse stood farther back. Most outhouses had two holes, one of which was small so children wouldn't fall through. Toilet paper could be purchased, but most used newspaper or anything similar. Because the shallow soil precluded cesspools, human waste fell into boxes under the holes. A designated plantation worker came around every day, lifted a flap in back of the outhouse, and threw lime in the box. Once a month, plantation employees assigned this task came by in a mule-drawn "honey wagon," lifted the flap, slid out the box, and replaced it with an empty one. The load of boxes was taken to various places near the foothills above the cane fields and dumped. This service was provided by the plantation. The few locks used in Kōloa in the 1930s were on clean outhouses so others wouldn't mess them up.

Houses were provided free with basic furniture. The lots were eight to ten thousand feet square so workers could grow vegetables and raise chickens. Virtually every family raised chickens, which were allowed to range freely. A small coop was built for them near the house where they were fed scraps each evening. Children collected the eggs; because the hens nested in the underbrush, there was a trick to finding eggs. A child would hold a hen after it had fed until it was flapping frantically to get back to its nest. The child would let the hen go, follow it through the underbrush to the nest, and retrieve the eggs.

Wood-burning stoves came with each camp house, and approximately a cord of cut firewood was delivered by mule-drawn wagon to each worker and his family every month. This was not enough wood for Japanese who had *furo*, so they were given tools and told where to cut more. A worker put his *bāngo* number on the cut pile of wood and it was delivered to his house.

Starting in 1910, employees were offered kerosene stoves, and over the next decade or two most had converted. Every month, each worker was given two 5-gallon cans of kerosene, which was also used in the lamps.

There were no washing machines for workers, so the women washed clothes in a large oil drum. They filled it with water, added the harsh but cheap yellow soap from the plantation store, then boiled and stirred the clothes over a fire. They took out the clothes, laid them on a clean area of concrete, and "hit 'em widda stick." When clean, the women rinsed the clothes and hung them out on a line to dry. They ironed with a charcoal iron, using hand bellows to get the coals hot before putting them into the iron.

Workers had some choice in purchasing food and other supplies. There were small stores in some camps, usually run by Chinese or Japanese, stores that catered to the preferences of their own ethnic groups, and a few larger stores and the plantation store in town. Workers had no transportation of their own, except perhaps a horse, and it would have been difficult to carry the purchases home. Because of this, an order-and-delivery system developed. Every afternoon, salesmen from the larger stores in town circulated in the camps taking orders, then deliveries were made by wagon or truck the next day. All of the stores followed the lead of the Kōloa plantation store and allowed employees to charge their purchases. Accounts were settled on payday.

The plantation dairy kept milk cows to supply the hospital and managers. The latter had milk delivered to them free. Workers, if they brought their own containers, could buy any milk left over at a low price.

Before 1922, water was supplied by tanks, usually one to a camp. Water had to be carried in buckets to individual homes. In that year, a concrete conduit was constructed from Ku'ia Stream and potable water piped to all the stores and houses. It was provided free by the plantation.

Electricity was slow in coming to Kaua'i and Kōloa. McBryde Sugar Company put in the first system on the island in 1906, bringing power to their pumps and mill from Wainiha. This was gradually extended to the homes in Numila Camp. It was available in Līhu'e by 1913, but not in the more remote areas of Kaua'i until much later. In 1918, a 120-kilowatt hydroelectric power plant was built north of Kōloa on "powerhouse hill," taking water from the Wai'ahi-Ku'ia aqueduct. This supplied electric power to the town of Kōloa, the camps nearby, and the well pumps. A small generator powered by bagasse supplied electricity to the mill and offices, but Mill Camp did not have electricity until 1931 when a larger generator was installed at the mill. Electricity was also furnished free by the plantation.

Refrigerators could be purchased but were prohibitively expensive for the workers. Iceboxes were cheaper and most houses had them. Ice was brought to the camps from Kōloa and at times from Waimea, by horse-drawn wagon for sale. In homes without iceboxes, food was kept in a cupboard open to cooler air underneath the house. Meat was eaten the day it was purchased, or salted so it would keep.

There were few telephones in Kōloa in the 1930s. George N. Wilcox put in the first line in 1880 so Dr. James Smith could be reached from Līhu'e, but the system grew slowly until the

The home of Dr. Herbert Waterhouse in Kōloa, 1910.

The Smith-Waterhouse family collection

1920s. By 1930, Kōloa Plantation officials had them, as did the hospital, pump stations, and certain stores. Radios were also few. The first reception from Honolulu was a concert in 1922, the year the "wireless," as it was called, came to Hawai'i. In the 1930s plantation officials and others with electricity who could afford to buy radios received KGMB and KGU from Honolulu until these stations shifted to low power at 6 P.M. Kaua'i did not acquire its first radio station, KTOH, until 1940. The remains of its antenna can still be seen near Jack Harter's helicopter office near the airport. It seems that no one remembers what the call letters stood for, but they must have been for "Kaua'i, Territory of Hawai'i."

Women made clothing from bolt cloth purchased at the plantation store. For some women, sewing became a specialized skill that made it worthwhile to purchase a treadle sewing machine. The workers wore *'āhina*, or blue denim, made into trousers much like our blue jeans today, and either denim or *palaka* (plaid) shirts. They sometimes wore the same clothes for days because they couldn't afford to have their clothes washed every day. However, those doing *hāpai kō* or other dirty work found it necessary to have them washed daily. In the fields, workers wore wide-brimmed straw hats for protection from the sun and wrapped bandannas over their faces to filter out the red dust.

Medical care was provided free to workers. Because of language barriers, some Japanese obtained care for a fee from a Japanese physician in private practice in Kōloa. The hospital/dispensary built by the plantation in 1911 consisted of a clinic for outpatients and an attached hospital with an operating room. Wives of workers regarded childbirth as a natural phenomenon and not really a medical event. Births were at home with hired midwives. The usual rate was $10 for midwife care (about a fourth of the average worker's monthly pay). The plantation sent a nurse from the dispensary afterwards to check up on the mother and child.

The physician and nurses were paid by the plantation and also by the Hawaiian government for performing public-health services. Dr. Herbert Waterhouse was the plantation physician until 1933, when he was let go for political reasons. He was replaced by Dr. Marvin Brennecke. Thereafter, Dr. Waterhouse maintained a private practice in a clinic at his home. More often than not he treated patients without charge. If a person appeared to be poorly nourished, he gave them a few eggs or other food.

Plantation workers received dental care from itinerant dentists at a small clinic next to the courthouse (now the Kōloa Civic Center).

While their parents worked, the children attended school. During the summers they could work in the fields and earn money to help their families, so most did by age 9 or 10. Their starting job was picking up "small cane," the cut cane that had fallen off cane cars. When they were bigger they hoed weeds and planted seed cane. St. Raphael Catholic School had closed long before, so all children attended Kōloa School, where classes were held in open bungalows. The students walked to school barefoot. Those who came from farther away than the camps (Kukui'ula, 'Ōma'o, and Lāwa'i) rode bareback on a horse, as many as could stay on.

Students brought food from home for lunch. They gathered in the orchard next to the school or on the rock wall behind the school, sharing strange foods with one another. *Musubi* and rice balls with pickled red plums inside were exchanged for salted fish or Korean *kimchi* (pickled cabbage spiced with garlic and hot pepper). Portuguese children were delighted their ordinary sandwiches were regarded as exotic and in demand, but they would still ask their parents for a bit of *pão doce* (sweet bread) or *linguica* (Portuguese spicy sausage) just in case. Hawaiian children found their *laulau* had great trading value. Some students could afford to buy ethnic food at the stores across the street and joined in the swapping and Pidgin conversation. These shared lunchtimes every school day throughout childhood may have had much to do with the racial harmony in Kōloa.

The Pidgin they spoke was another bond. At home, all the students heard and used was either the native tongue of their parents or Pidgin. Although a few of the teachers were *haole*, and others had been educated at the Normal School in Honolulu, most teachers of the early grades spoke Pidgin, so many younger children believed that Pidgin was really English. If they heard a *haole* speaking correct English, one might say, "Huy, wassamalla dis haole . . . he no can spik *haole!*"

School let out at two in the afternoon. After that, children might sneak into the orchard of Dr. Waterhouse to steal fruit. Guavas and mangos grew wild all around Kōloa, but stolen fruit tasted much better. Boys liked to play marbles, five hole and fish (knock 'em out of a fish drawn on the ground, keep 'em). They swam in ditches, various water holes, and Waitā Reservoir. One of the best swimming holes was at the old bridge in town, but ladies walking by there sometimes complained about the nudity. The boys saved Bull Durham sacks from "roll your own" tobacco for such situations, pulled them on and tied them in the obvious place. This caused more hilarity than indignation, so they could soon return to swimming nude. One game the boys liked was a top fight. They put nails in the tips of their tops, then tried to split each other's tops. On rainy days, all of the kids headed for favorite hills to slide down in the mud on a bundle of *ti* leaves.

Japanese children had to attend Japanese-language school. There were two one-hour classes after English school let out every day. The first hour was for grades 1 through 4, and the second hour for grades 5 through 8. Saturday morning was split similarly with two-hour classes. The teachers were *bon-san*, or priests, from the two nearby Hongwanji and Jodo Buddhist temples.

Only a small portion of the elementary-school students went on to the single high school on the island, Kaua'i High School, in Līhu'e. Mr. Yamaguchi ran the Waimea Stables bus from Waimea to and from the high school, but it was costly for workers. The income from work the children did was needed by many families, and boarding in Līhu'e was prohibitively expensive. Some managerial officials, mostly *haole*, had automobiles, and parents arranged car-sharing to Līhu'e. The upper level of officials and merchants sent their children to Punahou, a private school in Honolulu, where they boarded and returned on holidays. The Japanese believed so strongly in education that many sent their children to Honolulu, where they lived with relatives or friends while attending the one public high school there, McKinley High School, which became known as "Tokyo High."

Religion was an important part of life. Kōloa Plantation leased land to churches and temples for a dollar a year, contributed to their construction, and helped to support their activities. The various religions and sects that existed in Kōloa are described in previous chapters.

For adults, recreation in Kōloa consisted mostly of socializing with friends. Everyone knew everyone else, and despite the hard work there was time to talk story. Frequently, movies were shown outdoors in the camps. In town, the Shinagawa Theater showed mostly Japanese films, but the Old Plantation Theater near the ballpark had a wider variety. After it burned down in 1936, the New Plantation Theater was built near the site of the Old Mill. In the evenings, men often drank "swipe wine" they made by fermenting molasses. They might throw in whatever fruit was available, which sometimes gave it a distinctive flavor. Some had learned to distill it, which made "swipe" as potent as any bottled liquor. The origin of the name "swipe" is obscure, but one suspects it had something to do with the way the molasses was acquired. Prohibition was in effect until 1933, but this just added to the enjoyment. Japanese played *go,* which is similar to chess. Filipinos had weekend cockfights where they loved to gamble. Filipinos also were fond of fishing with long bamboo poles along the shore. "Taxi" dances were arranged for them at least once a month, with women from Honolulu who charged a dime for each dance. The dances were brief, lasting only a minute or so. More discreetly, the women were available for other purposes at certain establishments. One was surprisingly close to the missionary residences.

Recreation was supported in many ways by the plantation. It had built the Old Plantation Theater where movies were provided free for small *keiki* and for workers who had not missed a day during the previous month. For others, the charge was a dime for children under 12, and a quarter for adults. After it burned down, the New Plantation Theater was built and admission was the same. The plantation cleared and maintained ball fields and organized games with leagues for barefoot baseball, soccer, and football. It also furnished musical instruments and organized performances of the music of all ethnic groups.

Holidays were great occasions for all. The Chinese still living in Kōloa gathered with friends and celebrated Chinese New Year, usually in February, by hanging banners and flags, and setting off strings of firecrackers.

The Japanese celebrated a number of holidays. They observed Boy's Day by flying brightly-colored *koi* kites on a bamboo pole nailed to their homes; and Girl's Day by dressing girls in beautiful new clothes, when they could afford them. As described in the last chapter, *O-Bon* ceremonies were held in mid-summer. The celebration of Japanese New Year was their most popular annual festival. The traditions connected with it reflected its original association with the coming of spring and a time of rebirth. The festival is called *ji oshogatsu* in Japanese and was celebrated with feasting and the exchange of visits and gifts. The house gateway or entrance was hung with a *shimenawa* (a sacred rope made of rice straw) to keep out evil spirits; it was decorated with fern, bitter orange, and lobster, which respectively signified good fortune, prosperity, and longevity. Foods special to the holiday were *mochi* (cakes of sweet rice paste wrapped around azuki beans) and *zoni* (a soup of vegetables and mochi). The traditional amusements on Japanese New Year were shuttlecock and *utagaruta,* a card game that involved matching lines of 100 poems.

The emperor's birthday, *Tencho-setsu,* was celebrated with *sumo* wrestling and music, often played on *samisens* made out of tin cans. Japanese workers were given the day off and the

Japanese-language school was closed. Each family worshiped at their home shrines and bowed as one of them read the emperor's prescript. Although the youngsters dutifully participated, some wondered why they were not bowing to President Roosevelt instead of the emperor.

On December 30, Rizal Day was the celebration of the Filipinos commemorating the execution of Dr. Jose Rizal in the Spanish Revolution of 1896. There was a great gathering of Filipinos and others in the old ballpark with music and dancing. Kōloa Plantation donated a cow, which was barbecued, and a great feast was held.

The Holy Ghost Feast of the Portuguese, honoring the Holy Ghost on Pentecost Sunday, had come with the immigrants from the Azores. In Kōloa, it stretched over sequential Sundays for seven weeks. There was a different host family for each week where *chamarritas* were performed, and the family offered food and entertainment. The person who held the *dominga*, or crown, was decided by lottery the previous year, and that family hosted the seventh week. On the final day there was a procession from their home to St. Raphael Church where High Mass was held, followed by a banquet, games, dances, and auctions. Then a drawing was held for the person to be queen and hold the *dominga* the next year.

One event remembered by all the older residents of Kōloa was the picnic Dr. Herbert Waterhouse sponsored every July fourth for the plantation workers. He was patriotic but it also happened to be his wedding anniversary. He arranged for the train to wait behind the old plantation theater until all were aboard. Then it set off at 8 A.M., paused in New Mill Camp to pick up others, and came to a stop where the track curved to go along the shore. Everyone walked the half-mile with picnic baskets to what is now Poʻipū Beach Park and spent the day there. Dr. Waterhouse had a supply of iced fruit drink waiting that never ran out. He organized games and the kids swam and splashed in the ocean. The one event those living today remember most clearly was catching a greased pig. Whoever caught the pig could keep it. The smartest kids waited until the pig was exhausted and then grabbed it. About 4 P.M., the train took everyone back to Kōloa. Older faces soften as they tell of it today. Their voices do, too.

During the thirties the work was hard and the recreation simple. In the words of one who lived and worked on Kōloa Plantation, "We struggled, no suffered."

Chapter Eleven

By The Wind Grieved

This chapter takes up the story of the sugar industry in Kōloa from the mid-1930s, the point it was interrupted at the end of the chapter "Tall Cane," in order to tell about the immigrants who came to Hawai'i to work on the plantations. During the late 1930's, mechanisms were set in motion that would result in the demise of sugar production in Kōloa. That is not what the title of this chapter laments. The true loss is the passing of the way of life. In some ways the loss of a way of life is similar to the loss of a life itself. The title is from Thomas Wolfe's *Look Homeward, Angel* in which the death of a loved one was mourned with the words, "O lost, and by the wind grieved, ghost, come back again."

In the mid-thirties, life in Kōloa was far from sophisticated, but it had a worth that ours in America lacks today. Families were close, and there was more than enough love for children and the elderly. All religions were accepted, and beliefs were an integral part of the lives of their adherents. Hard work and character were respected, as were other old-fashioned values such as cleanliness, decency and courtesy. Crime was virtually unknown.

Of course, not all of the ethnic groups that had come to Kōloa over the span of more than a hundred years and created the way of life were still there in the 1930s, but descendants of most still were. The people of Kōloa represented a wide spectrum of ethnicity and cultures, and their interpersonal relationships were good. They did not have to contend with the negative aspects we have in so many parts of our country today: illegitimacy, drug use, senseless violence at a presumed slight, or the rioting and looting that destroy a community. A person walked the streets at night without fear and enjoyed meeting and talking with friends. Joshing about appearance, race, or anything else was received as it was intended, and the banter was returned with the same good humor. If it were possible to return to Kōloa in the 1930s and tell those living there then about our troubled times, our description would be met with a look of disbelief and shushed by a wave of the hand and a quiet smile.

Someday, as social scientists study this place and time, we may learn more about what made it work so well. Many vestiges remain, but those who were old enough to remember Kōloa as children and are still with us agree the high-water mark was in the thirties; and the tide has been receding slowly since.

As this account of the sugar industry resumes, the shadow of World War II looms and world events are becoming paramount; before it concludes, young men from Kōloa will be fighting and dying halfway around the globe.

Kōloa Plantation had struggled to operate at a profit through all of its history. As this effort continued into the early thirties, there were as many years of loss as of profit. In 1935, the plantation had an unusually good year, with 2,531 acres under cultivation and a profit of $86,768. That year everyone celebrated the plantation's centennial, attending the varied events in 1835 period costume. Those in managerial ranks did not join fully in the levity. The year before, the National Labor Relations Act passed by Congress allowed unions to organize in the workplace without interference by management. In addition to all their other problems, Kōloa Plantation officials had to worry about what organization of their workers would mean.

Management had been aware, since the arrival of the first Japanese on the plantation, of their cultural cohesiveness and propensity for refusing to work if certain conditions were not acceptable to them. At the time of Annexation, Japanese workers had been the most recent to arrive and received the lowest wages. Over the following years, small groups engaged in a series of unorganized strikes, but up to 1935 the Japanese on Kaua'i had neither organized effectively nor involved significant numbers in their strikes. A factor that management was not as aware of was the effect of the increasing proportion of nisei educated in the Islands, which brought the literacy rate of the Japanese in Hawai'i to approximately 80 percent, either in their own language, or English, or both. A major impediment to labor organization on the plantations had been the difficulty of travel between them because of their wide dispersal. By 1935, Japanese-language newspapers were read by nearly all issei and had become a remarkably efficient medium of communication well suited to organization.

The labor disturbances that had occurred on Oʻahu up to then were only rumblings across the water, like thunder over the far horizon. By 1908, the Japanese had become 70 percent of the territory's plantation labor force. On Oʻahu that year, leaders arose to form The Japanese Higher Wages Association, which called a strike of Japanese workers in 1909 on six Oʻahu plantations. The strike was not well planned and lasted less than a month without obtaining the higher wages sought. However, this strike triggered the planters into intensified recruitment of Filipino and other workers, so that ten years later the Japanese amounted to only 44 percent of the Islands' plantation labor force. In 1920, the Japanese, in a loose alliance with Filipinos, struck again on Oʻahu plantations and tried to extend the strike to the neighbor islands. This effort also was poorly planned and failed to attain its goals.

Although these rumblings were distant, plantation officials on Kauaʻi viewed the latter strike as an ominous harbinger because two ethnic groups had united, however ineffectively, for the first time. Together, the Japanese and Filipinos made up approximately 77 percent of the labor force on Kauaʻi. Some Filipino workers had yet to learn how strikes were to be carried out, and on at least one occasion armed themselves as if they were going into battle. This had unfortunate consequences in a small strike at Makaweli Plantation on Kauaʻi in 1924. It involved only 133 Filipino workers, but they took up arms and captured two strikebreakers. The sheriff, as should have been expected, formed a posse in order to free the two. This turned into a small war near Hanapēpē as gunfire erupted; sixteen Filipinos and four policemen were killed.

Federal agencies began to enter the island labor scene in 1937. The National Labor Relations Board held extensive inquiries to accumulate information. In that same year the Jones-Costigan Act was passed by Congress, authorizing the Agricultural Adjustment Administration to establish the wages of sugar workers at "minimal annual averages." Thus, a stroke of the pen accomplished what the workers had failed to do up to that time. The Internal Revenue Service and Social Security Agency also began to investigate the traditional perquisites given the workers in lieu of wages.

Mainland unions began to organize various urban and rural workers in the 1930s. The CIO chartered an affiliate in Hawaiʻi with the cumbersome name of United Cannery, Agricultural, Packing, and Allied Workers of America. Its first successes organizing sugar and pineapple workers on Kaua'i were on McBryde Plantation and Kaua'i Pineapple. Under the auspices of the UCAPAWA, The Kaua'i Progressive League was formed to enter the political arena in opposition to the Republican planter-representatives in the territorial legislature. In 1939 it succeeded in ousting the two longtime Kaua'i representatives, Lindsay Faye of the Kekaha Sugar Company from the Senate, and Elsie Wilcox of Grove Farm Plantation from the House of Representatives.

The International Longshoremen's and Warehousemen's Union, headquartered in San Francisco, saw the potential in Hawai'i and decided to make its mark. In 1939, representatives were sent to the Islands with instructions to concentrate first on longshoremen at all Hawaiian ports. The ILWU had many categories of workers under its aegis on the mainland and could have competed in organizing urban and rural workers; however, it chose this route of attack because of the Islands' unique vulnerability arising from dependence on shipping and the docks. An added advantage was the longshoremen were few in number and would be easier to organize. The ILWU signed up these relatively unsophisticated workers rapidly. Union control was weakest on the Big Island, in part because its ports were so widely dispersed, and strongest at Ahukini and Port Allen on Kaua'i, posing a threat to that island.

In 1940, the ILWU called a strike on Kaua'i, closing all ports. Oil tankers were permitted to come and go because the island depended upon oil for most of its electricity, and some vessels of the Interisland Steamship Company were allowed to unload a limited supply of food and other essentials. The only air service to the island was provided by Inter-Island Airways (to become Hawaiian Airlines), which consisted of twice-weekly flights of eight-passenger amphibious aircraft operating from Burns Field in Hanapēpē. Larger DC-3s and an adequate airport near Līhu'e were more than a year in the future. The results of this strike were disastrous. Kaua'i was isolated and the people suffered greatly as the strike dragged on for nine months. When it ended, the union had gained little, but the dockworkers learned much under its tutelage. An ILWU representative later admitted this was the main purpose of the strike. The union then turned to organizing workers on the sugar and pineapple plantations, and plans were made for an island-wide strike of all agricultural and dockworkers. When World War II began, martial law was declared, halting further union organization.

It was crucial to know what was in the hearts and minds of the Japanese immigrants and their offspring when the war started so dramatically. More than half a century later, it is still the most important theme in telling the story of how the war affected the Japanese in Kōloa. The sheer numbers of Japanese in Hawai'i give some idea of the importance. The total population in 1940 was 423,330, of which 157,905, or 37 percent, were Japanese. Of the 35,636 inhabitants of Kaua'i, 14,611, or 41 percent, were of Japanese ancestry. In Kōloa, because the plantation had been recruiting Filipinos preferentially, the proportion of Japanese was somewhat lower. Of 1,903 persons living in Kōloa, 704, or 37 percent, were of Japanese ancestry, but this was significantly more than the 533 Filipinos at 28 percent.

How the nisei born in Hawai'i reacted after Pearl Harbor was attacked, and much of what they thought and felt in the years leading up to that momentous event, is well-known today, so this can be deferred and dealt with later in this chapter. The real mystery, then as now, was the confusion and conflict that must have gone on within the issei in the months preceding, and on "the date that will live in infamy." Most of their thoughts and feelings were unknown before the war, remained so after it started, and have been so ever since. Undoubtedly they were complex and varied from person to person, yet they are worth an attempt to understand. Instead of definitive answers, only some guidance through events will be offered. The author's qualifications consist of being raised in an area where he knew Japanese well before the war, living in Japan after the war where he learned something of their language and customs, and having longtime Japanese friends in Kōloa. So the reader will have to draw his or her own conclusions as the events are related.

To provide background, the centuries of feudalism and even factors prevailing in Japan before then must be considered. The Japanese were a people living on islands of limited land area who had to adopt rigid rules of behavior to avoid disorder and conflict. Their isolation reinforced these rules. As anthropologist Ruth Benedict wrote while attempting to understand the cultural context that led to the war, "Throughout its history Japan has been a strong class and caste society. Any attempt to understand the Japanese must begin with their version of what it means 'to take one's proper station.' Their feudal society was elaborately stratified, and each person's status was fixed by inheritance."

In feudal times there were four castes. The *samurai*, or warriors, were at the top, and beneath them were the farmers, artisans, and merchants, in that order. Below all were the outcasts. This caste system formed the foundation of Japanese societal structure when the Meiji Restoration took place and the migration to Hawai'i began. By the start of World War II the edges of the caste system had become blurred below the level of the *samurai,* but one's rank was still firmly fixed by caste. We hear a lot about racial discrimination in our country, but it does not begin to compare with the social discrimination in Japan either then or now. It still underlies Japanese behavior, although the devastation of the war, the reforms of the occupation, and Western influences since have made its manifestations more subtle. Japanese are merely quieter about it, and one has to live there for years to become fully aware.

Two events occurred in Japan in 1868 that were to affect the issei immigrants in Hawai'i. The Tokugawa Shōgunate still ruled at the start of the year, as it had since 1603; during all that time the emperor had been little more than a shadowy figurehead isolated within his court in Kyoto. In that year, a group of *daimyo,* or feudal lords, overthrew the Tokugawa *shōgun* and his samurai retinue, replacing them with an imperial government under emperor Meiji. During the confusion of this transition, the first group of 148 Japanese workers left Yokohama bound for Hawai'i. The latter event had little significance except as a marker to bear in mind, because Japanese immigration did not peak until 1885 to 1908. However, the former would change the course of world history and affect all Japanese immigrants to Hawai'i.

At this point, our purpose might be better served by creating a hypothetical immigrant. Almost all were males in their early twenties, so assuming he emigrated to Hawai'i in 1900, his year of birth would be about 1880. Our hypothetical immigrant would not yet be born in 1868. The Meiji Period (1868—1912) was characterized by several factors, only a few of which will be given here. Supreme authority was vested in the emperor, the government was relocated to Tokyo (formerly Edo), and an era ensued of major political, economic, and social change. Western industrial standards were adopted, and intensive efforts were undertaken in all sectors of society to make Japan the military equal of Western powers. Elementary education was made mandatory, the curricula were standardized, and academic freedom vanished. Students were taught to venerate their emperor as a god and indoctrinated with the glorious destiny of their nation. All of this would be in place when our immigrant was born. In 1871, a national army was formed and strengthened by universal conscription beginning in 1873. Japan was strong enough by 1874 to launch a punitive expedition against Taiwan, and in 1879 it wrested the Ryukyus from China.

In his earliest years after his birth in 1880 our hypothetical immigrant would have learned the values of Japanese society at home. First would have been *ko*, respect for one's parents; then *gaman*, enduring without complaint; and he would have been taught to observe Japanese proprieties so as not to bring *haji*, or shame, upon himself. It may be a generality, to say this, but the Japanese do not feel guilt as most Westerners do from a censuring conscience within, but rather shame when they violate sanctions imposed from without. His parents would have acted as trustees of the hierarchical tradition in which he was expected to take his place. As he approached school age, he would have learned *shuyo*, self-discipline; *on*, moral obligation to family and forbears; *otagai*, moral obligation to others; *giri*, the maintenance of one's honor; and *chu*, absolute loyalty to the emperor.

From both school and community he would have absorbed the prevalent nationalism, and worship of the emperor as a god would have been strengthened. With the emperor at the top of the hierarchy, the place of all those beneath was known, which brought stability and order to Japanese society. This reliance upon order and hierarchy is in sharp contrast to Western freedom and equality before the law. When Thomas Jefferson wrote the Declaration of Independence he knew that no two human beings are created equal or identical, not even homozygous twins. What he meant was the concept of equal *rights* for all, in opposition to Alexander Hamilton, who wished to establish an aristocratic societal system.

During his school years our immigrant would have learned the language of respect, with different words and modes of address, to use with those above him in the hierarchy. His behavior to them, even the depth and number of bows, was governed by meticulous rules. Likewise, the ways in which he would relate to those below him in the hierarchy also would have been learned.

Because most immigrants were recruited from poor farming prefectures, we may assume his formal schooling did not continue past the elementary level. The few years before emigration to Hawai'i probably were spent farming, which would reinforce his position in the hierarchical pattern he had been taught. He would become accustomed to hard work and the necessity for it.

He was in his teens during the first Sino-Japanese War of 1894-1895, so this would have had a powerful impact upon him. This war grew out of Japan's desire for the resources of coal and iron on the Korean peninsula, at the time a protectorate of China. In 1894, Japan sent troops to Korea, and by 1895 had invaded Shantung (Shandong) and Manchuria. China sued for peace and withdrew from Korea, Taiwan, the Pescadores, and the Liaotung (Liaodong) Peninsula. Japanese garrison troops remained in these areas. If one wonders how Japan could so casually invade another country in pursuit of its own interests, the author would like to put forth a theory. The hierarchy of individuals the Japanese internalize from the time they leave their mothers' breast is easily projected into the realm of international relations where they would perceive their nation as naturally at the top of a hierarchy of nations. Therefore, what Japan wants is there to be taken and whatever means may be necessary are justified.

In 1895 there were 140,000 Japanese already in Hawai'i older than our hypothetical issei. He would join them soon, they would have an influence upon him, so their reaction to this war is significant. Here is what we know. Plantation workers took the day off, those with businesses closed them, and all held a daylong victory celebration that lasted into the night. They decorated their homes with flags and lanterns, cheered the emperor, and sang the national anthem. In Honolulu and Hilo they paraded in the streets. Those who had served in the imperial armed services proudly wore their Japanese uniforms.

In 1900, our issei immigrant would arrive and live in Kōloa Japanese Camp. There those of Japanese ancestry followed the customs of their homeland and had formed a traditional Japanese community. Even the celebrations and holidays in Japanese Camp were similar to those in Japan. All had ties through both religion and culture to Japan. The links with family members left behind were especially strong. There were no Buddhist temples in Kōloa until 1910, but worship in homes took place before then. A photograph of the emperor undoubtedly hung on our immigrant's wall, and he would have bowed to it every day.

Our issei immigrant, like the others, would have kept in touch with events in Japan through letters, newspapers and other publications. All were unsophisticated people of rural origin, with only an elementary education, who could read and write Japanese, but few had learned to speak English. Nisei children were coming of age at that time with a completely different outlook and spoke English well. Most of them did not speak enough Japanese to communicate with their own parents. Our representative issei, although not yet married, was probably looking at photographs of prospective brides, and his marriage would have taken place around 1910.

The Russo-Japanese War of 1904-1905 would have affected him profoundly. This war developed out of the rivalry between Russia and Japan in Manchuria. Russia previously had leased from China the Liaotung Peninsula and the strategically important port of Port Arthur (Lü-shun) at the tip of the peninsula. Russia had also won the rights to extend its Trans-Siberian Railway across

Chinese-held Manchuria to the Russian seaport of Vladivostok, thus gaining control of an important strip of Manchurian territory.

On February 8, 1904, the Japanese fleet launched a surprise attack on the Russian naval squadron at Port Arthur using the same strategy it would at Pearl Harbor, absent air power. Then Japan landed a large army in Korea that quickly overran that country. In May another Japanese army landed on the Liaotung Peninsula, cutting off the Port Arthur garrison from the main body of Russian forces in Manchuria, and Port Arthur's commander surrendered. The final battle of the land war was fought at Mukden (Shen-yang). After heavy casualties on both sides, the Russians withdrew and Mukden fell to the Japanese.

The naval Battle of Tsushima Strait ended the conflict. The Russian Baltic Fleet had sailed from the Baltic to relieve the forces at Port Arthur, but Admiral Togo's main Japanese fleet lay in wait. His ships were superior in both speed and armament, his crews were better trained, and he succeeded in the classic maneuver of "crossing the T." In the two-day battle in 1905, two-thirds of the Russian Fleet was sunk. It was a dramatic and decisive victory for Japan, which gained undisputed control of the Liaotung Peninsula, Port Arthur, the South Manchurian Railway which led to Port Arthur, and half of Sakhalin Island. Russia also evacuated southern Manchuria, which was restored to China, and Russia recognized Japan's control of Korea as a protectorate.

The results of the Russo-Japanese War stunned the Americans and Europeans in Hawai'i. They had believed Russia to be a major power, and this was the first defeat of any European army by an Asian one in modern times. Russia's true political and military condition would not be revealed to the world until the First World War. Upon this victory the issei throughout Hawai'i celebrated wildly for days and brought activities in the Islands to a halt. The enthusiasm with which they celebrated was to haunt them in the future. It is safe to say that our young immigrant joined in.

Japan maintained its Kwantung Army on the Liaotung Peninsula, which effectively removed Chinese and Russian influence from the Korean Peninsula. In 1910, Japan annexed Korea as a prefecture and colonized it as a source of labor and natural resources. In 1912, emperor Meiji died, and Japan was thereafter ruled by the parliamentary government the 1899 Constitution had established. During the 1920s, Japanese militarism continued to rise, both in the Kwantung Army and in Tokyo. Neither the cabinet nor the Diet dared to quell this militarism, and governments fell in rapid succession. Prime Minister Hamaguchi, who tried to curtail the military activists, was assassinated in 1930.

The "Manchurian Incident" occurred in the night of September 18, 1931, launching further Japanese aggression in East Asia. Officers of the Japanese Kwantung Army, acting on their own volition, blew up a small section of the South Manchurian Railway near Mukden. They blamed the act on China, invaded Manchuria, and established the Japanese-dominated state of Manchukuo. In Tokyo, the high command of the Japanese army and the government reacted to public opinion after the fact by sanctioning the invasion. The League of Nations condemned the action, upon which Japan withdrew from the League. Japanese domination later was extended to Inner Mongolia and North China. Militarism continued to increase in Japan between 1932 and 1936, and more prominent statesmen, among them Prime Minister Inukai, were assassinated by young army activists. We can only speculate on the reaction of our now middle-aged hypothetical immigrant to these events; it is not at all clear what it would have been.

On the night of July 7, 1937, a small Japanese force on maneuvers near the Marco Polo Bridge outside Peking (Beijing) demanded entry into the tiny town of Wan-p'ing in order to search for one of their soldiers. The Chinese garrison in the town refused, and the incident escalated into the second Sino-Japanese war. As the fighting spread into central China, Japan scored successive victories. It took Peking and Tientsin (Tianjin), blockaded the South China coast, and captured Shanghai with a savagery seldom seen in war.

Nanking (Nanjing) fell on December 13, 1937. Because the Chinese had mounted such strong resistence in Shanghai, the commanding general of the Japanese army in China ordered the annihilation of everyone in Nanking and the city to be burned to the ground. For two months after its seizure the Japanese army indulged in mass mutilation and killing of Chinese civilians and the soldiers who had surrendered. According to Iris Chang's meticulously researched book *The Rape of Nanking*, some 90,000 Chinese soldiers were systematically slaughtered and an estimated 260,000 citizens murdered, including the elderly, women, and children. Japanese soldiers, with the approval of their officers, repeatedly raped 30,000 women, then murdered them to keep them from talking. The total deaths exceeded those from both atomic bombs dropped on Hiroshima and Nagasaki in 1945.

There simply is no way of knowing what the reaction of our hypothetical issei was to all this. Not being able to read English-language newspapers or understand radio broadcasts, he would have relied upon censored Japanese-language newspapers. Mail, both from Japan and the war fronts, was heavily censored. Our issei would have had mature children by the 1930s who could speak enough Japanese to convey the essentials to him and his wife. One way or another, the news did manage to get through in such situations.

It is a matter of record the majority of issei in Kōloa refused to believe the atrocities reported in English-language sources, calling it "Chinese propaganda." Their memories were of an earlier peaceful Japan, and they were unable to reconcile the two. Yet they did not openly celebrate these later Japanese conquests, which by itself tells us something. The day before Nanking fell, the U.S.S. *Panay*, while evacuating American civilian and diplomatic personnel, was sunk by Japanese air attack in spite of the large flags painted on it. The British gunboat H.M.S. *Ladybird* was sunk under similar circumstances. Still, many issei in Hawai'i continued to buy Japanese war bonds and send *imon bukuro,* or "comfort kits," to Japanese soldiers in the field.

One factor that undoubtedly played a role in the reaction of the issei in Hawai'i was that they were still Japanese citizens and prevented from becoming American citizens. The U.S. Naturalization Act of 1790 had not anticipated Asian immigration because there was none at the time. It contained the phrase "free white persons," which had been interpreted in various ways by the courts, but definitely excluded Japanese. It was not until the Walter-McCarran Act of 1952 amended the immigration law that issei became eligible for U.S. citizenship.

The rest of the story leading up to Pearl Harbor is well-known, so it can be presented even more briefly. In 1939, President Roosevelt announced the U.S. would terminate its commercial treaty with Japan on January 1, 1940 and thereby cut off vital raw materials to the Japanese war machine. The Japanese entry into northern Indochina in 1940 by an agreement extorted from the Vichy government of France caused Roosevelt to freeze Japanese assets in the United States.

Japan then had plans for both a "Northern Strategy" (invasion of Russia) and a "Southern Strategy." The latter was designed to acquire oil in the Dutch East Indies and other vital materials in Southeast Asia. Its government concluded that it was forced to choose one or the other. After the German victories over The Netherlands and France in the summer of 1940, Japan looked southward at the colonies of those defeated powers, and at those of Great Britain, which was facing possible invasion by Germany. With the colonies of these three nations, and selected possessions of the U.S. in the Pacific, a bulwark could be formed against efforts to retake them. Japan would become virtually self-sufficient and dominant in the Pacific. If only the United States were held in check while these acquisitions were being consolidated, Japan believed it could hold out indefinitely. The elimination of the U.S. Pacific Fleet was necessary for the Southern Strategy to succeed.

On December 7, 1941 Japan attacked Pearl Harbor, less than a hundred miles from Kōloa, and the two nations were at war. Martial law was declared the same afternoon. All Japanese-language schools and newspapers on Kaua'i were closed, as were the four Shinto temples and eleven of the fifteen Buddhist temples. The issei were shocked into silence, and most remained in their homes. At one stroke they had been denied their newspapers, the temples in which they had worshiped, and their roles of leadership in the family and community. By definition they were enemy aliens. Andrew Lind wrote in *Hawaii's Japanese*, "[the] sudden forfeiture of respect and authority in the eyes of their own children [was] one of the most cruel by-products of the war." Their grown children assumed leadership roles at once. They had to.

Now with all of the foregoing, let's try to visualize our issei sitting on the porch of his home in Japanese Camp, quietly watching the sun set on that fateful Sunday while he pondered his situation and that of his family. He had already hidden or burned all evidence of Japanese fealty, such as his Japanese flag and portrait of the emperor. His wife had put away their Japanese clothing. He had watched her as she sadly folded and wrapped her beautiful kimonos and *obi* sashes and placed them in their lacquered *tansu* with camphor in each corner of the drawers.

What could have been going through his mind? Almost certainly, the realization came that both of them had lived in Hawai'i for 40 years, almost all of their adult lives. They had long since given up thoughts of returning to Japan except to visit. They had adopted too many customs that had been foreign to them on their arrival. Even if it were possible to return to Japan, they would have been strangers in their own land. The responsibility for the aggression and atrocities in China was not theirs, nor did either of them feel *haji*, or shame, for the attack upon Pearl Harbor. Instead, they felt anger at the act by the country of their birth, which was a new and strange sensation.

He must have realized that Hawai'i had, in fact, become their home. Their duty was to be loyal to the United States. The proper role for them now would be to set about living their lives so as to avoid any personal disgrace during the war. What their proper places and conduct would have been in Japan were less than memories. In Hawai'i, he and his family were free at last from its hierarchy and to live in their adopted country accordingly. Perhaps he could not express this realization to her, nor she to him, but somehow each would know. Nor could the torn feeling inside, the deep pain, be shown to each other or to anyone else. That was one thing neither knew how to do.

⌒ ⌒ ⌒

The story of the nisei in Hawai'i is quite different. Military intelligence and the FBI were at first uncertain about their allegiance because of the strong Japanese tradition of family loyalty. An additional factor not often mentioned is that approximately 70 percent of the nisei had dual citizenship because of a conflict in nationality laws. United States law held the concept of *jus soli* (right of the soil) whereby those born in the U.S. automatically became U.S. citizens. This applied to all nisei born in Hawai'i after it was annexed. Japanese law adhered to the concept of *jus sanguinis*, which gave citizenship automatically to children of its male citizens, no matter where they were born. In 1924, the Diet had amended this law in two ways. Those of Japanese ancestry born in the U.S. before 1924 could renounce Japanese citizenship through an expatriation process, and those born after 1924 became subjects of Japan only if their births were registered within 14 days at the Japanese consulate. Issei parents who had strong attachments to Japan at that time, still hoping to return with their children who would then have rights there, did this, and in Hawai'i, local priests acted as registrars. When these nisei with dual citizenship became adults, few of them bothered to expatriate and thus retained their dual citizenship.

Many nisei children had been sent to Japan for their education under the care of relatives and did not return until their teens or early adulthood. They were known as *kibei, ki* meaning intention, and *bei*, America. When they came back to Hawai'i they were almost unable to speak English. The emotional ties with their parents and siblings had been strained or severed, and they had little understanding or appreciation of American culture. While in Japan, they had been indoctrinated under the militaristic regime and were believed to be the highest risk.

Starting in 1939, military intelligence and the FBI in Hawai'i had been maintaining a list of those they believed to be a security risk. At the outbreak of war, 8,391 Japanese were on the list, with 93 Germans and 13 Italians. After an initial hearing, about half of the Germans and Italians and 1,441 Japanese were interned in a hastily built detention camp on Sand Island on O'ahu. The Japanese group consisted of 879 issei, 534 *kibei,* and 28 nisei. A

180

more thorough screening was done there. As a result 981 Japanese (almost evenly divided between issei and *kibei)* were shipped to mainland relocation centers where some 1,000 family members later joined them. As time went on, many of this number were cleared. By 1944, only 534 remained interned, most of them *kibei.*

It is interesting to contrast the Japanese in Hawai'i with those in California. The 1940 census gave the number of Japanese in Hawai'i as 157,905, and because of undercounting most authorities believed at the onset of war it was at least 160,000, or 37 percent of the population. In the multicultural society of Hawai'i, most Japanese had woven into the social fabric and were regarded as "locals," not "Japs." The limited land area in Hawai'i, and their large numbers, meant that constant interaction with others was unavoidable.

In California, most of those of Japanese ancestry had remained culturally isolated from the predominantly white population, and 110,000 (of whom 70,000 were U.S. citizens) were interned. General Delos Emmons, military governor of Hawai'i, understood the differences and resisted the War Department's urging him to do the same, saying, "prevailing socio-cultural values precluded internment in Hawai'i." He was supported by the fact that there was no sabotage or espionage by any Japanese other than those in their consulate. In any event, the relocation to the mainland of such a large number would have been a monumental task, and shipping was required for more urgent tasks.

General George Marshall also had evaluated the loyalty of the nisei, and in May, 1942, he issued orders establishing an all-nisei army unit. The Hawaiian Provisional Infantry Battalion was formed from former University of Hawai'i ROTC students and nisei who had been in the National Guard. It was designated the "100th Infantry Battalion (separate)" and shipped on June 5, 1943 to Camp McCoy in Wisconsin for basic training. Its famous motto "Go for broke" came from plantation gambling and meant the gambler was willing to risk all he had. After combat training at Camp Shelby in Mississippi, the 100th was shipped to Oran, North Africa, where it was made part of the 34th Division. On September 22, 1943 it landed at Salerno with that division and fought with it all the way to Rome.

The War Department was so favorably impressed with the 100th Infantry Battalion that it decided to form a larger unit consisting entirely of nisei. It was to be designated the 442nd Regimental Combat Team and would be made up of both mainland and Hawaiian nisei. The call for 1,500 volunteers in Hawai'i brought out 9,507. This was 40 percent of all nisei in the Islands in the specified age bracket of 21 to 38. The limit therefore was raised, and 2,686 were selected to joined the 1,500 nisei who had volunteered from mainland internment camps. After combat training, the 442nd was sent to Italy in 1943, where it absorbed the 100th.

The "One Puka Puka" did not lose its hard-won identity, however, because the combination was officially designated the 100th/442nd Regimental Combat Team. The easy camaraderie of those from Hawai'i spread to the mainlanders, whom they called "kotonks," which supposedly was the sound their heads made when knocked together. In turn, those from the mainland called the Hawaiians "buddhaheads," the "buddha" part being a distortion of the Japanese word *buta*, meaning pig. By the time the war ended, most of the officers were nisei and the 100th/442nd had become the army's most decorated unit for its size and length of time in combat. They received 9,486 Purple Hearts and 18,143 individual decorations for bravery. Of their number, 680 did not return.

In March 1943, all nisei in the United States were reclassified as eligible for the draft and thereafter many either volunteered or were drafted. Nisei also made up the 6,000-member Military Intelligence Service, half of whom were officers. Most were from Hawai'i and had acquired their language skills in the Japanese Language Schools. They served as interpreters and interrogated Japanese prisoners of war in all theaters of the Pacific.

The 1399th Engineering Construction Battalion had been formed before the war and was composed entirely of nisei. Because of the fame of the 442nd, they called themselves "the forgotten battalion." The 1399th performed many essential construction tasks for the military in Hawai'i during the war.

In all, a total of 33,000 nisei served in the armed forces. Because of the relatively low population of Kaua'i, only 1,300 were from the island and the precise number from Kōloa is not available. Of these, 250 served with the 100th/442nd. The 63 Kaua'i war dead, 51 of whom were Americans of Japanese Ancestry, are memorialized in the Veterans Memorial Convention Hall in Līhu'e.

When the veterans returned to Hawai'i, most took advantage of the GI Bill to further their education. Almost half became lawyers and the rest took teaching, government and other influential positions. Up to World War II the "Big Five" corporations—Castle & Cooke, Alexander & Baldwin, Theo H. Davies, C. Brewer, and American Factors—had dominated both the Hawaiian economy and the Republican Party. The nisei veterans became active in politics. Most became Democrats and took control of the party on all the Islands.

As mentioned before, the Political Action Committee of the ILWU had established a political beachhead in Hawai'i by 1939, but because of the war Republicans ran unopposed on Kaua'i in 1942 for the Territorial House of Representatives. After the war and the return of the veterans, the pendulum swung back and in 1946 all four Kaua'i representatives were of Japanese ancestry. When the issei were able to become citizens under the McCarran Act in 1952, they joined the nisei to form 40 percent of the electorate and the two voted as a bloc. In 1954, the Democrats won the state legislature for the first time, and Hawai'i has been strongly Democratic ever since. There have been a nisei governor of the state, U.S. representatives, and U.S. senators. Nisei also have been prominent in business and in the professions since World War II.

There is something for us to learn from their success story. The parents of the nisei had come to Hawai'i on crowded ships as indentured laborers, bound for years. Their appearance was different, they had strange customs, did not speak the language, were unable to become citizens, could not own property, and were unable to vote. Most immigrants came without their families and did not know anyone at their destinations. This has been compared to the slave trade from Africa centuries before. Yet many Japanese achieved middle-class status and higher in only one generation. Immigrant groups of all races, creeds, and colors that came to Hawai'i and remained did as well; it merely took longer because the Japanese had the advantage of their distinguished war service. There was no need for affirmative action or other racial preferences, which renews our faith in American institutions amid the accusations that roil around us today.

Now we can return to Kōloa Plantation before, during, and after the war. The shortage of workers had become severe years before Pearl Harbor. The United States had begun to gear up its defense industry, and the salaries offered in California and on O'ahu by "cost plus" contractors had lured workers of all races from Kōloa Plantation. The armed forces were expanding at the same time and drew still more. The resulting labor shortage precipitated a crisis on all the plantations. It was not until a year after the war started that the sugar industry was declared vital to national defense and the workers were frozen in their jobs. Wages were frozen at the same time, as were sugar prices.

Kōloa Plantation was in dire straits all during the war. Mechanization was intensified, but because equipment was difficult to obtain, much of it was manufactured by workers at the mill. They accomplished minor miracles making cane cutters, rakes, grabbers, and cranes from whatever material was at hand. A plantation official found a two-line mechanical planter on O'ahu. Any trucks that could be procured began replacing the old, inefficient rail system, and gravel roads were built on the former rail beds. Well aware that union organization of the workers would soon resume, the mood of the managers was gloomy as they contemplated the future.

On March 10, 1943, martial law was partially lifted by presidential decree. The ILWU intensified its organizational efforts on the docks and plantations, as the AFL and CIO did in other industries. Martial law in Hawai'i was lifted entirely on October 24, 1944. By then, the ILWU had organized the sugar and pineapple plantations as well as the docks so vital to these industries.

On September 1, 1946, the ILWU called a strike of all plantation workers in Hawai'i. Some 28,000 workers on 33 plantations were involved. The independence of the Philippines had cut off that source of labor except for those allowed under the national quota system and certain exceptions. The Islands were brought to a complete standstill for 79 days until an agreement was reached. Kōloa Plantation, along with the others, agreed to convert the perquisites they had been giving their employees into wages. The workers then found that they were the highest-paid agricultural workers in the world. The demand for conversion of the perquisites into wages seemed odd to plantation managers. They had been a financial drain and cause of conflict with the IRS and SSA, so they were glad to eliminate them. Only later was it learned that this was an ideological demand on the part of the ILWU intended to destroy the paternalistic influence of the plantation system.

On Kōloa Plantation free housing was discontinued, and the plantation houses were rented or offered for sale to the workers. Free fuel and electricity were stopped, as were all other benefits, including free medical care. The fees charged for these services were low out of compassion for workers unaccustomed to budgeting for them; the fees often went uncollected for the same reason. More mechanization was put in place and greater efficiency was sought wherever possible. Maintenance of equipment was allowed to slide. Still, by 1946 Kōloa Plantation was over $1,000,000 in debt and could not sustain the financial drain indefinitely. Its demise was only a matter of time.

Grove Farm Plantation had the same labor problems, but its land was less rocky, so it was able to mechanize more. Its major financial drain was the cost of having cane processed at the Līhu'e Plantation mill. Gaylord Wilcox, the manager and president of Grove Farm, came to the conclusion that Grove Farm not only needed its own mill to survive, but more land as well. He knew that Kōloa Plantation was having difficulty converting to mechanical equipment because of its rocky soil and did not have the funds necessary to clear the land. Fortunately, the founder of Grove Farm, George N. Wilcox, had left his stock in trust to the Wilcox family and they approved the proposed merger of the two. In 1948, Grove Farm bought Kōloa Plantation. Grove Farm had its own mill and doubled the size of its cane fields.

The struggle between the ILWU and the sugar industry in Hawai'i reached a climax when the union called a strike of longshoremen on May 1, 1949. This had a devastating effect upon the Islands. Although food and medicine were not boycotted, shipowners found it impossible to load their vessels with only these products yet remain profitable. As a result the number of ships calling at Hawaiian ports dropped to a fraction of what it had been before the strike.

Almost in panic, people hoarded whatever they could find. The empty shelves in the stores, the ruined cargo on the docks, and the sense of desperation that was felt still haunt the memories of those who lived in Hawai'i then, as the author did. More than a third of the businesses in Hawai'i became insolvent and unemployment soared. The governor reacted by seizing the Honolulu docks and hiring volunteers to load and unload the ships. The ILWU responded by ordering their members at West Coast ports not to touch the ships. For added measure, the same orders were given to longshoremen at Gulf and East Coast ports. Honolulu businessmen chartered ships and hired their own crews and longshoremen at wages dictated by the union, and this brought some supplies. Interisland shipping was excluded from the strike, but there was little on O'ahu for the ships to bring. All the neighbor islands, including Kaua'i, were devastated. After 177 days, the strike was settled for a relatively small wage gain.

Earlier, in 1947, Ichiro Izuka, president of an ILWU local on Kaua'i, had left the union and wrote a pamphlet detailing how Communists dominated the ILWU and intended to take over the Democratic Party and then the government of Hawai'i. After the strike an investigation by the FBI and the U.S. House of Representatives Committee on Un-American Activities revealed, with the Cold War at its height and threatening the nation, many of the ILWU leaders were active Communists. At hearings in Honolulu, 39 of those in the top echelons took the Fifth Amendment. Seven were indicted and convicted under the Smith Act for conspiring to overthrow the government by force and violence. Subsequent legal maneuvering resulted in the overturn of the conviction of six of them on appeal. Later, Lawrence Fuchs reviewed all the evidence, and in his leftward-leaning book *Hawai'i Pono: An Ethnic and Political History* concluded, "The evidence is overwhelming that Hall and other key ILWU leaders were active Communist party members."

Threats of strikes in the sugar industry continued, capped by an industry-wide strike in 1958 and a smaller one in 1961. The

The Kōloa Mill in Pāʻā after its closure in 1996.

eventual end of sugar in Hawai'i could clearly be seen. It was impossible to compete with other sugar-producing areas in the world with the wages prevailing in Hawai'i. Edward Beechert, in another leftward-leaning book, *Working in Hawaii,* wrote that "the sugar worker had almost become a white-collar worker in terms of benefits and job security."

On Kaua'i, Grove Farm decided to get out of the sugar business completely. In 1974, when its interests in quarrying and land development had matured sufficiently, it discontinued sugar operations. Grove Farm leased its Ha'ikū land to Līhu'e Plantation, and its Kīpū and Kōloa lands to McBryde, which by that time had become a subsidiary of Alexander & Baldwin.

McBryde's management believed, backed by resources of one of the biggest of the Big Five, and with modern management, their operation could succeed despite inflated labor costs. Economy of scale was favorable, with 7,000 acres added to its previous 6,000. McBryde closed its mill in Numila, transferred the best equipment to the Kōloa mill, and upgraded the equipment there. It also mechanized its operations as completely as possible and converted to the more efficient drip irrigation system. Despite these efforts it still operated at a loss. During this period federal price supports were being steadily lowered.

Although the handwriting was on the wall, only the date was unknown. Fate stepped in to make this decision for McBryde. In 1982, its cane fields were damaged by Hurricane 'Iwa, but it was able to surmount this and put much of its acreage into macadamia nuts, coffee, and other crops. Then these were destroyed, along with its sugar cane, by the more severe Hurricane 'Iniki in 1992. The coffee plants had withstood the hurricane best, so McBryde planted more coffee, abandoned sugar, and began looking for a way out. Its parent corporation, Alexander & Baldwin, took over, expanded coffee cultivation and now markets the product as Kaua'i Coffee. A visitor center was created at the former McBryde headquarters in Numila, near 'Ele'ele, where you can taste what may be the agricultural future for Kaua'i.

In 1996, McBryde, the last company to grow sugar cane in Kōloa where it had all started so long ago, went out of existence. It did so as such things are done only in Hawai'i: with a party under an immense white tent for all their workers. Music, song, hula . . . and unashamed tears.

An era had ended.

Chapter Twelve

A Tour of Kōloa and Poʻipū Today

This chapter will be quite different from those you have read so far. We are going to explore Kōloa and Poʻipū together, so it is more of a "guide book" than history, but the latter is not left out. It is also less formal than the preceding chapters. As I will be your "guide," the first-person singular will jump at you from the page now and then.

Almost everyone who comes to Kauaʻi enters either at the airport or the harbor near Līhuʻe, so before starting the tour of Kōloa itself, let's assume you are driving there from Līhuʻe on Highway 50, Kaumualiʻi Highway. This will allow me to share with you some items of information important to Kōloa as you drive along.

In the distance on your left is the Hāʻupu (recollection) Range dominating the skyline. The fragrant anise-scented *mokihana* that grows only on Kauaʻi is found on its slopes. The vines and berries are intertwined with *maile* to make the traditional lei of the island. *Mokihana* was loved by the Hawaiians of old, is still loved by all today, and is referred to in many chants:

> *Maikaʻi wale nō Kauaʻi*
> *Hemolele wale i ka mālie*
> *Kuahiwi nani, Waiʻaleʻale,*
> *Lei ana i ka mokihana*

> So very perfect is Kauaʻi
> So perfect in its calm
> Beautiful Mountain, Waiʻaleʻale
> Wears a lei of mokihana

The land on either side of Kaumualiʻi Highway was linked to Kōloa in several ways. When you pass through Puhi (puff or blow) you see Kauaʻi Community College *mauka*, and the Grove Farm headquarters building *makai*. You are surrounded by the ahupuaʻa of Haʻikū (sharp break), which is bounded on the *makai* side by the Hulēʻia (pushed through) River, and inland by the mountain range. Grove Farm had owned this land and the western tip of Kīpū (hold back) at the time it took over Kōloa Plantation. The *ahupuaʻa* of Kīpū lies beyond the river to the shore, from Māhāʻulepū on the west all the way to Nāwiliwili on the east. This *ahupuaʻa* is divided by the Hāʻupu Range into two parts. The portion you can see is called Kīpū Uka (inland Kīpū), or just Kīpū. William Hyde Rice, the son of missionary William Harrison Rice, started a cattle ranch in Kīpū in 1867 that is still run by the Rice family.

The Rices are related to the most prominent family in the history of Kōloa, and this is how that came about: William Hyde Rice married Mary Waterhouse, the daughter of John Thomas Waterhouse and his wife Eleanor. William Hyde Rice and Mary were more influential in Līhuʻe than in Kōloa; but Mary's brother, William Waterhouse, married Melicent Philena Smith, the daughter of Dr. James W. Smith, the missionary who had been so notable in Kōloa during the early years. Melicent and William's son was Dr. Alfred Herbert Waterhouse, about whom you will hear a great deal more later. Notice that he is referred to as Herbert and not Alfred, because that was how he preferred to be known during his lifetime.

For another turn of the Waterhouse tale, we go in our imagination over the ridge of the Hāʻupu Range to the other part of the *ahupuaʻa*, Kīpū Kai (seaward Kīpū). The gravel road through the old Rice camp in Kīpū leads up and over the range along an ancient Hawaiian trail. Parts of this trail can still be seen, cobbled with smooth water-worn rocks. This road is the only land access to the beautiful valley of Kīpū Kai nestled between two arms of the range. Mary Kawena Pukui composed a chant when she visited there:

No Kīpū Kai ke aloha
Home i ka pili kahakai
I laila au i ʻike ai
I ka nui loko maikaʻi.

For Kīpū Kai is my affection
Where there is a home beside the sea
It was there that I found
Such unbounded hospitality.

A cattle ranch formerly owned by Jack Waterhouse, now deceased, occupies the entire valley of Kīpū Kai. He was a son of John Thomas and Eleanor Waterhouse (referred to above), and, of course, was Mary and William's brother. Their parents had come from Tasmania in 1851 and settled in Honolulu, where John Thomas Waterhouse became wealthy as a merchant.

Jack's name was actually John Thomas Waterhouse, Jr., but he preferred to be called "Keaka," which is the Hawaiian way of saying Jack. If you have followed all of this genealogy, you may realize that Jack and Dr. Herbert Waterhouse were cousins. It is enough to know the prominent families of both Kīpū and Kīpū Kai are related to the Smiths and Waterhouses, who were so notable in the early years of Kōloa. Jack died in 1984, and his will stipulated that the valley be deeded to the state upon the death of his four nieces and nephew. The terms of his will are that Kīpū Kai will then become "a nature, animal, and wildlife preserve."

Let's get another matter out of the way before we reach Kōloa. Two legal entities own most of the land in and around Kōloa, and some concept of these is necessary to understand what you are going to see. These are the Knudsen Trust and the Smith-Waterhouse Family Partnership. The latter traces its origin to the arrival in 1842 of missionary James W. Smith, M.D., and his wife, Melicent Knapp Smith. At that time all of the land of Kōloa was controlled by the Hawaiian monarchy; after the Great Mahele, or land division, of 1848, it was owned by royal heirs. From them, Dr. Smith both bought and leased land south of Kōloa Road to grow cane and raise cattle. Through the years, he gave much of his land away or sold it for a low price to those whom he felt were deserving.

Dr. Herbert Waterhouse had married Mabel Palmer in California and brought her to Kōloa in 1907, where he practiced medicine for over forty years. During that time he purchased portions of the land his grandfather had owned. At his death in 1948, these holdings consisted of two and a half acres in the heart of Kōloa, plus some *makai* parcels. His widow formed the Mabel Palmer Waterhouse Trust in 1950, with their children as beneficiaries. The children in turn passed their interests to their children, who established the Smith-Waterhouse Family Partnership in 1953. Because some Smith-Waterhouse descendants on the mainland do not own an interest in this entity, the name was legally changed in 1995 to "The Smith-Waterhouse Family of Kōloa, A Partnership." At this writing neither the official tax maps nor residents of the area have adopted the correct terminology and it is still common to refer to the partnership as the Waterhouse Trust.

The story of the Knudsen Trust is less complicated, and again only the outline will be given. Valdemar Knudsen came to Kauaʻi from Norway by way of California in 1852, built a home in Kekaha, which he named "Waiʻawa" (bitter water), and started a cattle ranch there. In 1865, he married Anne Sinclair, daughter of Eliza Sinclair, who owned the island of Niʻihau and the *ahupuaʻa* of Makaweli (fearful features). Eliza bought most of the Kōloa *ahupuaʻa* in 1870 and gave it to Anne that year as a dowry. When Valdemar died, Anne set up a trust and through it leased her land first to Kōloa Plantation, then to Grove Farm, and finally to McBryde. Anne died in 1920, and Knudsen descendants formed trusts in their own names. First Hawaiian Bank manages the activities of all of them. Rather than speaking of the several trusts, it is customary to use the generic term Knudsen Trust, as we will here.

One last bit of Kōloa history is especially important to know before starting the tour. After Kōloa was bypassed by Kaumualiʻi Highway in 1935, the town entered a period of lassitude. The somnolence deepened after Kōloa Plantation was sold to Grove Farm in 1948. However, the town began to be rejuvenated when tourism on the nearby Poʻipū shore increased in the early 1960s. During the sixties and seventies, establishments in Kōloa that formerly served plantation personnel shifted their orientation toward tourists, who enjoyed shopping and dining in the authentic plantation surroundings.

Kōloa began to thrive again, yet managed to retain much of its early character. In 1982, Hurricane ʻIwa damaged many of the older structures, and an opportunistic group stepped in to bring about changes you will see at every turn. Robert Gerrell organized a group called Kōloa Town Associates (KTA) and persuaded the Smith-Waterhouse Family Partnership to grant the group a long-term lease on the property comprising the core of the town. KTA engaged a Honolulu architect, Spencer Leinenweber, to design a shopping center on this property to be under one management. The stated intention was to restore the historic structures in this part of Kōloa. As the project progressed over a two-year period starting in 1983, it became evident Kōloa Town Associates was tearing down the historic buildings and rebuilding, not restoring them.

The enclosed maps, one of Kōloa as it was in the 1930s, and the other as it was in the 1990s, have footprints that show the larger size, altered shape, and in some cases the different locations of the new buildings. What the 1990s map does not show is the wooden walkway along Kōloa Road in front of the buildings, added

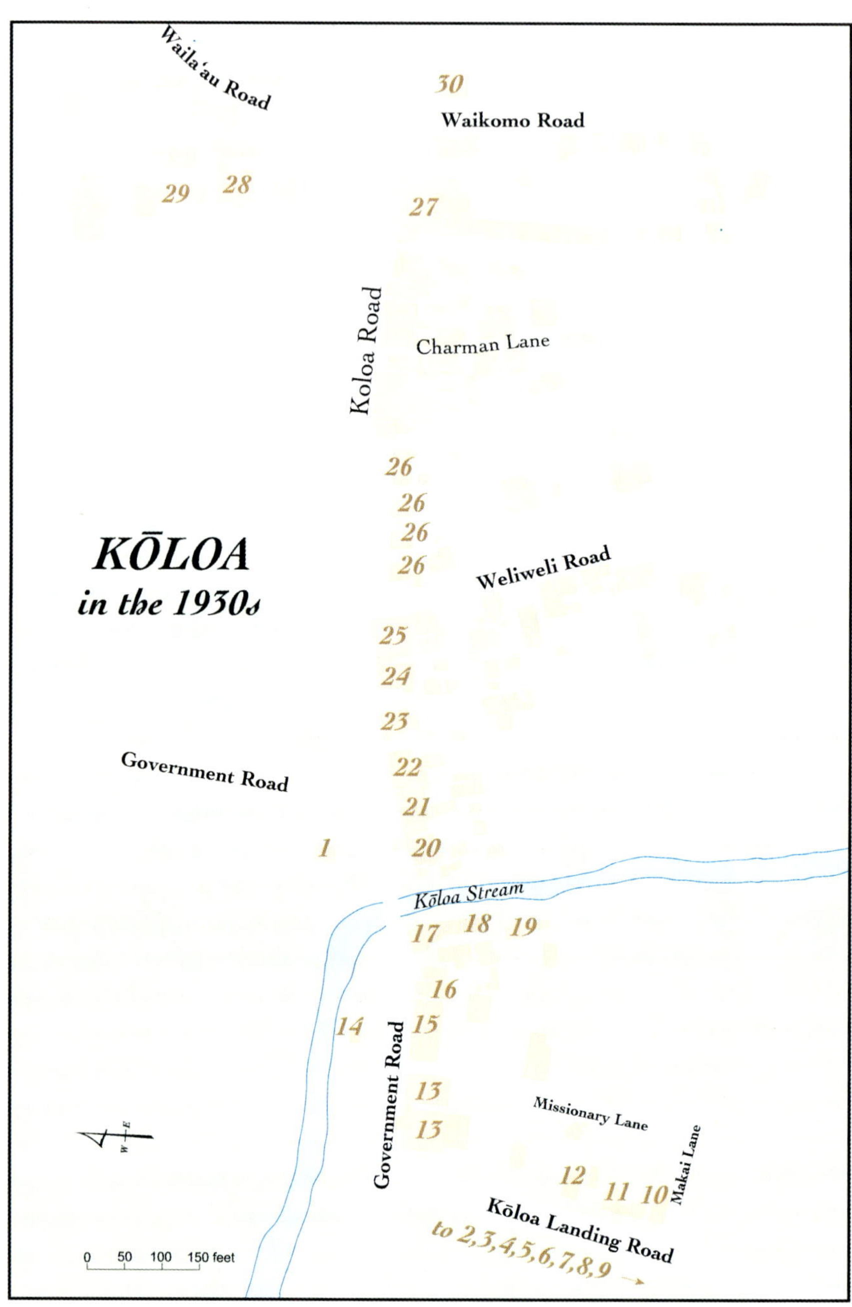

Kōloa Map in the 1930s

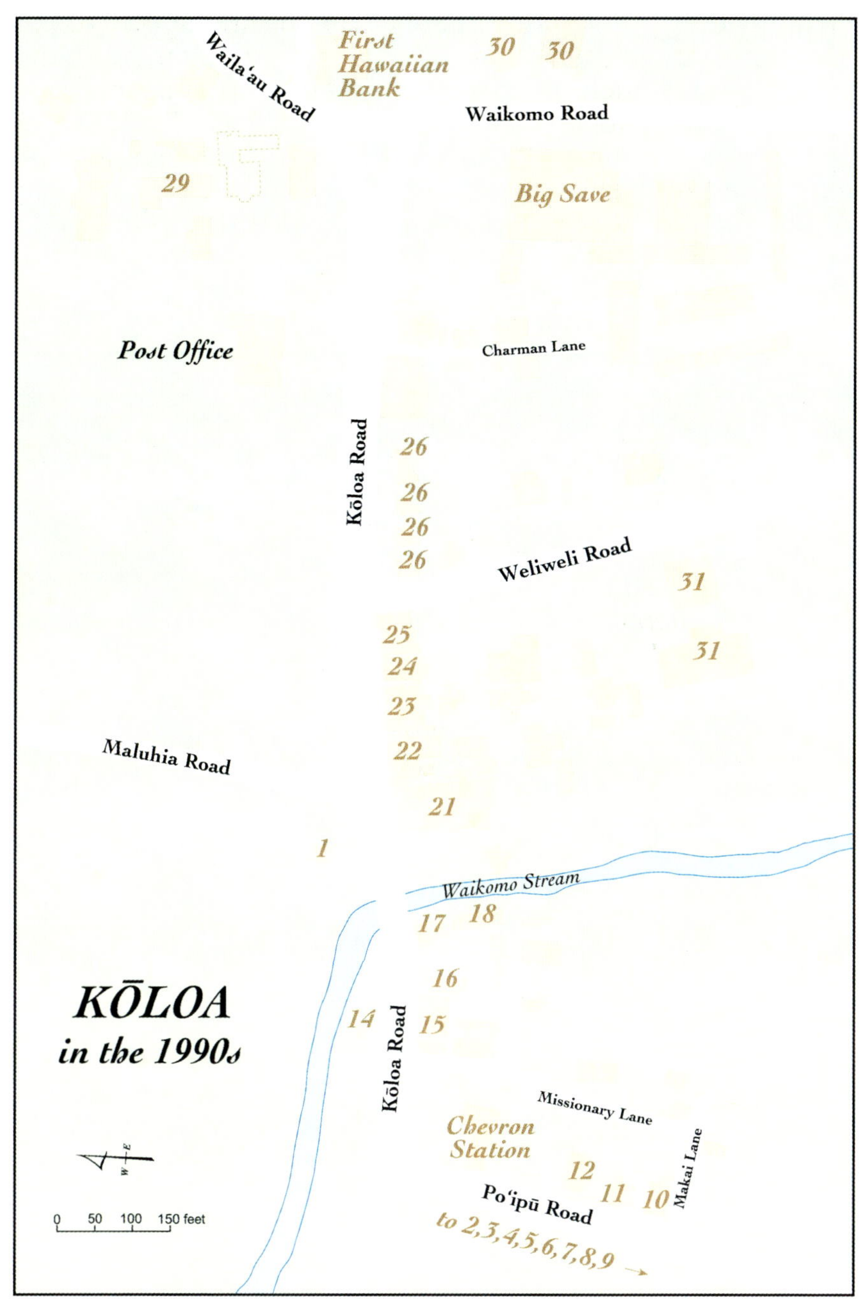

Kōloa Map in the 1990s

to facilitate tourist shopping. There is not one original board in any of the buildings "restored" by KTA. Some attention was paid to exterior features such as false fronts to give an appearance from the street similar to the original, but that was all. Kōloa Town Associates named the resulting group of *new* buildings *"Old Kōloa Town"* (italics are mine) and leased them to businesses catering to tourists. The effects were compounded as other historic structures were rebuilt at the same time to compete with the shopping center in the tourist trade. But not all were rebuilt, and we will indicate several that are authentic.

Kōloa, with a fascinating history, thus lost much that was redolent of its past. Nothing can replace the real thing. That is why the tour will not dwell overmuch on the buildings themselves, but on the people, their lives, and times past. And upon your imagination; let's start.

Note: All the locations in boldface below have historical interest, but the actual structures now on most of the sites do not. The symbol "★" is used to denote those structures that still have intrinsic historical interest. When numbers are given, they correspond to the numbers on the two maps, the one of Kōloa in the 1930s and the other in the 1990s.

Kōloa Gap, also called Knudsen Gap, is the pass to the southwest side of the island between the Hā'upu Range and Kāhili (feather standard) Ridge. It is best indicated by the junction of Maluhia (peaceful) Road and Kaumuali'i Highway. *Mauka* from this pass, the two peaks of Kawaikini (the multitudinous water) and Wai'ale'ale (rippling or overflowing water) soar to the sky. Wai'ale'ale is often cited as "the wettest spot on earth," but it is actually second, behind a peak in the foothills of the Himalayas near Assam, in India.

The Tree Tunnel on the first part of Maluhia Road into Kōloa is formed from a variety of eucalyptus called "swamp mahogany." Walter McBryde donated and helped plant them in 1911. The dirt road into Kōloa was often muddy and the roots of the trees absorbed moisture, adding stability. Maluhia Road was part of the old Government Road along the south shore, which once led to Kōloa. It turned right, and then curved inland to 'Ōma'o and Lāwa'i, before going on to Hanapēpē. The original Tree Tunnel was nearly three times as long. When Kaumuali'i Highway bypassed Kōloa, it cut off the *mauka* two-thirds of the tunnel. Grove Farm cut down most of the trees on this *mauka* portion in 1959 because their shade hindered the growth of cane, but some can still be seen wending their way toward Līhu'e almost to Halfway Bridge.

Puʻu-o-hewa is an ancient tuff cone located on the right about two miles down Maluhia Road. This name has an interesting origin. One of the early maps hanging on the wall of the Kōloa Plantation office gave an erroneous name to this hill. An unknown Hawaiian had crossed this out and written *hewa*, or "wrong," above it. No one bothered to find out what the name really was. Everyone has called the hill Puʻu-o-hewa, or "hill of wrong," ever since. The true name has long been lost. From the Kōloa side you can see an x-shaped scar on the hill made by Hawaiians for one of their favorite sports, *heʻe hōlua*—sledding. They carved out two paths that crossed, which added to the excitement, and laid *pili* grass on them for greater speed. One such sled is preserved in the Bishop Museum in Honolulu.

★ **1. The Old Kōloa Mill**, built in 1841, is at the intersection with Kōloa Road as you enter town and is the only structure in Kōloa still listed on the National Register of Historic Places. Its location is just below the confluence of the ʻŌmaʻo (green) and Waihohonu (deep water) streams that form Waikomo (entering water) Stream. On the banks of Waikomo Stream are remnants of the dam and mill race that powered the mill. The stone stack was the base for the tall boiler chimney and the foundation of the boiler room is behind it.

Park and look around. Note the monument depicting the different races of sugar workers, with a brief inscribed history. It is known as "the sugar monument" and was unveiled to commemorate the sesquicentennial of the sugar industry in Hawaiʻi. Nearby are examples of the different types of sugar cane grown on Kōloa Plantation.

One thing might strike you as you view the town of Kōloa from here. It appears to be somewhat lopsided, with most of the buildings on the south side of Kōloa Road. The land north of Kōloa Road to Kōloa Gap is Knudsen Trust land and was in sugar cane until recently. Most of the developed property immediately south of Kōloa Road is owned by the Smith-Waterhouse Family Partnership. Then it is largely Knudsen Trust land once again all the way to the shore.

The Kōloa History Center behind the Crazy Shirts store across the street has a collection of exhibits and old photographs worth seeing before starting our tour of Kōloa. They give a feeling for the town's past. Clean public restrooms are available.

The town of Kōloa is best explored on foot, so the first part of the tour will be a walking one. The best place to start is at Kōloa School. From the old mill turn right on Kōloa Road, then left on Poʻipū Road at the Chevron station.

Kōloa School was the first on Kauaʻi to teach in English. In this 1917 photo children are singing the National Anthem to the music from the gramophone seen at the right.

☞ Hawaiʻi State Archives

Have you noticed that some of the roads in Kōloa are still named for where they take you? For example, early in this century Kōloa Landing Road led south to Kōloa Landing and stopped there. There was as yet no Poʻipū Road; no Poʻipū Beach Road to Poʻipū Beach; no Lāwaʻi Beach Road to Lāwaʻi Beach (although footpaths existed along these routes). Waikomo Road went to the first mill site at Maulili, so was named Maulili Road. The first part of Weliweli Road led to the Courthouse, so that was its name. When the new mill was built, the extension of Courthouse Road was called New Mill Road. Then the Courthouse was moved to Līhuʻe in the 1930s, and both sections were renamed Weliweli Road.

Kōloa School is on the west side of Poʻipū Road, about 0.4 of a mile south of Kōloa Road. The school is difficult to miss as you drive toward the ocean. A road there veers to the southwest. This was formerly Kukuiʻula Road, which led to Kukuiʻula Harbor. Then it was cut off, later paved, and still later, renamed Paʻanau Road because it ended at a low rise Hawaiians called Paʻanau, where there was once a village. A housing development by that name is there now.

2. Kōloa Elementary School has a parking lot, and there is also ample room on the shoulders of Poʻipū Road for you to park. The history of Kōloa School was described in the chapter that related the story of the missionaries in Waimea and Kōloa. It is significant because the events and people involved with the school also made much of the history of Kōloa.

To recapitulate briefly, the Gulicks were transferred from Waimea to Kōloa in 1834 to establish the second missionary station on Kauaʻi. They lived in a thatched house near Maulili (constant rippling) Pond where the first and second mills were built. Near their home they started a small school in a thatch structure for Hawaiian children. The story of the burning of their home in 1837 was told in that chapter.

After that, they built a more substantial adobe home where the Kōloa Church parsonage is now and an adobe chapel where Kōloa Church stands today. Both had thatch roofs. The Gulicks built a second school of the same materials a short distance *mauka* of the present Kōloa School in 1841. Although Gulick started the first two schools in Kōloa, neither is regarded as a forerunner of Kōloa School because students were taught in Hawaiian. Gulick's second school closed in 1884 when English became the official language of instruction. Students then attended Dole's "English school" next door.

Reverend Daniel Dole's role in establishing a school in Kōloa was also told in the chapter about the missionaries. His 1855 school is regarded as the start of Kōloa School. In 1860, Dole built an English day school on the spot where the Kōloa Public and School Library is now.

Dr. James W. Smith also played an important part in education during the early years. In 1861, he established a boarding school for Hawaiian girls on the east side of Poʻipū Road just *makai* of what is now the Kōloa Missionary Church. His daughters, Emma and Charlotte (Lottie) taught the girls in English, assisted by their aunt Deborah Knapp until the school closed in 1871. Dr. Smith headed the group who petitioned the kingdom's Board of Education in 1877 to establish Kōloa School as the first government school on Kauaʻi to teach in English. When the petition was approved, he became the first commissioner of Kōloa School.

In late plantation times, there were several cottages where the parking lot is now. One was where the principal lived and others were for teachers and various school purposes. North of the cottages, across the playground, was the large L-shaped main building with a flagpole in front. Students gathered there every morning to raise the flag, pledge allegiance, and sing the National Anthem accompanied by a wind-up gramophone. There were a few bungalows to the west for overflow classes, and then a stone wall running roughly north and south, which marked the boundary of McBryde Plantation. Behind that was a spur of the McBryde railroad. Cane cars were sometimes parked there. One favorite activity of the students was to pull the pin to detach a car, release the brake, "geeve wan shove" to get the car going, hop on, and enjoy a hair-raising ride all the way down to Kukuiʻula, more than two miles away.

The main building burned down in 1973, so "temporary" portable classrooms were brought in that are still in use today. The library was finished in 1976 and the cafeteria soon afterwards. In 1982, the seventh and eighth grades were transferred to Kauaʻi High and Intermediate School in Līhuʻe; since then its official name has been Kōloa Elementary School.

Let's start the walking part of our tour of Kōloa by taking a short detour south to see where Dole's home and school were located.

3. The Dole home site is now occupied by a mortuary on the east side of Poʻipū Road, beside a large gray building.

Reverend Dr. James W. Smith and his congregation built Kōloa Church in 1859. It was remodeled in 1929-30 through the generosity of George N. Wilcox.

Although the home itself no longer exists, history happened there, as has been recounted. Dole's son Sanford was raised there, attended his father's school next to the home, and became president of the Republic, then first governor of the Territory of Hawai'i. When Dole's wife died in 1874 he sold the property and moved to Honolulu to live with his son. Dole died there two years later.

The person Dole sold the property to was George Charman, an English sailor who had come ashore from a whaler to engage in trade with ships that called at Kōloa Landing. When that trade tapered off, he went into cattle and cane and became wealthy. Dole's old house burned to the ground in 1907, and Charman built another home in Kōloa. The tropical style of the mortuary is somewhat reminiscent of the Dole home with a covered *lānai*, but without the second story.

Now walk north on Po'ipū Road.

4. Nakatsuka General Store was directly across from Kōloa School and sold all sorts of things to the school children, as well as general merchandise to residents of Kōloa. Next to it was Kurasaki Bakery which sold *sushi*, bread, and *manju* to the students for their lunch. Both are gone now, but the memories of them remain.

5. Tao Garage was on the south corner of Waikomo Road and Po'ipū Road in the twenties and early thirties. Part of the concrete slab is all that remains; the building there now is new. The smaller building *makai* of the concrete slab, where Tao had dispensed gas and oil, was rebuilt as Snorkel Bob's and looks much like the original. In the early 1930s, Tao moved to the west corner of Kōloa and Po'ipū Roads, where he continued to sell Shell gasoline and repair cars.

After Tao left the location on the corner of Waikomo Road, Yamamoto set up a Union Oil service station in the same building. It had one gasoline pump with a glass cylinder on top that was filled with a wiggle-waggle hand pump to the requested amount from a large tank in back of the building. The gas was dispensed from the cylinder to the car by gravity through a hose. Oil was kept in a large drum next to the gas pump. A copper container with a snout was filled from it with a hand rotary pump, and the snout lowered to put oil into the cars. When the larger and more modern Chevron station opened in town, Yamamoto's operation closed.

★ **6. Kōloa Church**, in classic New England style, is on the west side of Po'ipū Road. It is the custom on Kaua'i as elsewhere in Hawaiʻi to use the name of the congregation for the name of the church, but this would be too confusing for visitors. I can recall at least half a dozen names that have been used for this church. It is much simpler to use the original name for this and other churches we will see. Dr. Smith with his congregation built Kōloa Church in 1859 on the site of Gulick's 1837 adobe chapel. When it was rebuilt in 1929, the cornice with oculus window and the Doric columns were added. Otherwise, the church is in the same steepled style as the original and is still known as the "White Church." After Rowell's discharge, Dr. Smith's parish extended from Waimea to Wailua. He continued as pastor of Kōloa Church until resigning in 1869. At the last general meeting of the American Board of Commissioners for Foreign Missions at Boston in 1863, it was decided that all mission stations should become financially independent and that churches have native pastors. Dr. Smith continued to support himself, his family, and the church by raising cattle and cane.

Isabella Bird, an enthusiastic English traveler and a "young woman of exceptional intelligence and energy," wrote to her younger sister, Henrietta, about her stay with the Smiths in 1873. Her description almost makes Kauaʻi at that time come alive:

> The view is a pleasant one. The rains have been abundant, and the land, which here rises rather gradually from the sea, is dotted with houses, abounds in signs of cultivation, and then spreads up into a rolling country between precipitous ranges of mountains. The hills look something like those of Oahu, but their wonderful greenness denotes a cooler climate and more copious rains, also their slopes and valleys are densely wooded . . .

> It is a wild, lonely, picturesque coast, and the Pacific moans along it, casting itself on it in heavy surges . . .There is no inn or boarding house on the island . . . Mrs. Smith met me courteously at the door . . . the 'guest house,' where I am lodged, is a dobe house, and a very thick grass comes down six feet all around to shade the windows.

> Kauai is much out of the island world . . . strangers visit it seldom . . . It is called the 'Garden Island,' and has no great wastes of black lava and red ash like its neighbors . . . The valleys of Kauai are long, and widen to the sea, and their dark rich soil is often ten feet deep . . .

> The scenery in the Kōloa woods is exquisitely beautiful. Such supreme beauty produces on me some of the effects which fine music has . . .

Dr. Smith and his wife spent the remainder of their lives in the service of the people of Kōloa and Kaua'i. He died on December 11, 1887, Melicent on September 24, 1891. They lie side by side in the small private Smith-Waterhouse graveyard off Malino (calm) Road.

7. Kōloa Union Church, with its lava-rock exterior, stands beside the White Church. Early in this century, two services were conducted at Kōloa Church; one for plantation managers and other *haoles*, and a second for Hawaiians and plantation workers. In 1923 the Hawaiians and plantation workers separated, adopted the name Kōloa Union Church, and began to worship in the fellowship hall next door.

George N. Wilcox paid for the reconstruction of Kōloa Church in 1929. At the same time, he built a wooden church between it and Kōloa School for the Hawaiians and plantation workers. Because it was painted brown, it became known as the "Brown Church." The lava-rock church presently *mauka* of Kōloa Church was built in 1961 on land donated by Dr. Herbert Waterhouse and his wife, Mabel. The Brown Church was then used for other purposes until it was damaged by Hurricane 'Iniki in 1992. It was demolished in 1995 and replaced by the white educational/social building there today.

★ **8. Kōloa Missionary Church** is on the east side of Po'ipū Road. The building is an indirect descendant of the frame two-story school Dr. James W. Smith and his wife erected in 1861. They made it their home in 1871, then enlarged and changed it in many other ways over the years. Their son, Dr. Jared Smith, returned to Kōloa upon becoming a physician to assist his father in his later years. After the death of his parents Jared inherited the house, and in 1896 completely remodeled it for his bride-to-be. One night, before the wedding could take place, he answered a knock at the door and was shot in the face. The father and boyfriend of a young Hawaiian lady with leprosy killed him, hoping to prevent her from being sent to Kalaupapa. In a community almost without serious crime, this shocked everyone for months.

John K. Farley occupied the house until Dr. Herbert Waterhouse arrived in Kōloa with his wife Mabel in 1907. The Waterhouses lived in the home for nearly 40 years and continued to care for the large fruit orchard planted around it by Dr. James Smith. A few of the trees remain today, including a stately

The Kōloa Plantation Hospital/Dispensary, built in 1911.

Photograph by author, 1999.

tamarind tree near Waikomo Road from which Dr. James Smith gave cuttings to Queen Emma when she lived at Lāwaʻi Kai. One tamarind tree Queen Emma planted, toppled by Hurricane ʻIwa but still growing, is beside the Allerton home and another is near the Diana Fountain.

Dr. Waterhouse was the Kōloa Plantation physician until 1933, and then operated a clinic from the house until his death in 1948. In 1953, his widow Mabel moved to their Poʻipū beach house and sold the Kōloa property to the Kōloa Missionary Church. The Smith-Waterhouse home was torn down and the present church was constructed in 1955. Perhaps because many timbers in the White Church built in 1859 were found to be in excellent condition at the time of its remodeling in 1929 and were put back into that structure, the belief persists in Kōloa that material from the Smith-Waterhouse home was incorporated into the Missionary Church. This may be true, but records of the latter church do not mention this, whereas records of the White Church are specific on this point. Waterhouse descendants today are unable to say with certainty if the Missionary Church contains elements of their ancestral home. They do point to the garage and attached structure in back of the Missionary Church as original. These, and the benefit of the doubt, were sufficient to put a "★" beside the name above.

★ **9. The Kōloa Plantation Hospital and Dispensary**, built by Kōloa Plantation in 1911, is on the west side of Poʻipū Road, across from the Kōloa Missionary Church. An unmarked driveway between two rows of royal palms leads to the two attached buildings, which are now boarded up. It was fortunate that I looked around inside in 1946, because after the strike that year, free medical care was one of the perquisites that was discontinued and the hospital/dispensary was closed.

One building had been the clinic or dispensary and had three examination rooms, an office, and a small pharmacy. The hospital next to it had four private rooms and a large ward with ten beds for both men and women. Curtains provided the only privacy. An operating room was at one end of the hospital. The cottages along the driveway, former nurses' quarters, are now rented out as homes by Grove Farm.

Now you are about to enter commercial "Old Kōloa Town." On the east side of Poʻipū Road, as you approach the intersection with Kōloa Road, are four relatively new buildings. The three closest to the Chevron station are separated from the fourth by a narrow road that acquired the name *Makai* Lane in the 1920s when it marked the *makai* boundary of the town. The three buildings north of the lane have historic interest although they were rebuilt by KTA. The fourth, to the south across the lane, does not.

10. USA Store is the first of the three semi-historic structures as you walk north. Originally, it had been a plantation house built about 1920 by Kōloa Plantation. Later in that decade, Dr. Waterhouse purchased the property and leased it at a low rate to Toko Usa, a Japanese immigrant, who lived in it with his picture bride from Japan. Toko had worked in the fields for many years past his contract until he had saved enough to lease the house and open a store in the front part of it. Usa Store carried groceries and assorted household items; a sign in the window advertised "Bicycles and Diamond Rings." Mrs. Usa turned out to be quite a remarkable lady. She was famous locally as a marriage broker, spiritual counselor, and *O-Kamisama* prayer lady. She also repaired bicycles. At the start of World War II, a friend suggested the Usas capitalize the name, USA, to give the store a patriotic connotation. They did, customers smiled, and the Usas smiled in return.

11. The Nishita Building is the red building next to it, also originally a plantation house dating from around 1920. It was the home of the Kataokas, with his furniture and upholstery shop in the front and family living quarters in back. Mrs. Kataoka made and sold *tofu.* The property was purchased about 1930 by Dr. Waterhouse, at which time Masato Nishita and his wife, Tokie, moved in. Masato was a tailor who enjoyed a reputation as the best one in town. Tokie sewed and had ladies who lived nearby do piecework. The tailor shop was in the front for over 40 years; the family lived in back, as had the Kataokas.

12. Okumura Store is the two-story building next, on the north. It was originally built in 1905 by Matsuichi Okumura on land leased from Kōloa Plantation. His store, where he sold general merchandise, was on the first floor. The Okumura family lived on the second floor, and later added a kitchen and bedroom on the first floor in back. At that time, there was only a small plantation store in Lāwaʻi. As Matsuichi was willing to take orders and deliver that far away, much of his business was with the pineapple workers. The exterior of the building now on the site resembles the original more so than the other two just described.

13. Kauaʻi Motors was the first and only automobile dealer in Kōloa. In 1924, the company opened its doors in the building now occupied by Sueoka Store. Two years later, Kauaʻi Motors built two structures at the east corner of Poʻipū Road and Kōloa Road and moved there. The larger of the two buildings on the corner had a showroom in front where General Motors automobiles were sold, and a service/parts department in back. The smaller struc-

The Kōloa Telephone Exchange, built about 1912.

☙ Photograph by author, 1999.

The New Plantation Theater as it appeared in 1962 on the corner near the old mill site. It was the main source of entertainment for the residents of Kōloa from 1936 until it closed with the advent of television in 1963.

☞ Photograph taken about 1960.

ture to the east, attached by an office, was for body repairs and painting, with a one-pump Chevron station on Kōloa Road.

In 1970, Kaua'i Motors moved to Līhu'e, and the larger of the two buildings was replaced by the modern Chevron service station on the corner today. The body repair and painting shop was demolished by Kōloa Town Associates and a new structure was built behind the Kahalewai Building as a restaurant. This is the building just east of the Chevron station with the large sign "The Old Paint Shop," which it isn't. Kōloa Town Associates did this to enclose the landscaped area of the History Center and to provide parking for "Old Kōloa Town."

★ **14. The Telephone Exchange** was in the small green building on the north side of Kōloa Road, opposite the Chevron station. As everyone knows, Don Ameche and his assistant Henry Fonda invented the telephone in 1876, but it was slow in coming to Kaua'i.

The first telephone was installed on the island in 1880 by George N. Wilcox to link Dr. James Smith, the only physician on the island, to Līhu'e. The system was extended in Līhu'e and elsewhere but did not reach other residents of Kōloa, the hospital/dispensary, and plantation officials until 1900. During the thirties telephones were still rather rare in town and nonexistent in the camps.

Radiotelephone service to the other islands and the mainland was available from the Kōloa exchange in 1931. Workers came there, waited their turn, and went into one of the small booths to make a call. Operators knew almost everyone, and many stories are told about the services they performed. The exchange closed in 1948 and is now a modest private home.

The New Plantation Theater is no longer on the corner near the old mill, across Kōloa Road from Sueoka Store, but it had been so much a part of plantation life that it should be described. Try to imagine a 594-seat theater in art-deco style, with a neon-lit marquee, in the center of a rustic plantation town. Admission price: twenty-five cents. A photograph from the Hawai'i State Archives is in this book if the idea is too much to imagine.

When the Old Plantation Theater burned down, Kōloa Plantation built the new one in 1936. It was operated by Manuel Teves, who had operated the old one. By then office manager for the plantation, Manuel Teves lived near the new theater in what is now the Kōloa branch of the Kaua'i Medical Clinic. It is almost worth having a minor ailment to visit the clinic and look around inside this building.

Yamamoto Store, built in 1898. It was the oldest store in Kōloa when it was torn down in 1983.

Television could be received from Honolulu on the east side of Kaua'i as early as 1952, but did not affect attendance at the movies in Kōloa. In 1960, VHF-UHF transponders on Mount Kāhili brought television to this part of the island. The new theater closed in 1963, and in 1971 the building burned to the ground under mysterious circumstances. When you drive around the town after the walking tour you will see where the Old Plantation Theater had been located.

Now continue east along Kōloa Road on the south side.

15. The Kahalewai Building is on Kōloa Road in front of "The Old Paint Shop." The original building was put up by Dr. Waterhouse in 1927; Kahalewai means "the water house." It first contained a small post office at the west end; a general store operated by the Ornellas in the middle; and a tailor shop at the east end. Later on, it held Mr. Iwai's watch-repair shop; Mrs. Tanaka's beauty shop; a Filipino's tailor shop; and Dulce's Dress Shop. During World War II, the entire building except for the post office was taken over as an Army bakery.

For almost thirty years after that, Awa Store was the sole occupant. Johnny Awa was Chinese and had the best "crack seed" in town. He carried so much general merchandise only he could find anything. The Kahalewai Building was razed and rebuilt by KTA. Fortunately, the interesting design of the front on Kōloa Road was retained. It has a shed roof behind its false front and four bays defined by Tuscan pilasters. A hipped canopy of corrugated metal extends over the four bays. The building today is occupied by tourist-oriented shops and a pharmacy.

★ **16. The Salvation Army Chapel** was built in 1906 and, though repaired several times, is still essentially the original building. The inside has remained unchanged over the better part of a century. Mabel P. Waterhouse quitclaimed the property to the Salvation Army for as long as it is used for Salvation Army purposes. Services are held there every Sunday morning and are fascinating to attend. The Salvation Army plays an important role in charitable activities on Kaua'i, more than most visitors expect.

17. Yamamoto Store is on the bank of Waikomo Stream. The original store dates from 1898, when Yamashiroya (shortened to Yamaka which everyone called him; nobody now living recalls his first name) leased the building and sold liquor, groceries and general merchandise. Starting about 1915, he also operated a service station of sorts with one pump.

The Yamamotos took over in the early 1920s and ran the business along the same lines. They lived in a frame house (now gone) in the space between the store and the Salvation Army

Kōloa Street scene, 1963. All buildings shown were built in the early 1920s.

☞ *Hawai'i State Archives*

Chapel. The monkeypod tree by the stream was planted by Howard Yamamoto in 1925, and thereafter the store was often called Monkeypod Store. The porch was a favorite place in plantation days for people to gather and talk story. When the Kōloa Theater was across the street, movie patrons bought their snacks and soft drinks here. Children came after school for red coconut candy, *li hing mui*, dried abalone, and other treats. The historic store, then the oldest commercial building in Kōloa, was torn down in 1983, replaced with a slightly larger but similar structure designed to be a tourist shop, and leased to Crazy Shirts.

18. The Kōloa Hotel was the second hotel on Kaua'i. The first was the Fairview Hotel, which was opened in 1890 by Charles Spitz in Līhu'e. About two years later, Yamaka attached six small rooms to the back of his store and started the Kōloa Hotel. The Yamamotos continued to operate the hotel when they took over the store. The Kōloa Hotel was used mostly by salesmen who came over on the interisland steamer to obtain orders from stores in town and from plantation workers. Japanese players who gave open-air *shibai* performances in Japanese Camp also stayed there. In 1983, the hotel rooms were demolished and a larger structure, designed to contain a series of shops, was built at some distance farther back. Although that structure is an entirely different one, and in a different location, a plaque on it states it is The Kōloa Hotel and "believed to be Kaua'i's first hotel."

19. The Japanese Bath or *furo* was located approximately 20 feet in back of the hotel on the bank of the stream in a small building that also contained a laundry room. The exhibit now in the History Center is misleading as to its original location. The original bath/laundry was torn down at the same time as the store and hotel. For many years this *furo* and those in Japanese Camp were communal. Issei thought nothing of men and women bathing together, but nisei were somewhat more shy. A traditional hot bath with a scrub and long soak was a reward for the hard-working Japanese laborers and an opportunity to socialize in their own language. Japanese hotel guests also enjoyed the hotel *furo*.

20. Tanaka Fish Market was located where Sueoka's parking lot is now. Other than from fish peddlers who came to town and the camps, this was the best place in plantation days to buy fish. Tanaka got them fresh daily from Japanese fishermen who operated sampans out of Kukui'ula Harbor. A small Chinese dry-goods store was just east of the market and spanned the drainage ditch that ran along the south side of Kōloa Road. In 1960, the property occupied by both stores was acquired by the Sueokas and turned into a parking lot.

21. Sueoka Store first opened as a small shack in 1923 in Japanese Camp, where it thrived. In 1926, Kauaʻi Motors moved its showroom from the present location of Sueoka Store and consolidated its operations on the corner of Kōloa Road and Poʻipū Road. The building that is now Sueoka Store was then occupied by Mitsunami Store and the Bishop Bank. Mitsunami Store did not survive long, and in 1927, Mankichi Sueoka leased Mitsunami's half from Dr. Waterhouse. Sueoka's customers followed him from Japanese Camp to his new site. The Bishop Bank was renamed First Hawaiian Bank and moved down the street in 1935; Sueoka took over the whole building. He purchased the property in 1943 and improved the building.

The 1920s architecture that remains is interesting. The false front is distinguished by an articulating ogee curve and angled top, and a corrugated metal canopy is cantilevered over the sidewalk. Sueoka Store is the only privately owned business on the Kōloa Road frontage. It was not touched by Kōloa Town Associates.

22. The Yamada Building next to Sueoka originally had been built in 1921 but was razed and rebuilt by KTA. The front along Kōloa Road is similar to the original, with a shed roof behind a false front that is articulated into three bays by four pilasters and trim boards above a canopy along the entire front. It had various tenants over time, such as a small gas station, a beer hall, and a pool hall.

One tenant was Tadao "Barber" Kawamoto, who gave haircuts to the music of a wind-up Victrola and talked with customers about old times. He set up shop in 1932, bought the building in 1965, and remained until he was forced to leave in 1983. Even though he owned the building, the lease on the property was raised so high he had to sell and vacate. KTA demolished the structure and put up one almost twice as large as part of the "Old Kōloa Town" project. Because of Tadao's long occupation and ownership of it, the Yamada Building (its original name) is often called **The Kawamoto Building**. Tadao continued to give haircuts to some of his old customers, including the author of this book, in the carport of his home in Poʻipū, until he suffered a stroke at the age of 87.

23. Asahi Ice and Soda Works is next, to the east. Before the turn of the century, a small *poi* factory run by the Akona family was on the site, but it was replaced by a liquor store. In 1905, John Cockett, who had been variously employed by Kōloa Plantation, purchased the liquor store from his grand-uncle. Hawaiians had long brewed *ʻōkolehao* from *ti* root, and other plantation workers made "swipe wine" from molasses, as well as more disagreeable potions. Although this activity was against plantation regulations, and in violation of Prohibition until it was repealed, it was generally overlooked unless the products were sampled excessively. Cockett sold only brand-name bottled liquor. Yozaemon Yamamoto worked for him and the business did well until Prohibition came in 1918.

Cockett and Yamamoto then formed a partnership and started making soda near the cemetery across from Cockett's home at the corner of Maluhia and Waila'au Roads. They also brought ice in a wagon from Līhu'e (later from Waimea) and sold it in town and in the camps. The soda was made using syrup, gas, and bottles brought in at Kōloa Landing. The ingredients were mixed in each bottle by hand and capped with a device worked with a foot lever. Yamamoto was the one who suggested the name Asahi, perhaps because of the fame of Asahi brewery in Japan. The word means "rising sun" in Japanese, so he may have liked it for that reason. Although neither ice nor soda was actually made on the site in town, the business was called Asahi Ice and Soda Works because that was where both were sold.

They discontinued the sale of ice soon after 1918 when electricity—and refrigeration—arrived in Kōloa and the camps. The soda business went under in 1930 when Coca-Cola became popular. After Cockett died in 1931, other enterprises were located there, one of the last being a bar. KTA replaced the building with one nearly three times as large, extending farther back and almost touching the buildings on either side. It is now the Kōloa Broiler, and its bar is in approximately the same location as the bar in the former structure.

24. Chang Fook Store (sometimes called Chang Fook Kee, kee meaning store) is next on the east. It was started by the Changs in the 1920s as a general store, but it is most fondly remembered as the bakery it became in the 1930s, producing 'ono bread, apple pie, rice cakes, manapua, and a marvelous aroma that wafted far down the street. The local opinion of their products was "broke da mout, brah," meaning delicious! There was space in back where one could sit down to enjoy a treat while passing the time of day with friends. This area was developed into a restaurant by the Changs. In 1983-1984 the building was leveled and rebuilt by Kōloa Town Associates, but resembles the original more than most buildings "restored" by KTA.

25. The Tao Building on the corner of Weliweli Road was built by Mrs. Toyo Nii about 1920. Ichizo Tao leased it and with his family, operated a general store and ice-cream parlor there. They also sold ice cream and "shave ice" at the Po'ipū beaches and at festive occasions in town. After World War II, it housed a union hall, a dress shop, and a barber shop. Kōloa Town Associates replaced the Tao Building with one that bears little likeness to the original. What strikes an observer first is the missing shed roof that was so distinctive.

At Weliweli Road we have come to the end of "Old Kōloa Town" (which more properly should be called "New Kōloa Town"), and we can take leave of Kōloa Town Associates, except for one thing. The name "Old Kōloa Town" has caused confusion on the part of visitors and others who sometimes use the name for the entire town of Kōloa.

Behind all the buildings you have passed along Poʻipū Road and Kōloa Road were small family homes and vegetable gardens. Most of the gardens were near Waikomo Stream, and a large pipe ran from an intake by Tao Garage under Weliweli Road to irrigate them.

★ **26. Old plantation houses** are still to be found in Kōloa and four are east of Weliweli Road on Kōloa Road. They still bear their faded plantation numbers, as well as their newer addresses.

Then we come to a group of buildings that was rebuilt to compete with "Old Kōloa Town." Some of the previous occupants had been a Chinese barber, a series of Portuguese-operated stores, and a Korean tailor. The tailor was Ho Young Chun, whose shop was on the corner of the narrow gravel lane that is described next. The "Kōloa Cultural Center" is now located there with various shops on two levels.

Charman Lane is the small gravel lane directly across from the present post office. There is no sign, but the lane had been named for a crusty old salt who was mentioned before. He had lived in Dole's home until it burned down in 1907, and then built a large two-story house at the end of the lane. Although he was only a seaman when he came ashore from a whaler, he became wealthy and preferred to be addressed as Captain Charman. He owned all of the property between his home and Kōloa Road and also owned fine horses and an elegant carriage known locally as "Charman's chaise." When he sold portions of his land, he made sure the lane remained his so he could come and go in grand style. Although the lane is still there, his home is long gone.

Iwamura Theater was started in 1910 by Sadakichi Iwamura, in Charman Lane behind Ho Young Chun's tailor shop on the corner. He showed mostly Japanese films and some cowboy movies, all silent. There was a *benshi*, or narrator, for the Japanese films. This was before electricity came to Kōloa, so the Iwamuras ran the projector from the generator of an old Cadillac. The theater had no seats and patrons sat on cushions, as they would in Japan. They brought *bento* lunches and ate them at intermission.

The Shinagawa family made ice cream by hand in buckets across the lane and sold it to patrons of the theater. They saved for years, and in the late twenties they purchased the theater, which then became known as the **Shinagawa Theater**. They put in folding chairs, connected electricity which was available by then, and showed a wider variety of films, all of them in sound.

Japanese performances, *shibai* and *kabuki*, were also given there. For the touring Japanese shows they hired local youngsters to go around town with a narrator who extolled the virtues of the upcoming performance in Japanese. The youngsters beat a drum and passed out leaflets; the Shinagawas gave them free tickets for this. At least once a month they removed the chairs and held taxi dances for the single Filipino workers. They brought over women from Honolulu for the dances, and many of them remained for a few days on their own initiative for other purposes.

Nothing remains of the theater (by either name) today.

Along Kōloa Road beyond Charman Lane were small stores, Okutsu restaurant, plantation homes, a jewelry store, and a pool hall. These have all been rebuilt and now are occupied by various commercial enterprises. Out of curiosity, I dropped in to see the pool hall in 1952. It had four tables and a wobbly bench at one side for those who wanted to watch or wager. The pool hall was run by a diminutive and charming lady, Marcella Amoroso. When asked why she chose this occupation she replied, "Mo' bettah, no *luna* already." She added she could open the pool hall at hours "what feel like."

27. Kōloa Plantation Store had been at various locations since the first mill was built. In 1914, a wooden structure was erected for it at the end of Kōloa Road, where the First Hawaiian Bank is today. The post office moved and occupied part of the building. A warehouse was put up just north of the store where the railroad ran close by, and goods were brought in at Kōloa Landing. In 1927, a larger store incorporating the meat market, which had been near the plantation dairy until then, was built where the Big Save Market parking lot is now; and the old building became a Filipino social hall. By that time, goods were brought in at Port Allen or Nāwiliwili and delivered to the store by truck.

With their *bāngo* (metal tags bearing their numbers), plantation workers charged purchases at the Kōloa Plantation Store. Customers came to the counter and requested each item, which the clerks took down from the shelves and wrapped in a bundle to be carried home. Because the purchases were often heavy to carry, orders were also taken in the camps every afternoon and deliveries made the next day.

The Kōloa Japanese Language School, built in 1903.

Photograph by author, 1999.

The Kōloa Shingon-Shu Buddhist Mission, built in 1907, as it appeared in 1962.

The new Kōloa Plantation Store had a generator and refrigeration, so it carried meat brought from the dairy where cattle continued to be slaughtered. In 1918, the store acquired electricity, enlarged its meat market, and installed a freezer. Muranaka, the butcher, slaughtered three times a week. The older former plantation workers I talked to agree the upper echelons of the plantation hierarchy always got the best meat and workers were sold the rest. One old-timer said "Yeh . . . we got da rubbish." The only other choice was "old man Ono," who raised cattle north of Japanese Camp, slaughtered when he felt like it, and sold the meat that same day. Apparently, he was a grump, and if someone complained about something he growled, "no like, no stoppu," which was his way of saying, "if you don't like it, don't come."

The Plantation Store struggled after the 1946 strike and continued to do so after its takeover by Grove Farm in 1948. As plantation employees, the personnel belonged to the ILWU and received union wages, while the other stores in Kōloa were non-union and their prices were lower. Līhuʻe Plantation bought it in 1954 and remodeled it, but it continued to lose money and closed in 1959. Big Save intended to use the same building but it was damaged by fire. Big Save demolished the remains and put up a larger store behind it that is there today. The space formerly occupied by the Plantation Store became the Big Save parking lot.

The First Hawaiian Bank (formerly Bishop Bank), which had been in temporary locations, built its present structure at the east end of Kōloa Road in 1953. The Filipino social hall was removed to make room for it. The post office relocated at that time from the Kahalewai Building to occupy the south third of the new bank building, and had its own driveway and small parking lot on that side. The bank also had a driveway and parking lot on its side (north) of the building.

In 1983, federal funds were obtained for a new and larger post office erected on the north side of Kōloa Road, where it is now. The bank then expanded into the entire building. Part of the wall that formerly separated the post office from the bank can still be seen inside the bank. When the post office moved to its new location, the driveway and small parking lot it had used were taken over by the bank. The parking lot the bank had previously used looks somewhat strange today on the side of the building that has no entrance.

28. The Kōloa Hongwanji Mission is across the street north of Big Save Market. The large green structure is a combination social hall and auditorium and was first used by the Young Buddhist Association, or YBA, patterned after the YMCA. Next to it

The Kōloa Jodo Mission, built in 1910.

⌁ Photograph by author, 1999.

was the gorgeous Kōloa Hongwanji Mission Temple, built in 1910. It burned down in 1994, and services are presently conducted in the hall. The Early School is where martial arts were formerly taught.

★ **29. The Kōloa Japanese Language School** roof can be seen behind the Early School. Since the Early School leased the site and locked the access gate, the only way to get there on foot now is along a path that starts behind the post office. Park in the rear of the post office and you will see the path along the fence of the Early School playground. There is another way to get there by car that will be described later. The Kōloa Japanese Language School was built in 1903 and is the weary-looking building shaped like an L. In one classroom the blackboard still has writing on it from a lesson more than 50 years ago. If you are very quiet, you may hear the high-pitched voices reciting the lesson as reflected from the rafters above.

All Japanese children had to attend. The school was taught by priests from nearby temples, both Buddhist and Shinto. They were strict and physical in their discipline. If the kids went home and complained, they got more of the same from their fathers. The tuition was low and paid by the parents. The students learned the Japanese language, culture, and religion using texts printed in Japan. They were also taught loyalty to the emperor, which was why the school was closed after Pearl Harbor.

★ **30. The Kōloa Jodo Mission** across Waikomo Road from the Big Save Market on the east was the first Jodo sect mission on Kauaʻi. The smaller temple was built in 1910, and its classic details are exquisite. Note the beauty of the altar. When the congregation outgrew the small temple, the larger one next to it was built in 1985 and dedicated that year in a moving Buddhist ceremony. Both temples were built by master craftsmen brought from Japan for that purpose.

Now walk *makai* on Waikomo Road. Between the Jodo Temples and Waoke Road are the old Waiʻohai Hotel cottages dating from 1962, which were moved there and made into homes when the larger Waiʻohai Resort was built in 1981.

Turn right, and walk back towards town on Weliweli Road. If you had continued on Waikomo Road, **Maulili Pond**, the location of both the first and second Kōloa mills, is farther on at the Kapau Road turnoff, but there is little to see there now. This portion of Weliweli Road retains some of the atmosphere of old Kōloa, but most of the structures along it are shabby now.

The Shingon-Shu Mission is the small, battered green building immediately on the right as you walk back to town on

Weliweli Road. It was built in 1907 in Puhi Camp, moved by cane train to New Mill Camp in 1919, and then moved to this site in 1956.

The Shingon sect was perhaps the most peaceful of the Buddhist sects in plantation times, and not as nationalistic or militaristic as Shinto was in the thirties. It was the only Japanese temple in Kōloa not closed after Pearl Harbor. It was immaculately maintained by its congregation until damaged by Hurricane 'Iwa in 1982. By then, most of the adherents to this sect had aged or died, so it was not restored. A photograph taken in 1962 was found in the Hawai'i State Archives and included in this book to give you an idea of its appearance before it was abandoned.

There are some authentic plantation houses along Weliweli Road that are of interest. Before World War I, German workers occupied several houses on this road.

31. The Kōloa Civic Center on the left was built in 1977. Before then it had been a combined courthouse, sheriff's office, and jail, with a small dental clinic at one side.

When you reach Kōloa Road again, retrace your steps to your car near Kōloa School and pause along the way to look again at anything that interested you, or stop to shop in town. This is the end of the walking portion of your tour.

Now I would like to guide you in your car to some of the interesting sites around Kōloa. There are several, but most are on private property, so you can't see them. A word of explanation is in order.

The island tradition for centuries has been one of *aloha*. Private property/trespassing were almost alien concepts on Kaua'i until the late sixties, when careless people trashed many beautiful places on the island. Then came a series of liability suits. The result was the first "No Trespassing" signs that began to appear in the 1970s; gates were put across the cane-road entrances in the 1980s. Please don't hold this against those of us who live here. It is not the island way of life but was brought here from elsewhere.

This reduces us to so few sites that, by way of compensation, I'd like to suggest a side trip before we return to see them.

The maps included in this book are of the town of Kōloa and the Po'ipū shore. They do not cover this side trip, or the sites around the periphery of Kōloa for that matter. The area is so large the maps would have to be fold-outs with multiple folds. Fortunately, the places are not hard to find, and any of the free maps available anywhere on Kaua'i are all you will need. Stop in one of the tourist booths in Kōloa and ask for one. I'll try to make the directions clear enough so a map really won't be necessary.

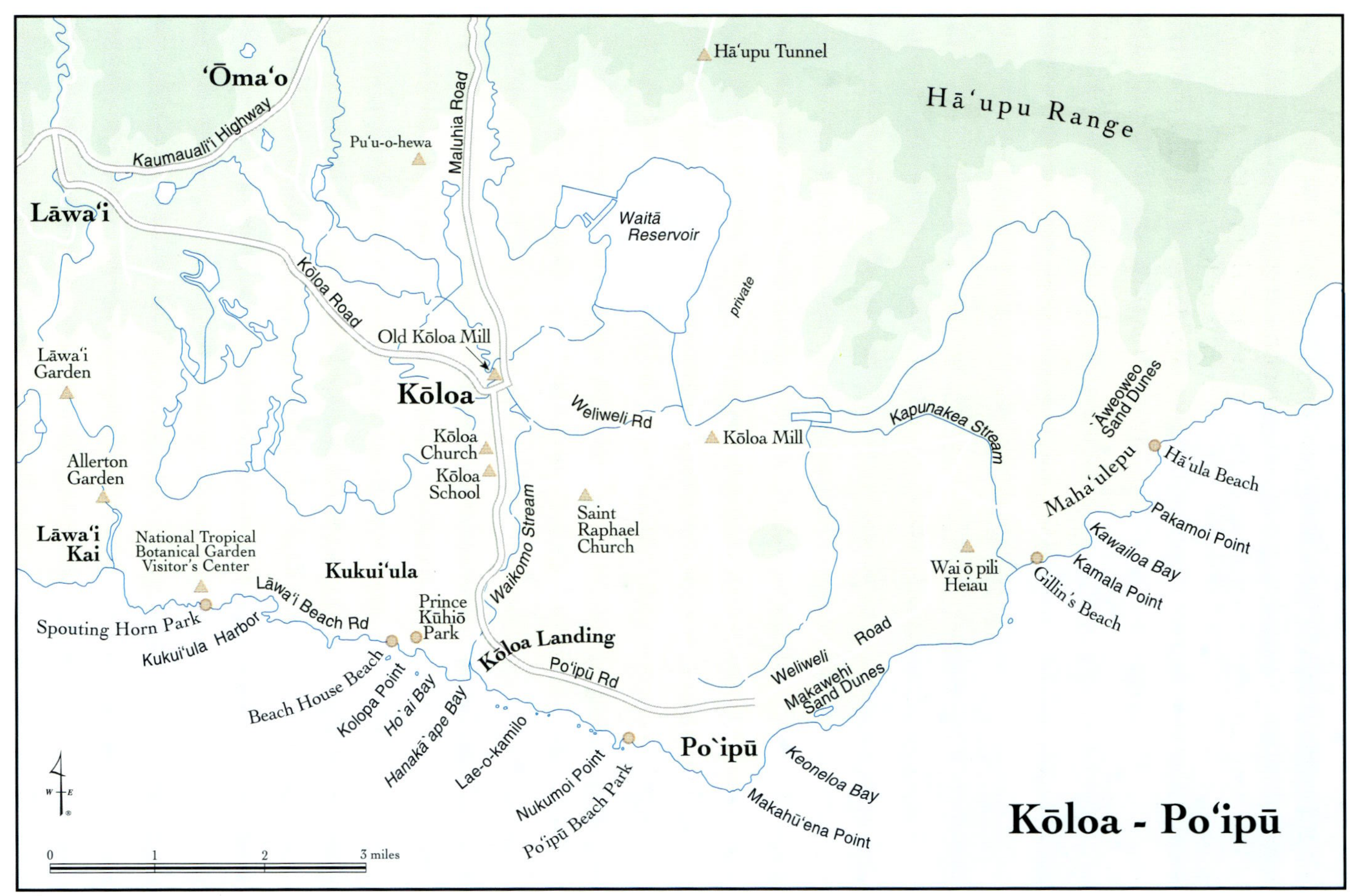

Kōloa - Poʻipū
Hāʻupu Range
Hāʻupu Tunnel
ʻŌmaʻo
Kaumualiʻi Highway
Maluhia Road
Puʻu-o-hewa
Lāwaʻi
Waitā Reservoir
private
Kōloa Road
Old Kōloa Mill
Kōloa
Lāwaʻi Garden
Weliweli Rd
Kapunakea Stream
ʻĀweoweo Sand Dunes
Hāʻula Beach
Allerton Garden
Kōloa Church
Kōloa School
Kōloa Mill
Māhāʻulepū
Pakamoi Point
Kawailoa Bay
Lāwaʻi Kai
National Tropical Botanical Garden Visitorʼs Center
Saint Raphael Church
Kamala Point
Kukuiʻula
Waikomo Stream
Wai ō pili Heiau
Gillinʼs Beach
Spouting Horn Park
Lāwaʻi Beach Rd
Prince Kūhiō Park
Kōloa Landing
Weliweli Road
Kukuiʻula Harbor
Poʻipū Rd
Makawehi Sand Dunes
Beach House Beach
Kolopa Point
Hoʻai Bay
Hanakāʻape Bay
Lae-o-kamilo
Poʻipū
W E
Nukumoi Point
Poʻipū Beach Park
Keoneloa Bay
Makahūʻena Point
0   1   2   3 miles
Kōloa - Poʻipū

This side trip will be to the adjacent *ahupua'a* of Lāwa'i and **Kukui-o-Lono**, a beautiful place made accessible to all by an unusual man, Walter McBryde. He purchased a large tract of land for the specific purpose of creating a park for the people to enjoy. Upon his death, title passed to the County of Kaua'i with his life savings to maintain it, and it will remain forever a public park. You have read about him before: he is the one who donated and helped plant the trees on Maluhia Road that now form the Tree Tunnel.

Drive north on Po'ipū Road to the intersection with Kōloa Road at the Chevron station, and turn left on Highway 530. This is a continuation of Kōloa Road leading to Lāwa'i. It was originally part of Government Road, then commonly referred to as "the belt road" even though it didn't go all the way around the island.

On the way, I will tell you about some sites as you pass them. They are on private property, so you can't explore them. This may be frustrating, but telling you about just these few has a purpose. It will give you an idea of what is "off limits" now around Kōloa and almost everywhere on Kaua'i and serve as a reminder for us to treat those that remain accessible with respect, or we may lose the right to visit them. For example, access to the last unspoiled stretch of the south shore, Māhā'ulepū, was prohibited for a time by its owner, Grove Farm, because of trash that visitors left behind and other thoughtless behavior. In response to public pleas, it was reopened and is presently patrolled and cleaned up with Grove Farm bearing the expense. That is an exception we can't often expect.

About a mile toward the ocean from where you are on Highway 530 is a heiau. It was reported in 1907 by an amateur archeologist in Thrum's *Hawaiian Annual*, but could not be located by anyone since then. This intrigued me, so I searched for it (with the permission of the owner) and found it in 1986. The heiau cannot be seen from the haul cane road that passes by it, or from anywhere around because of the overgrowth. Atop a hill is the magnificent **Niu-kapu-kapu heiau**. Only the three seaward sides remain, which are 3 to 4 feet wide, up to 5 feet high, and enclose an area 50 by 100 feet. The heiau commands an absolutely spectacular view of the entire southern shore.

The **Nōmilu Fishpond** can be seen from there. I have visited it only once, with the permission of the Palamas. This is one of the most famous in the Hawaiian Islands, is over 20 acres in size, and has been mentioned before. It is fed both by freshwater springs and saltwater from the ocean seeping under the sand, so the water is brackish. Hawaiians brought mullet and other fingerlings from

Lāwa'i Kai (fish would not breed at Nōmilu) and they thrived feeding off bottom growth. The fishpond, and the land around it, including Makaokaha'i Point to the west, was bequeathed by Walter McBryde to his close friend Philip Palama, Sr., and the Palama family uses it for recreation. Ancient salt pans are on the rocky ledge on the seaward side, a *heiau* is near the point, and in the bluffs surrounding the pond are several stone taro terraces and a burial cave.

From Niu-kapu-kapu *heiau* one can also see a beautiful half-mile-long beach east of the fishpond, where clear blue water breaks on crystal white sand. The beach is deserted because there is no access by land, and it is the sort of beach one dreams about. It has a Hawaiian name, Papalo'o, of uncertain origin, but because it is next to the Palama property it has been called **Palama Beach** since the 1930s.

Continuing along Highway 530, only three more sites that are inaccessible will be mentioned. A few miles after leaving Kōloa on Highway 530 you enter the ahupua'a of Lāwa'i, which means "the day to end the fishing tabu." The fields on either side were planted in pineapple from 1905 until 1964. Both the field and cannery workers were organized by the ILWU during World War II, as you have read elsewhere. Strikes after the war brought the pineapple industry to an end in 1965. It is more labor-intensive than sugar cane and received no price supports because pineapples were considered a luxury.

Just before you arrive at the old cannery, Iwipo'o Road leads off to the left. Behind the houses lining the road are two huge black monoliths with mysterious Hawaiian petroglyphs carved on them. These have never been reported or studied by archeologists. Again, I had the permission of the property owners to explore the thick growth and find them.

A little more than a mile farther along Iwipo'o road, a rough hike takes you to a dilapidated building dating from 1909. It once housed the Hop Sing Society, a secret Chinese fraternal organization, where Taoist ceremonies were held. An overgrown cemetery is beside it and it is completely surrounded by private property.

Lāwa'i was a small plantation town around the cannery where many of the pineapple workers lived. Today there are only a few stores to mark the spot. The Lāwa'i post office has been moved to Highway 50.

Next is the old cannery itself. Kaua'i Fruit and Land Company, Ltd. was formed by Walter McBryde in 1906. By 1925, production had reached 250,000 cases of canned pineapples annually. When Alexander & Baldwin bought the operation in

1930, its name was changed to Kaua'i Pineapple Company. The local people never paid much attention to the official names and always called it "Kaua'i Pine." The company, although relatively small compared to others in Hawai'i, was doing well until the strikes mentioned above caused it to go under. Kaua'i Pine stopped planting in 1962, and the last can of pineapple was sealed at the cannery on September 16, 1964. Its land in Lāwa'i was added to Grove Farm Plantation for growing sugar cane.

Turn left on Highway 50 carefully because this is a dangerous intersection. Almost immediately you will pass still another place of interest you won't be able to see. This is the Lāwa'i Shingon Temple, more often referred to as the **Kobo Dai Ishi Shrine**. Kobo Dai Ishi is the posthumous name of Kukai, who went to China from Japan in the eighth century, studied Chen-yen doctrine, and returned to found the Shingon sect in Japan. The original shrine was dedicated to him over a thousand years ago.

Between 1896 and 1900, many Japanese were brought from Shikoku to work for Kaua'i Pineapple Company. Walter McBryde gave the workers permission to build a place of worship here. On their own time they cleared away the growth, constructed a covered shrine with an altar, a caretaker's house, and a stone receptacle for ablutions fed from a small spring. I vividly recall my first visit when there were tokens and other offerings on the altar, paper prayers, and the scent of burning joss sticks in the air. The quiet surrounding forest, the trickle of water, and the view of the south shore gave me a small sense of what those first worshipers must have felt so far from their native land, clinging to their culture.

They also made 88 images nearly a foot tall and placed them on a path around the bluff, each in its own cast concrete structure. The figures represent the 88 sinful desires of man according to the Buddhist Sutra. Under each they put a bit of earth taken from the equivalent site of the original Kobo Dai Ishi Shrine on the island of Shikoku. The tradition is that if you walk the path you will not be tempted by any of the sins. I rather like to be tempted, so never walked the entire path.

By World War II, most of the original issei had died. After the caretaker died in 1947 the temple was all but abandoned. In 1990, nisei and sansei descendants of the original worshipers started to restore the site. The wooden structures were beyond repair, so they burned them and put the ashes in an urn which was buried nearby. Walter Zane, the new owner of the property, stopped them and commenced a condominium development on the location. Fortunately, two of the original worshipers had been buried there, and Hawaiian law prevents such desecration of graves, so the development was halted.

Today the site is so overgrown the original layout is obscured, and the path is impassable. Only a dozen of the housings for the images are still there, and these are empty. However, something about the site, an almost mystical quality, will always be there.

Continue on Kaumualiʻi Highway until you come to Kalāheo (the proud day). You can't miss Kalāheo—there is only one stoplight in town, and it is the first one you will encounter after your left turn onto the highway. Get ready to turn left at the light, and as you do glance to your right.

You will see a church with an unusual sign "Iglesia Ni Cristo." A McBryde Sugar Company camp for Filipino workers was formerly *mauka* of the highway, and this was their church. The camp was razed when McBryde consolidated its camps around 1960, but the church is still thriving. The name is Tagalog for "Church of Christ," which is the largest entirely indigenous Christian church in the Philippines, and it has a strong centralized organization. Unitarian in theology and Philippine in its languages, liturgy, and music, the church represents a popular Filipino nationalist movement and constitutes a substantial political power there today.

Turn left on Papalina Road at the light, continue 0.9 of a mile *makai* out of Kalāheo, then look to the right for a small sign reading "Kukuiolono." At the sign, angle back to your right to pass through the large gate into the park. The gate was designed by Walter McBryde and dedicated to his mother. A short distance past the gate, the road divides. Turn left and park in the oval parking lot where you will be able to read about the park and the man who created it.

The large hill on which you are parked has the ancient name **Kukui-o-Lono**, which means "Torch of the god Lono." An agreement between agricultural Hawaiians in the area and fishermen who lived along the shore was that a fire would be maintained on the hill every night to guide seafarers. The fire was near where the pavilion is now, which you will visit later. At that elevation the light could be seen at night all along the coast, and as far as 24 miles to sea.

The three-terraced Kukui-o-Lono *heiau* was once on top of the hill. Each terrace was between 50 and 100 feet on each side, and their combined length facing seaward was 246 feet. Human sacrifices to the war god Kū were offered there. The victims were killed at a nearby place called Na Pōhaku a Kiʻiloa so the altar would not be polluted by blood. Their bodies were then brought to the *heiau* and placed upon the altar. Thrum reported remnants of the *heiau* in 1907.

You were first introduced to Walter McBryde in the chapter "Tall Cane." He was mentioned again at the start of this section as the one who donated and helped to plant the trees on Maluhia Road leading into Kōloa that form the Tree Tunnel, and again in reference to Kaua'i Pine. But now you are at the site of his former home, and his greatest contribution to the Hawaiian people is all around you, so some details bear repetition. His father, Duncan McBryde, had come from Scotland around 1856. With his boundless energy he soon was raising cattle on a large tract of land that included the *ahupua'a* of Wahiawa he had purchased and land leased from the Crown in Kalāheo. Note this Wahiawa has the same stress on each "a" which gives it the meaning "place of milkfish." The better-known Wahiawā on O'ahu has the stress on the last "a" which means "place of noise."

Duncan married Elizabeth Moxley in 1860 and built a home in upper Wahiawa they named "Brydeswood." The couple had six children before Duncan died in 1878 at age 52. Walter was born on January 2, 1864 in the family home, the second of three sons. You will read more about Elizabeth, who acquired the *ahupua'a* of Lāwa'i from the estate of Queen Emma. When Elizabeth moved to California a few years later, two sons, Alexander and Walter, remained on Kaua'i.

Walter had inherited much of the energy and enterprise of his father. After his education on the mainland, he held a series of increasingly responsible positions both there and on O'ahu before returning to Kaua'i in 1895. He influenced his brother to abandon cattle and form McBryde Sugar Company, Ltd. in 1899. He was elected a Representative in the Territorial Legislature; when the county government was organized in 1905 he was on the Board of Supervisors (equivalent to the County Council of today) for the next 16 years. He formed the Kaua'i Fruit and Land Company in 1906, and continued as its manager until he died in 1930.

There was much more than this to the man. His institution of contract cultivation has been described, and he raised no objection when the HSPA claimed credit for the concept and began to advocate it for all sugar planters. He was busy with other ideas. Starting with some land obtained at auction in 1907, he acquired more parcels in upper Lāwa'i, Kalāheo, and at Kukui-o-Lono. Within a few years he held title to 346 acres and set aside 178 acres on the summit of the hill to be developed into a park. The remainder was planted in pineapple to support the project. Only then was it apparent this was the primary reason he had formed the Kauaʻi Fruit and Land Company. He in devoted much of his time over the next few years to landscaping the park at his own expense.

It was during this time he started the first homesteading project in the Hawaiian Islands. He knew the history of homesteading in the Midwest and decided to do the same for his pineapple and park workers. He held a long-term lease on a large tract of land in upper Kalāheo, and in 1907 turned this over to the Territorial Government with the agreement it would be given to the workers as homesteads. The terms varied somewhat as the project progressed; in general, they stipulated that if an applicant occupied the land for a period of three to five years, improved upon it, and then paid about a dollar an acre, title passed to him. The second wave of Portuguese was arriving then, and most of the applicants were Portuguese who had families. You have passed the well-kept homes and businesses of the Portuguese descendants in Kalāheo. For many years Kalāheo was known as "Homestead" before it received its present name in 1918. At the same time, the streets in Kalāheo were named, and you might like to know their rather exotic Hawaiian names translate into various body parts.

In 1913, Walter made another tract available for homesteading in lower Kalāheo, and this was occupied mostly by Japanese. The Territorial Government became interested at this point and initiated more homesteads on Kauaʻi and the other islands.

Prince Jonah Kūhiō, the non-voting Territorial Representative to Congress, had been deeply concerned about the plight of landless Hawaiians. He also observed the success of these efforts and was responsible for the passage of the Hawaiian Homes Act by Congress in 1920. Under the terms of this act, the Hawaiian Homes Commission was formed in 1921. Land was given to applicants with half or more Hawaiian blood. They could borrow from the Commission funds required to build a home and purchase farming equipment and livestock. Later on this tour we will pass the monument to Prince Kūhiō, who, after one two-year term filled by Robert W. Wilcox, was the delegate to Congress from 1902 until his death in 1922.

Walter built a modest home at Kukui-o-Lono in 1908. He had cleared and landscaped the park area sufficiently for public use by 1911, and the park was dedicated on October 13 of that year. It was not until August 20, 1918 that the 346 acres were deeded by him in trust as the Kukuiolono Park Trust Estate. Under the terms of the trust it was for the recreation of the public "regardless of race, color or creed," and during his lifetime he would be trustee and manage its affairs. He retained the right to have his home and live there. One old-timer, Thelma Hadley, recalls, "The magnificent gardens with peacocks strutting about was a favorite picnic site."

Walter completed construction of a larger home in 1929 on the rise just to the east of the Japanese Garden. Walter was a bachelor, and although the house had 17 rooms, there was only one bedroom. The same year, his Japanese workers completed the beautiful Japanese Garden there today and placed a large *torii* gate at the entrance to the garden. The *torii* was destroyed in 1982 by Hurricane 'Iwa. The park also was finished according to his original plans that year. It had a horse-racetrack around the periphery, a nine-hole golf course, and a field for playing either baseball or football.

Walter lived in his new home only a brief time until he died there on October 30, 1930. His close friend, Philip Palama Sr., lived in the house from then until World War II and supervised the gardeners who cared for the grounds.

At the onset of World War II the house and grounds were taken over by the U.S. Army. The house sustained such severe damage it was dismantled in 1954. I recall several graffiti that were scrawled on the walls by the troops. One that is printable read:

"They say the boid is on the wing,
But that's absoid,
Because the wing is on the boid."

Now let's walk back to the monument where the entry road meets the perimeter road. There is a bronze plaque on it. Philip Palama, Sr. brought the large slab of stone from Walter's former beach home at Nomilū. When Walter had stayed at Nomilū, he loved to get up early to watch the sunrise and have breakfast using this stone as a table. Palama also selected the site where the monument was placed. Walter frequently walked to this spot to enjoy the view up and down the coast. Trees now obstruct the view. The monument is not a posthumous one to Walter. It commemorates the irrevocable gift of the park to the people of Kaua'i on January 24, 1919.

A passing note. Little has been written about Walter McBryde, and he would be a fascinating subject for a biography. what you read here was laboriously obtained from those who knew him, and from others such as Philip Palama, Jr, who listened when his father told him about Walter. I am indebted to all who have helped me so much.

Next to the monument is the life-size statue of a male white-tailed deer. Even this has a story. On the base a plaque reads, "The iron deer, now in Kukuiolono Park, was manufactured by order of

Queen Victoria as part of a memorial to the Prince Consort. It was brought from England by the late John T. Waterhouse of Honolulu." The Prince Consort, of course, was Prince Albert, who died in 1861, and you know who John T. Waterhouse was. This is the last of several cast-iron animals and other outdoor ornaments that had been placed in the park by Walter McBryde. During World War II, the Army moved many of them to make room for trenches and barbed-wire barricades. Remnants of some have been found in nearby gulches. The others simply disappeared after World War II during the time the park received little care.

A stone Japanese lantern can be seen not far away, placed on a slight rise so it was silhouetted against the sky when viewed from the home. It, too, has a story. As you approach it, you will notice some parts are missing—even the round ball that should be on top has been broken off. Lanterns such as these are carved in sections, and both hurricanes blew the lantern over, scattering the sections and breaking some of them. This is not the story, however. On the lantern are some Japanese characters. I have had them translated, and they read, "To Walter McBryde. A gift from the Lawai Japanese People." The lantern was brought from Japan and erected by them in gratitude for Walter's homesteading project that gave the Japanese their homes in Lāwaʻi.

Now we are going to see something that will be puzzling to most Western minds. At first sight, it is just a bunch of rocks. They are located at the end of a path that leads up a gentle rise from the parking lot. A Hawaii Visitors Bureau sign reading "Hawaiiana Exhibit" indicates the path. The rocks are about 70 yards along this path where it curves to the right and ends.

It has been pointed out before that Hawaiians did less monumental rock carving than might be expected. Archeologist Wendell Bennett observed in *Archeology of Kauai,* "Very little carved work is represented in the artifacts from Kauai." This appears to be for reasons that may be difficult to understand. Elsewhere, such as on Rapa Nui, or Easter Island, Polynesians performed near-miracles when they carved, moved, and erected the many *moai* that stare inscrutably out to sea.

Porous basalt is readily available on Kauaʻi and is not difficult to carve with implements of harder basalt. The scarcity of stone carving probably has to do with the Hawaiian belief that all of nature is inhabited by spirits. Rocks of certain shapes stirred Hawaiians by suggesting the spirit within them, so were left untouched, or enhanced by as little carving as necessary so the spirit would be manifested more clearly. At the same time, they had no compunction about carving shapeless rocks into utilitarian objects such as bowls, pounders, grinders, and lamps. Most of these smaller implements are now in private collections, although many can be found in the Kaua'i Museum or the Bishop Museum in Honolulu.

Walter McBryde collected these unique stones and placed them here between 1919 and 1929. His original collection was much larger and was famous at the time. Ethel Damon wrote in *Koamalu,* "He had been born soon enough to touch something in thought and speech of the Hawaiian who felt himself kin to all forces of air and earth and sea." Yet it is not certain he understood the meaning of all of them. He loved to show the rocks to visitors and regale them with legends, but some guests noted the tales varied.

What you are about to see are almost all of the larger rocks still in existence that were carved by Kauaians. You will see smaller ones at Moir Garden, and these are representative of the contents of most private collections except for the one with the most, the Wilcox Collection.

There are 13 stones here extending to the west from the end of the path. The 14th is along the asphalt path that leads toward the pavilion. Walk generally to the west; the numbering is arbitrary. The Board of Trustees placed bronze signs on four of them in 1937, and nine plastic signs were put in place years later by a group of volunteers who helped to maintain the park. A few of the signs are in error, some conflict, and many are misspelled.

#1. The first rock on the left near a low rock wall is large, irregular, and has a knob on top. Walter's story about this one has not survived. It does serve as an introduction to the others, and the knob suggests the head of a sentry. It has no plaque or plastic sign.

#2. This is a large flat piece with a hook at the top, and has no sign. If the hook is thought of as a beak, the rest of the stone could be spread wings, and it may represent a bird. Some of these rocks are like a Rorschach test: they can mean just about anything you want them to.

#3. The third is an irregular rock with no bronze plaque or plastic sign. Even a fevered imagination fails to give an idea of what it might represent. Walter had a great sense of humor, and one might wonder if a rock here and there is a spoof, or perhaps a nondescript one he could use as a basis for whatever tale came to mind.

#4. A stone salt pan, used by Hawaiians for making salt. Its surface has been shaped by hand into two sections with a narrow raised divider between them: a larger deeper one and a smaller shallower one. Ocean water was bailed into the larger pan, allowed to evaporate in the sun, and then the slurry was scooped into the smaller one and spread out to dry.

#5. This stone has a plastic sign that says "Lamp." Stone lamps used by Hawaiians were hollowed out on top to hold sufficient oil and a wick. This does not have such a hollow. Bennett observed that stone lamps were of all shapes and sizes, and the only certain way to tell if one had been a lamp is if it is blackened from use. This stone is not blackened, either, so the sign may be incorrect.

#6. This is in the form of a bowl. It appears to have been shaped by hand, although there is no way of knowing what the natural shape was to start with. It may have been used to store water.

#7. The rock with tree molds. These are common, especially on the Big Island, and the plastic sign is correct except for the date:

Tree Molds
they were formed when lava from
Kukuiolono poured onto trees in
Lawai Valley about two million
years ago.

#8. The large roughly spherical stone with a bowl eccentrically placed is called *Pōhaku awa*, or the awa-fish stone. Originally, as used by Hawaiians, it was located about a mile west of "Brydeswood" on the trail to upper Wahiawa lands. Fishermen caught *awa* (milkfish) fingerlings by net at the shore, stopped off near this stone for the night, and kept their catch alive in the bowl. It was covered with vines to keep the water cool and the fish from jumping out. The next day the *awa* were taken to the mountains to replenish the stock maintained in a pool in Wahiawa stream.

#9. The Game Stone is a nearly spherical rock about 10 inches in diameter. The plastic sign states:

Stones like these were
used in games such as
shot-putting and bowling.

Actually, shot-putting was unknown in Hawaiʻi, and *ʻulu maika* discs were used in their game that resembled bowling. Smaller stone balls were thrown. Those of this size were used in games of balance with a person standing on them and rolling them. Still larger ones were lifted by warriors to show their strength.

#10. This stone has an adjacent plastic sign that states:

Kauai Iki
little Kauai
the stone is shaped like a map of Kauai.

The bronze plaque reads similarly. The stone was moved here from Wahiawa Valley. The story is that a Hawaiian family clearing their land of rocks to plant taro came across this stone. Because it resembled Kaua'i, they left it in place and named it. However, the story does not explain how they knew what Kaua'i looked like on a map or from the air.

#11. This stone bears a bronze plaque:

Pohakuhunaahuula
hiding place for chief's feather cloak.

A plastic sign reads:

Pohakuhunaahuula
The Feather Cloak Stone

During a battle Chief Ola hid his feather cloak under this stone to avoid capture and the loss of the engagement.

The stone was brought from the McBryde family home in Wahiawa. It was taken there previously from a level area in Kalāheo where a battle is said to have taken place. The rock is heavy, and one wonders if the men to lift it could have been spared if Chief Ola was so hard-pressed.

#12. This stone is named *Pōhaku loa* (tall rock), or The Fish God. Most of the south face has been dressed flat. The stone was found at the junction of two trails leading to the beach near the McBryde mill, where it had rocks around it to keep it erect. Fishermen on their way to the shore stopped to pray for a good catch, leaving 'awa root or other offering, and left fish on the way back as thanks if they were successful. The Japanese characters are not explained, but obviously were added much later.

#13. "Lono's Spoon" is a stone approximately 40 feet north of the nearest of the others. It looks somewhat like a spoon with a truncated handle. Hawaiians did not have spoons except for sections of coconut shell or gourd, which were used like scoops.

#14. Approximately 70 yards up the path from the parking area to the pavilion is one more stone. It has an almost circular hole through it. The legend is that it once moored Ni'ihau close to Kaua'i. Stones like this were used by Hawaiians to anchor their large canoes.

For a panoramic view of the south shore, continue on this path to the pavilion. It was built as a gift of gratitude by cannery and field workers on Walter's sixtieth birthday. The dedication in 1924 was attended by over 2,000 people and featured a parade with over 600 Japanese lanterns, according to *The Garden Island* newspaper. Don't linger too long to watch the sunset---the park gate closes at 6:30 PM.

A drive around the park to the other side will take you to the unprepossessing clubhouse of the Kukui-o-Lono Golf Course. This course is used mostly by locals, green fees are low, and a cart is not necessary. You can play barefoot and without a shirt if you wish. The atmosphere is laid-back and friendly.

A rough hike west through the brush would bring you to a place from which you could look down on Kalāheo Gulch. The taro terraces there look as if they had been left only yesterday. Many Hawaiian house sites and a *heiau* also are in the gulch. The most fascinating finding, never reported by archeologists, is a vertical bas-relief about 2 by 3 feet with contoured human forms, not the usual stick figures Hawaiians were wont to carve. The carving is so weatherworn it is difficult to tell exactly what it portrays.

As you leave the park, reflect that Walter McBryde's ashes are buried in an urn at the entrance to his former home. The bronze plaque that marks the spot is hidden under the flowers, and the fact that he is buried there is unknown to most park visitors.

As you can see, we could continue this side trip step-by-step all the way around the island. But now it is time to return to our tour of the few accessible sites of interest around Kōloa.

When you return to Kōloa and come to the Chevron station, continue on Kōloa Road through town and turn left at the First Hawaiian Bank. Keep to the right, and you will be on Wailaʻau Road passing through the neat homes that former Japanese plantation workers built when they were allowed to buy property after 1946. These sales marked the end of Japanese Camp. Curve left when the road does, and you will be as close to Waitā Reservoir as you are allowed. Locals take another turn or two, park by the huge rocks that bar the dirt road leading to the reservoir, and walk in to fish or gather small shellfish. But again, you are cautioned to respect private property, and this belongs to Grove Farm.

★ **Waitā Reservoir** can be glimpsed from Wailaʻau Road, to the east between the trees. It is the second-largest reservoir in Hawaiʻi, and, at 424 acres, it is also the second-largest lake in the Islands. First place on both counts goes to Wahiawā Reservoir, now called Lake Wilson, on Oʻahu. Waitā was originally named Kōloa Reservoir because Kōloa Marsh had been on the site, but was informally known as Marsh Reservoir. Grove Farm maintains the dam and regulates the water level in the reservoir, which is a good thing because the level is above the town of Kōloa and imagination can run rampant about a possible break or overflow on dark and stormy nights.

Now return towards town, and as you approach the First Hawaiian Bank, take the road near it that angles back sharply to your right. Check the sign to be sure you are on Wailani Road. It ends at the "crossing," which has been described before. Turn left on the gravel road, the former railroad bed; turn left again on the first gravel road and drive slowly for less than a quarter of a mile. Several old plantation houses are along here and you may see locals picking plumeria to make lei, or knocking down mangos with a stick. The people are open and friendly and you can talk story with them. Where the road ends, turn left and park near the buildings. **The Japanese Language School** described on the walking tour is the L-shaped one.

The Old Plantation Theater built by Kōloa Plantation as a social and recreational hall was just north of the Japanese language school. Manuel Teves showed movies there until it was damaged by fire in 1936. Because kids played barefoot ball and soccer in the **Old Ball Park** in front of the theater, George N. Wilcox remodeled it into a gymnasium called **Wilcox Gym**. It was blown down by Hurricane ʻIwa in 1982 and nothing remains on the site today.

Now we will continue working our way towards the shore and what may be the most interesting part of our tour, Poʻipū.

★ **The Kōloa Mill** is at the end of Weliweli Road, southeast of Kōloa. The road to the mill is barred by a yellow gate, but you can park close enough to see it. The gate that stops you has a sign reading "tennant access only" because the old houses around the mill are now rented out. The original 1913 mill has been substantially altered over the years, especially in 1948 and 1974, but what it represents is so historical it is marked above with a star.

The Kōloa Mill closed in September 1996. If you could have been there when it was in operation; to hear the huge trucks pull up with a thunderous roar; to watch the cranes unload immense bundles of cane; to actually *feel* the vibration of the mill machinery; to cough in the red dust; and to smell the fragrance of molasses in the air, you would have experienced an epoch that has passed in Kōloa, and is passing in all of Hawaiʻi. The mill is still an awesome sight in its solitude.

There is a tunnel through the Hāʻupu Range behind the mill that cannot be seen from the gate, but it has an interesting story. Once Grove Farm had acquired Kōloa Plantation with its land and mill in 1948, the problem presented itself of transporting cut cane by truck from Grove Farm lands in Haʻikū and Kīpū around the

Saint Raphael Church, Kōloa, dating from 1854. This was the first Catholic church on Kaua'i.

Photograph by author, 1999.

north end of Hā'upu Range to the Kōloa Mill. After calculating carefully, it was determined that a tunnel through the range would pay for itself within three or four years. Using surplus Army equipment found in a cave on O'ahu made it more economical. Elbert Gillin was put in charge of the project, the half-mile tunnel was cut through solid rock in 1948-1949, and the rubble was used for the approach roads.

The last place you will see before the Po'ipū tour is Saint Raphael Church. You passed the turnoff to it on Weliweli Road when you continued to the mill. Return towards town and look for a sign on your left. If you miss it, because it is placed to be seen most easily by those coming from town, don't despair, just turn around when you reach Waikomo Road and follow the directions below.

★ **Saint Raphael Church** is reached by driving east on Weliweli Road from Waikomo Road, then right on Hapa Road. A sign or two along the way will guide you. The church and associated structures have undergone many changes over the years and were so extensively repaired after each hurricane that although the site is truly historical, the buildings themselves are questionable.

The last additions, a beautiful parish hall and teaching center, were added in 1994-1995. However, a stroll around the grounds with Father Felix, who pointed out the original remnants and told how Catholicism had spread on Kaua'i from this spot, was convincing, so a ★ appears before the name.

One note about Hapa Road. In the early plantation years this was the path taken on foot or horseback by residents of Kōloa to Po'ipū Beach because it was more direct than going to Kōloa Landing and then east along the shore. By the middle 1910s, automobiles were used by many who wanted to enjoy Po'ipū Beach. They went on the better road by way of Kōloa Landing, and the section of Hapa Road beyond Saint Raphael Church became overgrown and impassable. In 1998, that part was cleared by volunteers from the Kōloa Community Association as a hiking and bicycle path. It intersects Po'ipū Road next to the Kiahuna Tennis Club.

Catholicism encountered resistance during its early years in Hawai'i. Although the first Catholic missionaries were nearly coterminous with the Protestants, their influence was less because the Protestants had arrived at a particularly propitious time soon after the *kapu* had been overthrown; the Catholics arrived later and in fewer numbers. The first three priests came from France to Honolulu in 1827. Ka'ahumanu accused them of idolatry and ordered them to be deported, but they quietly remained and built a small chapel. Bingham was furious and Kʻahumanu allowed no more ashore until her death in 1832.

The persecution of Catholics continued under both Kamehameha II and Kamehameha III. In 1839, during the latter's rule, Captain LaPlace arrived from France on the warship *L'Artemise* to set things right. Among other threats and demands, he vowed to destroy Honolulu with his cannon if Catholic missionaries were not allowed ashore. Kamehameha III found this argument, though not theological, to be persuasive and conceded to this and all the other demands made by LaPlace.

Father Arsenius Walsh, who came to Kōloa in 1841, was the first Catholic priest on Kauaʻi. On Christmas Day of that year he conducted the first mass ever held on the island at a crude stone altar near Kōloa Landing, and the mission of St. Raphael the Archangel was founded. In 1842, Walsh acquired three acres, extended in 1843 by an additional 17 acres, *mauka* of Kōloa Landing. The first Catholic church was completed there in 1854 and a small rectory in 1856. Some years later, he built a larger rectory and a school. In 1936, the church was lengthened and the bell tower added. More buildings were added to the complex as time went on and the older ones were rebuilt each time they were damaged by hurricanes. The first parishioners had been converted Hawaiians, then Puerto Ricans, Portuguese, and Filipinos. Almost all of those who lived nearby have moved away. Only a few descendants remain, and the complex stands today in near isolation between the town of Kōloa and the ocean. The church continues to be very active, however, and parishioners come by car.

The next part of our tour continues by car along the Poʻipū Shore.

Before we start, the law of the State of Hawaiʻi regarding shoreline access should be mentioned so we will not trespass on private property. The State owns all of the shoreline up to the "debris and vegetation line." This is defined as the highest place where the waves and tide deposit debris, and the lowest where natural vegetation grows. The public may use this State-owned strip of shore anywhere on Kauaʻi (and other islands) that lies between this line and the ocean, and, of course, the ocean itself. The difficulty at some desirable places is gaining access through private property to the shore. The State and County have solved this in most cases. Routes from the nearest roads have been made available for public use and are indicated by "Beach Access" signs.

The bond between Kōloa and the nearby shore has always been strong. In ancient times, before Kōloa existed as a settlement, Hawaiians lived and farmed on most of the land from the marsh area

The lava ledge on the southwest side of Makahūena Point. This ledge is the origin of the name Poʻipū.

☞ Photograph by author, 1999.

to the sea. Farmers exchanged their products with the fishermen who lived at the ocean's edge. With the coming of missionaries and the sugar plantation, Kōloa Landing was essential to both and the connection became even stronger. Residents of Kōloa and plantation workers used the beaches for recreation. When tourism arrived, Kōloa became dependent upon the tourists staying in Poʻipū and the increasing number of residents there. Today, development plans are underway for one community, reminiscent in some ways of the ancient pattern of the Hawaiians in the area. Residences and commercial centers will occupy all of the land between Kōloa and the shore, so the name may well be hyphenated in the future as Kōloa-Poʻipū.

If you look at maps you might ask where Poʻipū actually is because the location of that label is slightly different on each map. The name Poʻipū (covered as by crashing waves) was used by Hawaiians for the part of the shore along the western side of Makahūʻena (eyes overflowing with heat or rage) Point. On first thought this seems curious because this lava ledge where Hawaiians fished and gathered small shellfish is safe most of the time.

Winter storms arising in North Pacific lows produce waves reaching heights of twenty to thirty feet on the north shore, but not upon the southern coast. When it is winter in the southern hemisphere, most of the storms arising there are so far away they have little effect upon the south shore. But each year a few of these storms are so strong that waves, often augmented by *kona* or onshore winds that tend to occur in the same season, can arrive without warning on the south shore and make such activities on the ledge hazardous. So the name may have been given for a good reason. It might have been lost except it was used by *haoles* to refer to the adjacent beaches when they began using them.

One day in 1986, I met an old Hawaiian, Abraham Keliʻiokapalapala Aka, sitting on the rock wall at Brennecke Beach. He lived about a block inland from there and had been raised nearby. Keliʻi confirmed that Hawaiians had given the name Poʻipū to the lava ledge along the western side of Makahūʻena Point because "all of a sudden big waves break and *poʻi* (cover) you," and told of the danger of picking *ʻopihi* (limpets, small shellfish) there because of this. With a smile he said what is now Brennecke Beach, Poʻipū Beach Park, and much of the land *mauka* of these beaches was called Waiʻohai by Hawaiians because of the spring there. The beach in front of the Waiʻohai Resort was part of this, but the beach and land west of that, where the Kiahuna Plantation Resort is located, was called Milohaʻi. The meaning of this name is no longer known, but it could refer to swaying *milo* trees that once grew there. The name Waiʻohai

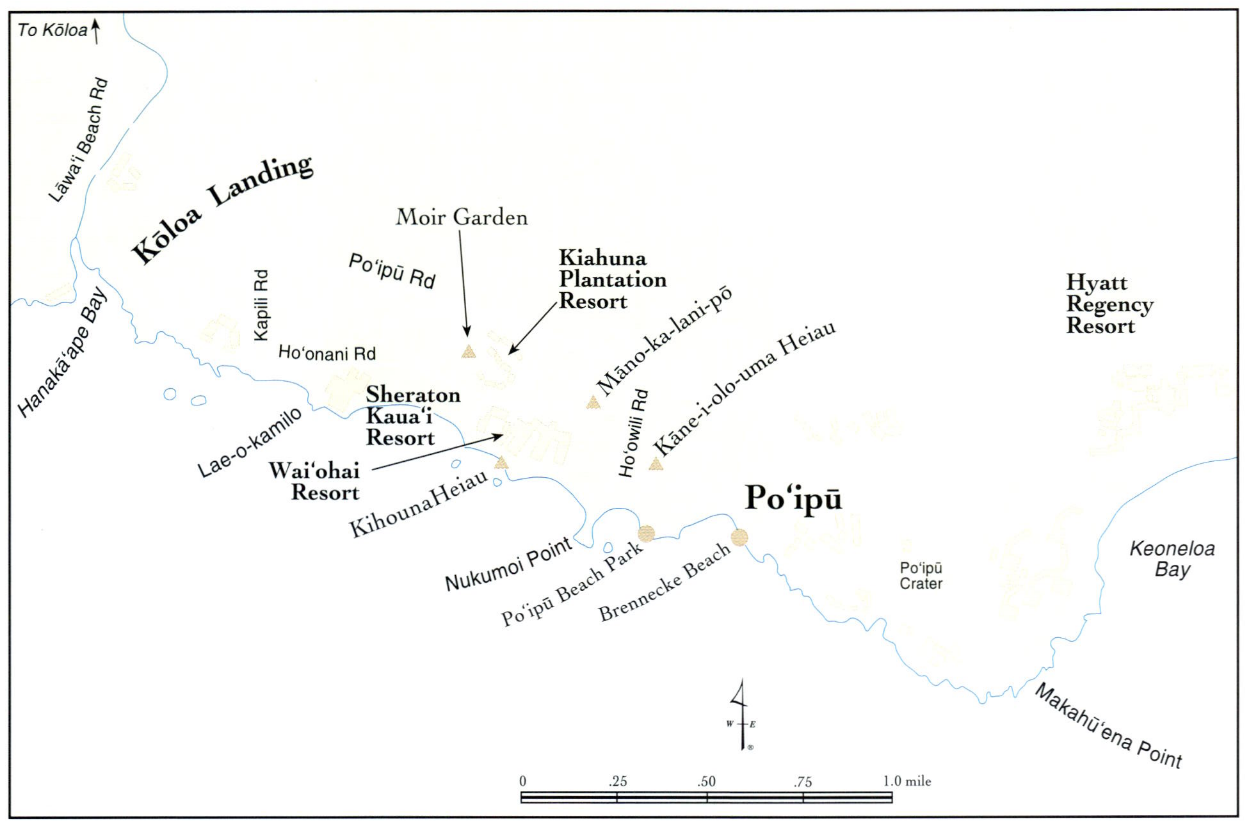

Kōloa Landing—Po'ipū

persists today only as that of the resort, and Milohaʻi is no longer used at all.

Keliʻi said he once knew all the old Hawaiian names for places along the coast. He learned them from his family, who had lived there since "old times," but had forgotten many. He told me about one name that is still used, Nukumoi (threadfish snout), the point on the west side of Poʻipū Beach Park. It is a tombolo, or sandbar, that connects to a small offshore island and does have the shape of a threadfish snout. A golden opportunity to learn more Hawaiian lore and names he still remembered was lost because I had to leave the island the next day. When this book was begun, I went to his home to learn more but his wife came to the door and told me he was too ill to talk.

I had heard about the series of interviews of local residents published in 1988 as *Kōloa: An Oral History of a Kauaʻi Community.* I hoped to make up for the lost opportunity by looking up the interview with Keliʻi. His jovial personality came through, and I found out more about him, but the interview had been unguided so the questions I wanted to ask went unanswered. It was the same with the interviews of others I had known for years. The individual oral histories were not well correlated with each other nor with facts that had been otherwise documented, so after reading the three-volume publication I knew little more about the history of Kōloa.

Throughout their centuries here, most Hawaiians lived within walking distance of where they were born. They gave names to the smallest topographic features, but most of these names have been lost. Fortunately, Western mariners recorded the names of prominent bays and points for their own purposes so these have come down to us. In a ten-year project ending in 1990, John Clark accomplished the most thorough work in this regard on the shores of the major Hawaiian Islands. He researched all of the available material in various archives and talked to hundreds of old-time residents. The four volumes are as definitive as it is possible to be. While we were working together on *Beaches of Kauaʻi and Niʻihau,* John made an observation that is particularly pertinent: Hawaiians did not have our penchant for enjoying beaches, so named these only if they had some practical value in their daily lives. Still, many of the beaches must have been named, and it is unfortunate that only a few of these traditional names are known. Most of the designations we use today for places along the shore came into being over the last 150 years or so.

The Poʻipū shore itself is a good example of this. In the latter half of the last century, the population of Kōloa began using what is now Poʻipū Beach Park for recreation. The name of the abutting rocky ledge on the western side of Makahū‘ena Point was incorporated in the name they gave the beach, Po‘ipū Beach.

Early in this century, the construction of Po‘ipū Beach Road from Kōloa Landing to Po‘ipū Beach had the effect of extending the name Po‘ipū somewhat fuzzily to the entire shoreline along its route. The Wai‘ohai Resort cottages were built in 1962, blocking off the last part of Po‘ipū Beach Road. A new road was built inland of the old one, from Kōloa Landing Road all the way to Makahū‘ena. It was named Po‘ipū Road and Kōloa Landing Road became part of it.

Thereafter, Po‘ipu even more fuzzily referred to all of the contiguous coastline from Kōloa Landing to Makahū‘ena. That portion of the old Po‘ipū Beach Road leading east from Kōloa Landing was renamed Ho‘onani (to beautify) Road. The end of this was cut off by the Kiahuna Plantation Resort and became the access to the Sheraton Resort when both were built later in the 1960s. During that decade, developers of these three major resorts began using the name Po‘ipū Beach in their promotion for the beach in front of the resorts, although it was nearly half a mile west of what had been called Po‘ipu Beach for almost a century. The small hotel between the Kiahuna and the Wai‘ohai was actually named the Po‘ipū Beach Hotel.

When the first Wai‘ohai cottages were built, management made a brief attempt to call the strip of sand in front of it Wai‘ohai Beach. Whether they knew the cottages and beach were in the area traditionally called Wai‘ohai is not known. But after the two larger resorts opened next to it their publicity proved to be overwhelming, and the Wai‘ohai ceased its efforts. All three resorts then called the beach in front of them Po‘ipū Beach.

The shopping complex inland of the resorts was first the Kiahuna Shopping Village and then became the Po‘ipū Shopping Village. Several condominiums with the word Po‘ipū worked into their names in various ways were built along Pe‘e Road on Makahū‘ena Point.

The name Po‘ipū was incorporated into other developments far from the original site. There is no recorded Hawaiian name for Pīhākekua Crater inland of Makahū‘ena Point, but it came to be called that more than a hundred years ago for a rather natural reason. Strong trade winds blew sand from a nearby stretch of beach bearing that old Hawaiian name and piled up dunes all the way from the shore to the side of the crater. In 1980, this sand was dumped into the crater, Po‘ipū Crater Resort was built inside of it, and the crater was thereafter referred to as Po‘ipū Crater.

Aerial view of Po'ipū Beach, circa 1928. The Knudsens' Beach House shown was taken down when the Wai'ohai Resort cottages were built on the site in 1962.

Hawai'i State Archives

The Hyatt Regency Kaua'i Resort was indirectly responsible for extending the name Po'ipū even farther east along the coast. Its golf course, which extends a mile and a half east to Māhā'ulepū, was known as the Hyatt Regency Kaua'i Resort Golf Course during its construction. However, when completed in 1991 it was given over to separate management. Even though there is no such thing as Po'ipū Bay, it was named the Po'ipū Bay Resort Golf Course!

Throughout all of this development, many Hawaiian names for areas and topographic features along the coast that were fading from the memories of long-time residents were lost completely. Exceptions are Makahū'ena, Kukui'ula, Lāwa'i Kai and those of major points and bays preserved on charts drawn up by the early mariners.

The tourist industry has been so successful in attaching the name Po'ipū Beach to the crescents of sand fronting the Wai'ohai, Kiahuna, and Sheraton that it has stuck. But if the name were to be restricted to just that stretch of shore, then the beach at Po'ipū Beach Park would be shorn of its century-old name. Fortunately, the two beaches meet at Nukumoi Point. Just as the name was extended west from the Makahū'ena ledge to the beach and park, development and tourism caused a second extension still farther west. It is *all* now referred to as Po'ipū Beach.

Of course, this is far from settled. Even if the above is accepted for Po'ipū *Beach*, the name Po'ipū alone is still in transition. It is generally agreed it now applies to the coast from Kōloa Landing east to Makahū'ena. But more and more it is applied to the coast from Kōloa Landing west to Lāwa'i Kai, ignoring Kukui'ula except as the harbor. The name Po'ipū will be used in this book, admittedly rather loosely, for the entire coast from Makahū'ena to Lāwa'i Kai because that usage appears to be inevitable in the future.

As you explore the shore, prepare yourself for a different experience from that of strolling along roads in Kōloa while reminiscing about the old plantation days. In Po'ipū, you will see modern resorts interspersed with ancient archeological sites, and this may require some mental shifting of gears. It is hard to believe now, but there was almost no development on the shoreline except for a few scattered houses before tourism soared in the 1960s.

As mentioned above, the first hotel, the Wai'ohai Resort, was built by the Kimball family in 1962. It was charming but modest, consisting of 24 two-bedroom cottages scattered in tropical landscaping. In 1981, the cottages were replaced by a modern

Aerial view of Kōloa Landing, 1931.

four-story structure with 461 rooms. The Sheraton Hotel came in 1965, and the first phase of the Kiahuna Plantation Resort went up in 1967. Condominiums that now crowd the shore mushroomed in the 1970s and 1980s, and the Hyatt Regency Resort opened in 1991. With these came shopping centers, golf courses, restaurants and houses. Most of the latter are vacation homes of part-time residents.

Time to start the tour. From Kōloa, drive south on Po'ipū Road about a mile, until the road divides east and west at a low rock wall with the sign "Welcome to Po'ipū Beach" on it.

★ **Kōloa Landing** is about two hundred yards *makai* of the rock wall. Continue left on Po'ipū Road after the rock wall, then angle right on Ho'onani Road to go along the shore. You will see a rocky road going down on your right leading to the landing. Rather than driving down this road it is more convenient to park at the widened place on Ho'onani Road and walk to where the landing can be seen. First, Hanaka'ape (headstrong) Bay comes into view. Near the mouth of Waikomo Stream is an indentation in the shore protected by rocky points on either side. This is Kōloa Landing, unbelievably small, and all that remains of what had been the major port of Kaua'i for nearly a hundred years.

The history of Kōloa Landing has been covered, but in segments, so a summary here is appropriate. After the publication of Captain Cook's journals in 1784, Waimea was the favored port of call on Kaua'i for decades. However, the currents and winds in Waimea Bay frequently caused dangerous conditions there, so Kōloa Landing became the main port of Kaua'i in the 1830s. A crude wooden wharf had been built at Kōloa Landing in whaling days; later, it was improved upon by Kōloa Plantation. It had a derrick for handling cargo and a warehouse. Buoys were placed in the bay where ships could moor while their boats plied to and from the landing.

Ele'ele Landing near Hanapēpē was remarkably similar until McBryde began a series of improvements in 1903, and in 1912 renamed it Port Allen. Kōloa Plantation began using Port Allen instead of Kōloa Landing for importing heavy equipment and exporting sugar. Kōloa Landing was still used by the plantation and others for light cargo, passengers, and mail until the derrick became unserviceable. Commercial use tapered, then ceased in 1928, and the wharf fell into disrepair. The section of railroad track along the shore leading to it was taken up in 1931. Since then, Kōloa Landing has been utilized only for recreational purposes. Activities such as snorkeling and introductory scuba-diving lessons are given at the site and outrigger canoes are launched there.

Moir Garden, Po'ipū. The garden was started by Alexandra Moir, daughter of Eric and Anne Knudsen around 1930 when she lived there with her husband, Hector Moir, the last manager of Kōloa Plantation.

★ **Moir Garden** is reached by continuing east on Poʻipū Road to a sign "Kiahuna Plantation" on your right, across the road from the Poʻipū Shopping Village. Turn down the entryway to Kiahuna Plantation, park under the huge monkeypod tree, and walk toward the ocean on the path by the restaurant.

Hector Moir, the last manager of Kōloa Plantation, lived here with his wife, Alexandra (Sandy) from 1930 to 1968. Sandy was the daughter of Eric and Anne Knudsen, who gave them four acres of land and built the large lava-rock home for them when the Moirs were married. She started an unusual garden of cacti and succulents on the grounds and named it *Pāʻū a Laka* (skirt of the goddess Laka), the Hawaiian name for the level area fronting their home where hula had been performed in ancient times. I learned this and more while walking on the grounds with their son Eric "Iki" Moir, who grew up in this house, and I am indebted to him.

Stroll through the Garden. You will see much more than cacti and succulents. Near the main path is a bowl Japanese immigrants carved by hand from lava rock. They used this as a mochi pot. Every New Year, *ji oshogatsu*, their tradition is to pound rice into a paste with a wooden mallet and mold the paste around sweet azuki beans. They give these as gifts or consume them in family celebrations.

A large granite mill roller is on the lawn in front of the restaurant. In the 1820s, enterprising Chinese brought this from China, and, with its missing counterpart, used it to grind sugar cane at Māhāʻulepū. I gave a brief account of this in the chapter "Tall Cane," told how the mill had been assembled for the centennial celebration in 1935, and was exhibited in the yard of the plantation office. When Grove Farm took over Kōloa Plantation in 1948, Hector Moir moved one grinder to this location, and Grove Farm took the other.

A mixing stone for Hawaiian herbal medicines is nearby. It has four nearly circular hollows of various sizes on top, which Hawaiians shaped with stone tools. Along the main path is a sharpening stone for adzes, standing on end so that you can see the hollows on either side. Near it is a mirror stone Hawaiians also made with stone tools. They filled the hollow with water to see their reflection.

Moir Garden continues to the west, where many plants are labeled. This is an area of refuge from the hustle and bustle of the nearby resorts. There is the old marble butcher-shop counter from the Kōloa Plantation Store made into a bench. Tucked in a corner is an old whaler's try-pot. On whaling ships the crew put pieces of blubber in pots such as this and reduced them to oil with fires built underneath on stacks of bricks. This one had been used for evaporating cane juice to molasses and brown granular sugar in the first Kōloa Mill at Maulili. Try-pots proved to be unsatisfactory for the purpose so copper boiling pans were used afterwards.

The main path in the Garden leads *makai* to the gateposts of the original entry to the Moir residence. On each gatepost is a granite bowl carved by hand in China with the artisan's name inscribed on the rims in Chinese characters. From 1948 to 1968, the Moirs conducted tours of this Garden and it became quite famous. Their home was converted into a restaurant in 1968.

The nearby portion of Poʻipū Beach is the most beautiful beach on the south shore. Public access (with restrooms) is at the end of Hoʻonani Road. Stroll down and enjoy the view.

Poʻipū Beach Park is a change from the serenity of Moir Garden. Continue east on Poʻipū Road and turn down Hoʻowili (to wind or curl) Road. Over the past few years, Kauaʻi County has acquired most of the land east of the original park to include Brennecke Beach. Because recent newspaper accounts have stated two of the lots are still under negotiation, I decided to check with the Mayor of Kauaʻi, Maryanne Kusaka. She told me, "You can inform your readers that all the land belongs to the County." I said I would quote her in this book, so there you are. Poʻipū Beach Park has become a major recreational area. It has the safest beach on the south shore, with a lifeguard and a protected shallow section for toddlers. Snorkeling is excellent on both sides of Nukumoi Point.

The Waiʻohai Resort is still battered from Hurricane ʻIniki, but its condition could be taken as a metaphor for a dispute that took place there in the late 1970s. The Kauaʻi Surf, an eleven-story hotel, had just been built at Kalapakī (which means "the double-yolk egg" that Nāwiliwili Bay resembled until it was improved as a harbor), and those who loved the unique beauty of Kauaʻi were appalled at the sight of the huge structure. In response, The County Council passed a Comprehensive Zoning Ordinance in 1963 restricting all buildings on the island to four stories, approximately the height of a mature coconut palm. At the same time it passed a billboard prohibition that you may have appreciated as you drove to Kōloa.

American Factors, or Amfac, planned to build the Waiʻohai Resort as an eight-story hotel to replace the cottages, and sought a variance from the CZO. This would have started a trend on the south shore toward another Waikīkī where hotels had already reached 40 stories. At public hearings, the residents of Kauaʻi were vehemently opposed, so the developer grudgingly gave ground and proposed a six-story hotel. Amfac, one of the "big five" corporations in the Islands, exerted its considerable influence so a variance for six stories was granted. Residents intensified their opposition; in the face of this the County Council backed down and withdrew approval of the variance. The CZO restricting the height of buildings and the billboard prohibition have done much to preserve the natural beauty of Kaua'i.

★ **Kihouna heiau** is in front of the Wai'ohai Resort and is equally battered. This heiau is the origin of the name Kiahuna, as in Kiahuna Plantation Resort and Kiahuna Tennis Club, with the spelling simplified for visitors. It was built under the direction of the district chief Kina in the late sixteenth century and dedicated to the gods of the sea. The *heiau* originally had walls four to six feet high in a rectangle 100 feet by 130 feet, with oracle towers, an altar, and several wooden images on its platform. Restoration of the *heiau* will almost certainly be a condition for the permit to rebuild the Wai'ohai Resort.

Most of the land along the shore from Waikomo Stream to Po'ipū Beach Park is still owned by the Knudsen Trust, which has leased it to the various developers and homeowners. About 1890, Anne Sinclair Knudsen, wife of Valdemar Knudsen, built a family beach house near the base of Nukumoi Point. It started as little more than a shack and was enlarged over the years. Their son, Eric "Kanuka" Knudsen, loved to stay at the beach house. When I first visited this area in 1947, the only structures there were this beach house and a few shacks nearby occupied by some Japanese who worked for him. In 1962, the Knudsen beach house was demolished so the first Wai'ohai Hotel could be built on the site.

A large portion of land to the east of Knudsen Trust property, including what is now Po'ipū Beach Park, Pīhākekua Crater inland, and Makahū'ena, was once owned by a Hawaiian named William Keaumaika'i Bacle, who had inherited it. A conversation with his *hānai* grandson, Keli'i, has been recounted. When asked how his family had acquired the property, he replied, "probably in the Mahele." This was the great land division of 1848 that divided ownership of the land in three roughly equal parts to the king, the government, and the chiefs and people.

William Bacle had a large home with five bedrooms inland near St. Raphael Church, and a smaller beach home where the Po'ipū Beach Park pavilion is today. The latter was a two-bedroom home set high on posts with a lānai along the entire seaward side of the house. Bacle grazed horses and cattle at Makahū'ena and watered them daily behind his beach home in the brackish water there. It is not clear if he knew this had been part of an old Hawaiian village (described below).

Until his death in 1921, Bacle sold many lots to poor Hawaiians for a dollar each. The area became something of a Hawaiian settlement, where fishing, farming, and just plain enjoying life were the main activities; *hukilau* were frequent. When he died, Bacle's descendants inherited the rest of the property and most of them soon sold their portions, which changed the character of that part of Poʻipū. The only reminder of Bacle is his headstone in the small family graveyard somewhat incongruously situated in Poʻipū Beach Park near where his beach house once stood.

★ **Manō-ka-lani-pō** was an ancient Hawaiian village inland from Poʻipū Beach Park. The remains are protected by the curve of Hoʻowili Road and covered with *koa haole* overgrowth. They include an *ʻauwai*; three *loʻi* that were irrigated by it; many rock platform house sites; a paved ceremonial platform; and a stone altar.

The spring around which *ʻōhai* (monkeypod trees) once grew is also there. This is what gave the Waiʻohai area its Hawaiian name and is the origin of the name of the Waiʻohai Resort. The runoff from the spring leads into four fishponds, each about 80 feet in diameter, with stone-faced walls. They are now filled with mud that comes up nearly to one's armpits. Yours, if you are not careful. Part of the village across Hoʻowili Road near the Waiʻohai Resort was eradicated by bulldozers. Workers were creating a small lagoon with an island for the resort to use for *lūʻau*, but this was stopped by public outcry. Too late, but the area is now a county park.

★ **Kāne-i-olo-uma heiau**, dedicated to the god Kāne, abuts the village on the east. It is behind the old YMCA building that is now a surf shop. The structure consists of three large sections enclosed by a rock wall three to five feet in height. The center section still has much of its limestone paving. The entire complex measures about 150 by 170 feet. One would never suspect so much was there, all but invisible in the overgrowth.

Brennecke Beach, a little farther to the east, is now part of Poʻipū Beach Park. It became famous over many years for body-surfing and bodyboarding. Since the two hurricanes removed much of the sand and exposed large rocks under water, these sports are enjoyed today mostly by locals who are aware of the dangers. Dr. Marvin Brennecke, the plantation physician who followed Dr. Waterhouse in Kōloa, built a beach home there in 1941. He worked for other plantations from 1942 until his retirement in 1972, and then settled in Waimea, where he died in 1996. His beach house was swept away by Hurricane ʻIwa in 1982 and only the slab remains.

Next on our tour is **Keoneloa Beach**. Return to Poʻipū Road and continue east. The Hyatt Regency Kauaʻi Resort faces Keoneloa

Bay, and public access to the beach is on the left side of the resort. The bay still appears on some maps as "Keoniloa," which is in error. Keoneloa means "the long sand," which is a perfect description of the half-mile-long beach. Keoneloa was the Hawaiian name for the *'ili* that included the beach. Both the beach and bay acquired their names from this ancient land division.

During the countercultural era of the 1960s and 1970s, hippies lived in the tall *naupaka* that grew down to the ocean's edge. I owned a condominium at the Kiahuna then and loved to stroll along the beach every day. Others did too, but we were put off by some of the antics of the hippies, the smell of marijuana in the air, and the trash they threw everywhere. They called the beach "Shipwreck" because the keel and ribs of a wrecked vessel had been there for several years. In 1982, the last remaining hippies were driven away by Hurricane 'Iwa. The hurricane also washed the wreckage out to sea, leaving only the rusty motor deep in the sand. We breathed a sigh of relief, but soon learned they had left something behind that was not washed away, the name "Shipwreck Beach." When the Hyatt was built, it installed a fake shipwreck as part of its landscaping, so the name lingered on. Then Hurricane 'Iniki washed the wreck away; management of the Hyatt by then was aware of the origin of the spurious name, and the fake shipwreck was not replaced. That name is now fading and it is hoped it soon will disappear.

At the western end of the bay, separated by rocks from Keoneloa Beach, is another beach that collects floating debris brought by the trade winds. Hawaiians called it **Pīhākekua**, which means "burdened with flotsam." I have often wondered at this because many other beaches on Kaua'i face the trade winds, also collecting their share of floating debris, yet this is the only one with that descriptive name. Since Hawaiians rarely named beaches and then only for practical purposes, there must be something unusual about this one. A noteworthy event could account for the name. It is possible Hawaiians found a quantity of iron in the wreckage from a Spanish galleon washed up on this beach. We will never know.

At the eastern end of the Bay is a group of petroglyphs on the limestone ledge at the shore, but you won't be able to see them. They have been observed on only one documented occasion, in 1897, when a series of severe southwest storms scoured out the sand. John Farley, a resident of Kōloa then, reported they were exposed for several days in June of that year. He counted 67 glyphs in an area 25 by 100 feet, made sketches and measurements, and took black-and-white photos. The Bishop Museum sent a representative, who took back a three-foot-square slab with glyphs. It is there today with a plaque that states "presented to the Museum by J. K. Farley, Esquire." Others since then have claimed to have seen these petroglyphs, but if we rely on reports documented by sketches, photographs, or similar evidence, we are left with just one: Farley's.

Farley also interviewed an old Hawaiian lady named Kauʻila who had been raised nearby. She told him she had seen the petroglyphs once in 1848 as a girl and described another group inland still under the sand. Her description of this second group was in such detail it almost certainly exists. Farley concluded that the shelf had subsided some six feet since the glyphs had been carved. His conclusion about subsidence is probably correct because the level of the ocean has not changed appreciably in the time the Islands have been inhabited.

The Makawehi Sand Dunes, beyond the point at the east end of Keoneloa Beach, is one place where Hawaiian commoners who lived nearby buried their dead. Their wooden tools made burial in the rocky soil elsewhere in Pāʻā difficult. Bone fragments are turned up even today by strong winds. Among the human remains are scattered those of many species of extinct birds, whose bones fascinate ornithologists. Please do not dig in the sand, but treat these dunes with the respect you would any graveyard.

Kawailoa Bay is reached by driving past the Hyatt, east on the graveled part of Poʻipū Road, then turning right at the junction of a cane road with utility poles along it. This is Māhāʻulepū Road, a dignified name for a series of bumps and holes. Pass the first turnoff on the right, which leads to a gravel quarry, and you will come to a gate and sentry shack. You should be waved through with an admonition not to remain after 6 p.m. when the gate closes. Grove Farm owns all the land from the end of the paving on Poʻipū Road. In fact, it owns the entire *ahupuaʻa* of Pāʻā, and the ahupuaʻa of Māhāʻulepū right up to the ridge of Hāʻupu Range. This is the last unspoiled coastline on the south shore, and the plans of Grove Farm to build four hotels and a golf course there are certain to be opposed.

Lithified sand characterizes much of the shoreline, so for those with a scientific interest, this is how it gets that way. Rain mixes with carbon dioxide in the air to form weak carbonic acid, which dissolves calcium carbonate from the coralline sand. This percolates some distance down, and after the rain evaporates, calcium carbonate crystals fuse the sand grains. Caves are undercut by waves because the lower levels have undergone less lithification.

The origin of the name Māhāʻulepū (and falling together) has been ascribed by some to an interesting story. When Kamehameha attempted his first invasion of Kaua'i in 1796, he set out from O'ahu with some 1200 war canoes headed for Kaua'i. Most turned back or sank in the stormy channel. According to the story, at least one canoe made the crossing; apparently blown off course, it landed at Māhā'ulepū. The exhausted O'ahu warriors collapsed beside their canoe and slept. This gave the Kaua'i defenders time to organize in the night and before dawn slaughtered all but a handful. The survivors succeeded in launching their canoe but, afraid to face Kamehameha on O'ahu, sailed all the way to the island of Hawai'i.

This tale told on Kaua'i may be credible because an identical one is told at Kawaihae where the canoe is supposed to have landed. It does not appear in any collection of legends, but this does not necessarily mean it did not happen. Even if the story is true, the incident could not be the origin of the name of the *ahupua'a*, which would have been named centuries before 1796.

Another source for the name is suggested by a legend published under the auspices of King Kalākaua in 1888. *The Legends and Myths of Hawaii* was one of his many efforts to restore interest in ancient Hawaiian culture. The legend in this compilation tells of a remarkably similar battle in the Māhā'ulepū area that took place in the 1300's, but with many canoes landing on the beach and mighty opposing armies. Apparently, it is a rewritten version of the story above, with the usual flourishes and magical elements of legends added. That such a battle actually occurred in prehistoric times is doubtful because other collections of myths and legends published prior to 1888, including the exhaustive *Papers by Lahainaluna Students after Interviews with Old Residents of Kauai, 1885*, would have mentioned such a major event. This suggests the legend in the 1888 compilation was composed, perhaps under royal pressure, for inclusion in it, and was based upon the story of the 1796 battle.

The only conclusion one can presently draw is that the name is derived from something else altogether. Perhaps it is a poetic allusion to those who "fell" and were buried there together in the burial ground. The true origin may never be known

There are three distinct beaches at Māhā'ulepū. The one farthest to the west is called Gillin's Beach and has an isolated house on it still owned by the Gillin family, although they no longer live there. Elbert Gillin was the civil engineer who supervised the Hā'upu Range Tunnel project.

Petroglyphs are under the sand in front of the Gillin home. Between January 7 and 9, 1980, a series of severe *kona* storms scoured out several vertical feet of sand and exposed three sandstone ledges with six groups of petroglyphs. People who happened to be on the beach to watch the storm saw them, the word spread, and residents of Kōloa photographed the glyphs in color. "Pila" Kikuchi, professor of anthropology at Kauaʻi Community College, documented them on this occasion with sketches, measurements, and photographs.

The petroglyphs are a mixture of stick figures, animals, and canoes with crab-claw sails. There are also carved Hawaiian names in Romanesque lettering, which had to have been carved after missionary schooling had begun on Kauaʻi. Such lettering is not found among the glyphs at Keoneloa, which tempts one to speculate on the age of this field relative to Keoneloa, but this is not justified. Adena Gillin, Elbert's widow, told me she had seen the glyphs several times over the years and added she didn't want her privacy disturbed so she had said nothing about it. This would indicate the ledge at Gillin's Beach has not undergone the same degree of subsidence Keoneloa has, and no conclusion can be drawn as to its age, relative or otherwise. Both areas await further study.

There is another intriguing site nearby, but you won't be able to see it. The story is interesting, however, so it is worth telling. At the west end of Gillin's Beach is small Kapunakea (the clear water) Stream. Inland about 100 yards is the entrance of a lava-tube cave. Just inside is a wide part Hawaiians used as a shelter, and farther into the cave is a sinkhole some 100 feet in diameter. The limestone ceiling collapsed about 7,000 years ago, and the 30 feet of sediment accumulated since then is being studied. Pollen and microfossils tell of the surrounding plant life over the millennia. The animal remains are almost unbelievable. One example is the bones of the extinct *moa-nalo,* a flightless oversized duck with a beak resembling the snout of a sea turtle. There are many lava-tube caves in Māhāʻulepū, and rare blind insects have been found in them.

Wai-o-pili *heiau* is near the Gillin house on the east side of Wai-o-pili (water of *pili* grass) spring. The quarry covers most of it. It had a rectangular wall 50 by 90 feet ten feet high and almost as thick. It was the largest of four major *heiau* on the south shore. Though only the southeast corner can be seen, the massive slabs of volcanic rock are impressive. According to an archeological survey in 1974, the *heiau* was the focus of a large Hawaiian community in the area. Excavation has yet to be done.

Kawailoa Beach is the central beach at Māhāʻulepū, taking its name from the bay which means "the long water." Because it receives almost all of the use it is more commonly referred to simply as **Māhāʻulepū Beach**. Walk back along the shore around

Kāmala Point or drive behind it to get to the beach, which stretches from Kāmala Point to Pakamoi Point. There is an amazing variety of colorful fish in the caves eroded into the shore, but currents make snorkeling rather hazardous. Much of Donovan's Reef was filmed here. This a favorite place for locals to come on weekends, fish, and cook out. Talk with some—they are friendly and you will enjoy the experience.

Farther east is a barbed-wire fence with "No Trespassing" signs, so don't. Grove Farm regards both the path beyond and the beach it leads to as treacherous, hence the fence and signs for your own protection. If your curiosity is stirred, perhaps telling you what lies beyond may sate it somewhat. A faint trail on the rocky slope leads to a bluff overlooking a small pocket beach. This is Ha'ula (hot sun) Beach, the third in the Māhā'ulepū area. Hawaiians also buried their dead in the Āweoweo (a type of seaweed) Sand Dunes behind it.

Before you leave Māhā'ulepū, look up to the head of Hā'upu Range looming over you at more than 2,000 feet. If the cloud cover is right, you will see why it got the nickname "Hoary Head."

Now return to the "Welcome to Po'ipū Beach" rock wall to Lāwa'i Beach Road, which will take you along the rest of the Po'ipū Shore to Lāwa'i Kai. Yes, the road signs read only "Lāwa'i Road," matching the signs on Po'ipū Road in not having the word "Beach" on them. This is the original road to Lāwa'i Beach and was named Lāwa'i Beach Road nearly a century ago. One wonders if perhaps there wasn't room for the extra word on the signs.

As soon as you make the sharp cutback from Po'ipū Road past the "Welcome to Po'ipū Beach" rock wall, pull over to the side of Lāwa'i Beach Road because there is something to tell you here.

Alexander & Baldwin, a large firm headquartered in Honolulu, is currently working on a huge 1,000-acre development, and you are at one corner of it. It will occupy all of the land *mauka* of Lāwa'i Beach Road to Kōloa, and from Po'ipū Road where you are parked to Lāwa'i Kai. The plans have been revised several times, but the development will include about 3,500 individual homes, several condominiums, an 18-hole golf course, a commercial center, and at least one 500-room hotel.

When occupied by over 10,000 residents, the development will unite Kōloa with the Po'ipū Shore and more than double the present population of the area. You may have noticed that traffic in Kōloa and Po'ipū is already a problem, the beaches and parks are used to their maximum capacity most of the time, the beauty that formerly was the primary attraction of Po'ipū has been blighted in many spots, and the tranquility that once was so

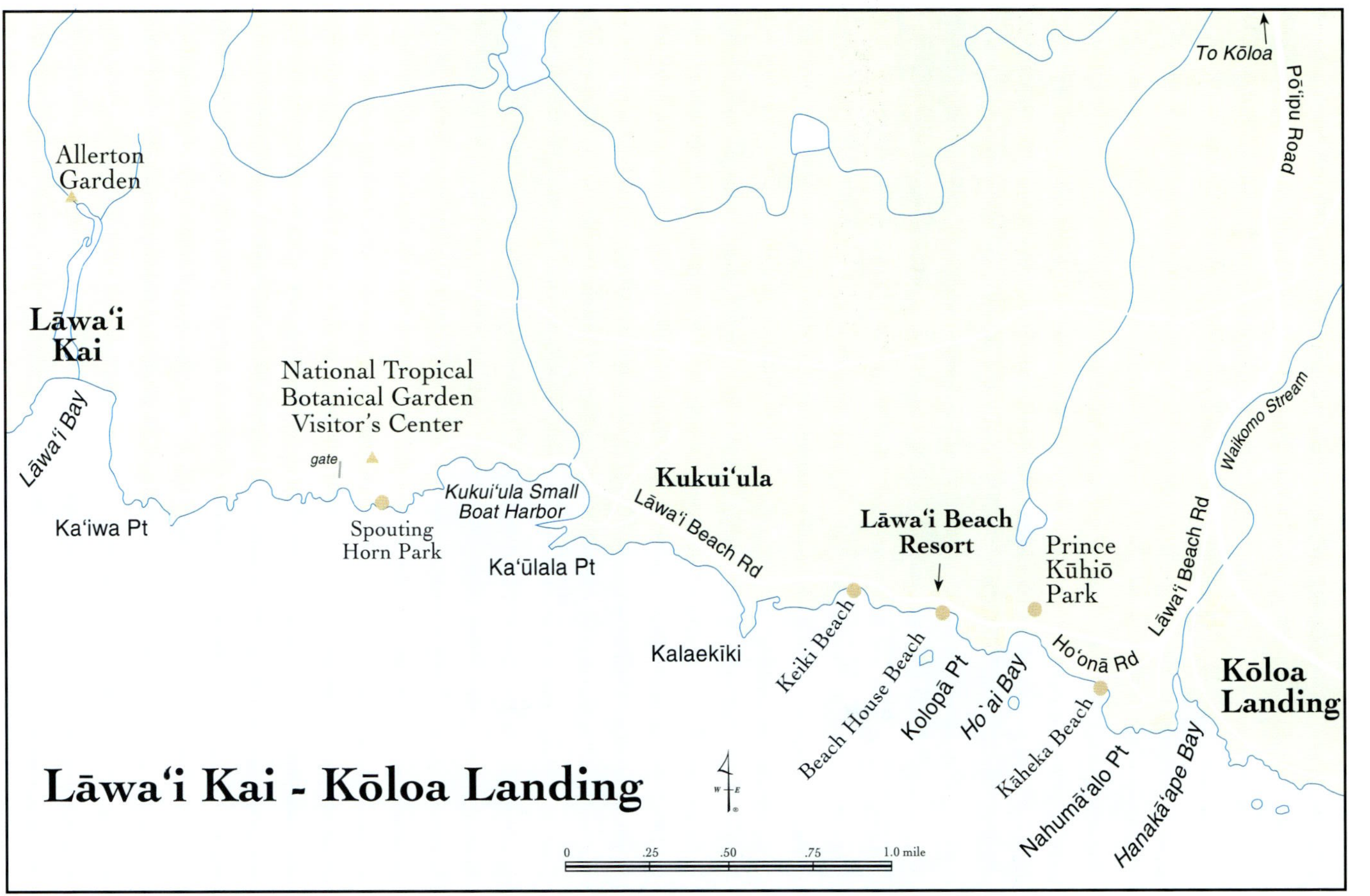

Lāwaʻi Kai - Kōloa Landing

Prince Kūhiō Monument and Park, dedicated in 1928 to commemorate
Prince Jonah Kūhiō Kalaniana'ole, who was born there.

⌒ Photograph by author, 1999.

characteristic of the shoreline is now gone. Most developers are after the dollar with no thought being given to the impact upon the natural beauty or the quality of life of all who visit or live here.

Now let's resume the tour; you will almost immediately take a turn left off Lāwaʻi Beach Road on Hoʻonā (calmed) Road which angles off to the left. Stay on Hoʻonā Road, which goes along the shore.

Kāheka Beach is along this road; public access to the beach is marked. The word Kāheka means a shallow rocky basin where the ocean washes in through an opening, which describes this beach perfectly. Hawaiians gathered shellfish and *limu* (edible seaweed) and made salt there well into historic times.

As mentioned often, Hawaiians did not customarily name beaches unless they had some practical value in their lives. This raises the possibility that here is one of the few named by them and the true name has come down to us. Kāheka is given as the name of the bay offshore on the earliest charts of the European navigators. Although they asked Hawaiians the names of such places, the navigators were less concerned with them than with the accuracy of their charting.

To clarify this, I asked Leilani Souza, an elderly Hawaiian lady born in Kōloa who had lived at the beach most of her life, whether the name was that of the beach or the bay. She replied "All same t'ing" and explained that Kāheka was the name of the beach and also the bay. This may be a rare instance in which Hawaiians did name the beach because shellfish and *limu* were gathered there. We know the name because it was recorded on the nautical charts of Western mariners as the name of the bay.

It is also sometimes called Waterhouse Beach because the Waterhouse family owns much of the land around it, including the point on the east. Some erroneously call it "baby beach," confusing it with Keiki (baby) Beach, a protected pond farther down the road beyond the Lāwaʻi Beach Resort. At Kāheka Beach, there are seashells to find, tide pools to explore and sand for building castles. It is probably the best beach on Kauaʻi for children aged two to six.

★ **Kūhiō Park** is on your right less than a mile beyond the rock wall. This park is owned and maintained by The Order of Kamehameha, a Hawaiian civic club founded by Prince Kūhiō in 1902 to preserve Hawaiian customs and traditions. Kahoʻai, a prominent Hawaiian fishing village in pre-contact times, occupied this site on Hoʻai Bay, and chiefs of Kauaʻi would often stay there.

Prince Jonah Kūhiō Kalanianaʻole was born here on March 26, 1871. He was a grandson of the last high chief of Kauaʻi, Kaumualiʻi. Kūhiō was adopted by Queen Kapiʻolani, wife of King

Kalākaua, raised in 'Iolani Palace in Honolulu, and made a prince by royal decree in 1884. After Hawai'i became a Territory of the United States, Kūhiō was elected second delegate to Congress. He served 10 consecutive terms from 1902 to 1922 and was responsible for passage of the Hawaiian Homes Act in 1920. He died in 1922 and was laid to rest in the Royal Mausoleum in Nu'uanu Valley on O'ahu. He was the last heir of the Hawaiian monarchy and is revered because of his heartfelt efforts on behalf of the Hawaiian people. His birthday on March 26 is a state holiday and the occasion for a week of celebration that concludes with a moving ceremony in this park.

The monument to Kūhiō placed there and dedicated in 1928 bears the inscription:

In memory of
Ke Ali'i a na maka'ainana
[the chief of the common people]
Jonah Kūhiō Kalaniana'ole
Delegate to Congress
1902-1922
March 26, 1871 January 7, 1922
Makua 'Aina Ho'opulapula
[father of the Homestead Lands]

There is much more of interest in the park than the monument. To the right as you face it is a square bed of rocks, which was the foundation of the grass house where Kūhiō was born. Near it are the walls of the cook house, with niches for food and implements. There are old stone taro terraces, house sites, and a well at the back. One stone enclosure was a pigpen of typical Hawaiian design. A low opening allowed small pigs to go out and forage, but they always returned at feeding time. When a pig got too large to squeeze out it was time for a *lū'au*.

A cleared area just behind the pond was a ceremonial and game ground. The pond is actually an ancient fishpond. In the northwest corner is a small *heiau*. Beyond the fence are remnants of irrigation ditches, taro terraces, walls, and many other structures. These will be preserved in the A&B development now underway. An archeological area is planned that will have a visitor center with an artifact display.

Behind the park a short distance is an impressive rock berm nearly 200 feet long and up to 20 feet high. It was once part of the old McBryde railroad.

Aerial view of Kukuiʻula Harbor, 1924. The town of Kōloa is in the background with Waitā Reservoir behind it.

Fishing sampans moored in Kukui'ula Harbor, about 1920. At that time Kukui'ula was commonly called "sampan harbor."

Just past the Beach House Restaurant in front of the Lāwaʻi Beach Resort is a small beach that looks as if it might go under when the time-share owners and guests of the resort gather there to sunbathe. Endangered monk seals often come ashore to bask as well. Snorkeling is fabulous because many snorkelers feed the brightly colored fish, although they shouldn't. The beach is usually safe, even in summer surf conditions, because of the protective reef. I first knew this as Longhouse Beach, named for the Tahiti Longhouse Restaurant on adjacent Kolopī (to pull away) Point. This was sold and renamed the Beach House Restaurant, so many started calling it **Beach House Beach**, a name that has stuck because the restaurant has been there for so many years. Three popular surfing spots are offshore and contests are often held here.

Farther down Lāwaʻi Beach Road, past the point with a Thai-style home, is tiny **Keiki Beach**. As the name implies, it is the best beach on the island for infants. "Keiki" is the Hawaiian word for baby or child. Old-timers call it Boyden's Pond because of a family that lived on the point next to it for many years. It seems almost everyone who was born on Kauaʻi learned to swim here. It has a totally protected pond only a foot or two deep, depending on the tide, a sandy bottom, brightly colored baby fish, and *aʻama* crabs to chase; toddlers can't wander more than a few feet away because of the walls on either side. Public access is by way of the stone stairs.

Kukuiʻula Small Boat Harbor is farther along Lāwaʻi Beach Road, reached by turning left on Āmio (narrow channel) Road. The word *kukuiʻula* means "red light of the kukui nut." The burning of kukui nuts by Hawaiians on shore guided late fishermen home. A Hawaiian fishing village was once near the stream, but the last evidence, a fishing shrine, was eradicated by Hurricane ʻIwa in 1982.

This is a natural harbor. McBryde built a stone wharf here and extended the point with a small breakwater about 1900. The reason cannot be determined at this date. Kōloa Landing belonged to Kōloa Plantation, and McBryde owned Eleʻele Landing. At the time both landings were rudimentary and boats had to be rowed to and from ships anchored offshore. The intention may have been to have an alternate landing closer to fields in the area, but the swells from the southwest during summer months would have made Kukuiʻula unsatisfactory for this purpose.

McBryde Camp #18 was located along Kukuiʻula Stream and extended to the railroad, which is now a large haul cane road. Starting about 1910, some Japanese who had worked out their contracts established a small fishing village on the shore

Japanese women returning to Kukui'ula after selling their fish in Kōloa, about 1924.

Bishop Museum

near camp #18 at Kukuiʻula. They built their own sampans and went out to fish every night. It was then called "sampan harbor" because they moored their sampans end-to behind the point. The pom-pom sound of their two-cycle motors as they departed at dusk and returned at dawn was a familiar one. There was no refrigeration then, so every morning the fishermen or their wives carried the night's catch slung from a pole on their shoulder to Kōloa and the camps to peddle them. During the 1930s as the fishermen aged, their offspring found better jobs in Kōloa and elsewhere, and fishing faded at Kukuiʻula. By World War II the village of shacks was gone.

Most of the film Islands in the Stream was made at Kukuiʻula Harbor in 1976. An entire Bahama-style village was constructed for the shooting.

You may have wondered why Kukuiʻula Store in Poʻipū Plaza at the junction of Lāwaʻi Beach Road and Poʻipū Road has that name when it is more than a mile from Kukuiʻula. It is a short but interesting story. Hajime "Jimmy" Kuribayashi started operating the plantation store in McBryde Camp #18 at Kukuiʻula Harbor in 1953, although he knew McBryde was consolidating its outlying camps. By the mid-1960s, McBryde's 30 camps had been demolished and all of their workers lived in one camp at Numila. Jimmy managed to stay in business under the name Kukuiʻula Store after Camp #18 closed by, as he says, "working hard" and adding items for tourists. In 1973, he moved to the present location; as this book is being written he is changing the name to Kukuiʻula Market. He still works in the store, helped by his family.

Spouting Horn Park can't be missed because the large parking lot next to the road was built to accommodate a dozen tour buses and at least twice that many automobiles. High swells enter a large lava tube open to the ocean and force a geyser out of a hole high into the air. The height of the spray varies from six feet on a calm day to sixty feet when the swells are high. Blowholes are common in the Islands, but what makes Spouting Horn unique is the air driven out of another opening close by, producing a moaning or wheezing sound. It is this awesome sound that gives it the "horn" part of its name. It was named by whalers calling at Kōloa Landing, which accounts for the "spouting" part.

Heed the warning signs and don't go near the openings—footing is slippery. Several people have been swept out to sea through the lava tube and drowned. Only one, in 1985, lived to tell about it! The commercial booths selling trinkets and Hawaiian souvenirs have a low overhead, so bargains are often to be found.

There is a story often heard on Kaua'i that Spouting Horn was dynamited around 1920 by the order of McBryde officials so the spray would not damage the sugar cane immediately inland. This is another example of the stories that abound about the Kōloa area and make writing the first history intriguing yet difficult.

The records of McBryde Sugar Company contain no mention of such an episode, but this is not persuasive either way. Spouting Horn had become an item of interest to visitors nearly a century before, and probably pains would have been taken not to leave a written account. These visitors, as well as missionaries and residents of Kōloa, had written about Spouting Horn in letters and diaries since 1835. Although most of their depictions are more touristic than precise, those written after 1920 are in accord with the ones before then. More importantly, none of the accounts written around 1920 contain any reference to dynamiting.

Three descriptions of Spouting Horn before 1900 sufficiently detailed to be convincing are found in various archives. The best, a letter from Sanford B. Dole on June 4, 1863 to his cousin, whom he addresses as "Dear Sister Mary," contains precise descriptions and carefully estimated measurements. All three accounts match the appearance of Spouting Horn today.

The Garden Island newspaper was searched for the ten-year period on either side of that date and nothing was reported in the only paper Kaua'i had at the time. Older residents who were alive then were asked if they had either witnessed the dynamiting or had noted a change in the appearance of Spouting Horn around that date. None had, but they had all heard the story.

Photographs would provide conclusive evidence. Fortunately, a large number have been taken by visitors, many are in archives, and those after 1860 are clear enough to reveal details. After reviewing these, the only conclusion possible is that no dynamiting ever took place and the story is false. Even the height the spout attains today appears to be unchanged, allowing for differences in swells and tide. Readers who are interested are referred to the best photos taken by Ray Jerome Baker in 1908, 1910, and 1925 in the archives of the Bishop Museum.

The motivation for starting such a story is not known. A possible one lies in the labor unrest of the time and the prevalent feelings of many workers against management.

From Spouting Horn Park you can look ahead on Lāwa'i Beach Road and see that the road ends a short distance beyond the park at a large gate. The gate marks the transition from a county road to a private one owned by the Allerton estate, portions of which beyond the gate have fallen into the ocean. So you can tell your tour is soon to end, and it will with the story of Lāwaʻi Kai and how the Allertons and others were involved.

Lāwaʻi Kai valley is one of the most gorgeous and interesting sites on Kauaʻi and should not be missed. Hollywood must agree, because parts of South Pacific, Jurassic Park, and many other movies were filmed there. Just *mauka* from Spouting Horn Park is a cluster of restored camp houses surrounded by plants and trees. This is the Visitor Center of the National Tropical Botanical Garden (NTBG), and the only way to see Lāwaʻi Kai is on a tour starting there. The telephone number is in the directory.

The headquarters of the **National Tropical Botanical Garden** and one of the four gardens that comprise it, 252-acre Lāwaʻi Garden, are in the upper valley. The other three gardens that make up the NTBG are Limahuli at Hāʻena on Kauaʻi; Kahanu near Hāna on Maui; and Kampong in Florida. The **Allerton Garden** in the lower 96 acres of Lāwaʻi Kai valley is owned by the Allerton estate and administered by NTBG. A self-guided tour around the Visitor Center itself is an interesting way to await the start of your tour. It has labeled plants and a vegetable garden typical of those grown by workers during plantation days.

In ancient times, the valley of Lāwaʻi Kai was filled with taro terraces watered by an intricate irrigation system. Water was diverted from both Lāwaʻi Stream and springs in the eastern cliff; remnants of the system can still be seen. A village site is visible by a water-fall and pool.

Lāwaʻi Kai was a favorite fishing place for Hawaiians who used the large cave near the beach on the west as a shelter. The black basalt hill at the mouth of the stream has an ancient name—Kaihoʻolale (encouraging the sea)—heard in chants, but at the time of contact Hawaiians commonly referred to the hill by the more utilitarian name of Puʻu-o-kilo-iʻa (hill of the fish watcher) because it was used by fish spotters to direct fishermen at sea in canoes. Other caves in the cliffs farther inland were used as burial sites and many artifacts have been found in them.

The story of how the National Tropical Botanical Garden came to be is rather convoluted. In the Great Mahele of 1848, when Kamehameha III awarded one-third of his land to the chiefs who had been loyal to him and his predecessors, James Young Kanehoa acquired the entire *ahupuaʻa* of Lāwaʻi. The valley of Lāwaʻi Kai is in the center of the *ahupuaʻa*. About 1850, he and his wife, Hikoni, built a home on the bluff above the east side of the valley and lived there. Title to all this passed to Hikoni upon Kanehoa's death.

Their niece, Queen Emma, or Kaleleonalani as Hawaiians prefer to call her, the bride of Alexander Liholiho (King Kamehameha IV), stayed with Hikoni on her Royal Progress Tour in 1856. Emma fell in love with the valley. Because of this, Hikoni deeded the entire Lāwaʻi *ahupuaʻa* to her and built a cottage next to her home for Emma's use when she visited her newly acquired land.

In 1862, Emma lost her only son Albert, then her husband the following year. Stricken with grief, she was inconsolable. Finally, in 1871, Emma gave up court life and came to live in the cottage. While there, she introduced many plants into Lāwaʻi Kai. The magenta bougainvillea that cascades down the east bluff was planted by her from cuttings she was given by Dr. James Smith of Kōloa. After her famous trip to Kōkeʻe and the Alakaʻi Swamp, she named her cottage on the bluff Mauna Kilohana after the lookout point she had reached. In 1872, Emma returned to her court duties in Honolulu at the request of King Kamehameha V.

In 1876, Emma leased the *ahupuaʻa* of Lāwaʻi, excluding her cottage and a few acres of loʻi in the valley, to Duncan McBryde. Emma died in 1885. By then Duncan McBryde had also died, and his widow Elizabeth purchased the *ahupuaʻa* of Lāwaʻi in 1886 from Emma's estate. When McBryde Sugar Company was formed in 1899, it planted sugar cane in the upper valley. Pump 6, taking power from Wainiha and still a landmark in the valley, was used to irrigate the cane. The lower valley was not suitable for sugar cane so was leased to Chinese tenant farmers to grow rice and other crops.

Of the two sons of Duncan McBryde, Alexander had botanical interests his brother Walter did not share and wanted to create a garden in the lower valley. Elizabeth gave the lower part to him while McBryde Sugar Company continued to grow cane in the upper valley. By 1906, the company needed land on the bluff above the valley for sugar cane. Alexander had wanted to live in the valley, so that year he moved Queen Emma's cottage down to its present location and lived in it until 1915 when he built a larger home next to it. He lived in that home until his death in 1930. During all these years, Alexander added a great number of exotic plants in the lower valley. Chinese, and later Japanese, plantation workers continued to grow rice as well as various fruits, watercress, and edible lotus, in the unused portions of the lower valley.

Now the story shifts to the Allertons. Robert Henry Allerton was the only son of a wealthy Chicago cattleman. He inherited a large tract of land near Monticello, 150 miles south of Chicago, built a mansion, and created extensive gardens. He traveled widely, acquiring art, and filled both the mansion and gardens with his collection. In 1922, when he was 49, he met John Wyatt Gregg, a 27-year-old student of architecture at the University of Illinois. The two formed a very close relationship and traveled together all over the world.

In 1937, Robert and John visited Lāwaʻi Kai. Robert bought the lower 96 acres from the Alexander McBryde estate the following year. Alexander's former home was torn down, and John designed and built a home for Robert and himself next to Queen Emma's cottage in a style similar to it and restored the cottage itself. Over the next 20 years, Robert and John created the Allerton Garden by adding exotic species to those that had been introduced by Alexander McBryde. The Allerton Garden extends from just *makai* of Pump 6 on both sides of Lāwaʻi Stream to the ocean. Robert also brought art pieces from Monticello and placed them at strategic places in the Garden. Other works of art were collected on their trips together over the years, and they added these as well. Because of the scandal their close relationship engendered at the time, Robert had Illinois law changed so he could adopt John in 1960.

In 1964, the last year of his life, Robert Allerton established the Pacific Tropical Botanical Garden (PTBG) and donated $1,000,000 to purchase the land for it in the valley *mauka* of Pump 6, and to provide initial funding for its operations. Upon its creation, Robert stated the purpose of the PTBG was to study and preserve tropical plants, and it was chartered by Congress in 1969. He died at the age of 91 and his ashes were scattered in Lāwaʻi Bay. John inherited a life estate in both the home and Allerton Garden and lived there until his death in 1986. After that, Allerton Garden was administered (but not owned) by the Pacific Tropical Botanical Garden.

By 1989, the Pacific Tropical Botanical Garden had acquired the three additional sites, as previously mentioned, one of which was in Florida. The acquisition of the latter made its name inappropriate, so it was changed that year to the National Tropical Botanical Garden.

All of Lāwaʻi Kai, especially the Allerton Garden nearest the ocean, was badly damaged by Hurricane ʻIniki in 1992, but it had recovered sufficiently to be reopened in early 1996. While reviewing plans for the re-opening, Dr. Bill Klein, then Director, was struck by the incongruity of referring to the upper valley as the National Tropical Botanical Garden, when the NTBG actually included the upper valley and three other gardens. The 252-acre upper portion was then renamed Lāwaʻi Garden. The headquarters of the National

Tropical Botanical Garden remained where it had been, but its location from then on was called Lāwa'i Garden. The NTBG continues to administer the Allerton Garden in the lower 96 acres of Lāwa'i Kai.

Lāwa'i Beach is a beautiful crescent of sand divided by Lāwa'i Stream. Green sea turtles are a frequent sight here. It is one of only two places on the island where sea turtles feel safe enough to lay their eggs. Gazing down upon the valley from the bluffs above, one is reminded of the chant:

> *Ua nani Lāwa'i e waiho nei*
> *I ke ala kike'e a ka manu.*

> *Lāwa'i lies beautifully below*
> *The winding trail of the birds.*

Ethel Damon, who grew up on Kaua'i, wrote in *Koamalu* a fitting ending to the tour and to this book:

> Koloa is a small place on the map of the Pacific and even on the map of Kaua'i, yet there is something about it, intangible, but very real, which is often felt by passing strangers and which has riveted many who expected to be transients . . . without any apparent explanation its kama'aina, or children of the soil who have grown up there, as likewise many newcomers, feel for it an intense loyalty and attachment.

References

Chapter One

"Beautiful Kaua'i"

Armstrong, Atlas of Hawai'i, 1983.
Beaglehole, The Journals of Captain James Cook, 1967.
Donohugh, Kaua'i, 1992.
Green, "Settlement pattern archeology in Polynesia," 1970.
Kirch, Feathered Gods and Fishhooks, 1985.
________, The Wet and the Dry: Irrigation and Agricultural Intensification in Polynesia, 1994.
Kikuchi, "Archeological Survey and Excavations on the Island of Kaua'i," 1963.
Landrum, Archeological Reconnaissance of . . . Kōloa, Kauai, 1984.

Chapter Two

An Island is Born

Armstrong, *Atlas of Hawai'i*, 1983.
Blay and Siemers, *Various Aspects of the Geology of Hawai'i and the Island of Kaua'i*, 1997.
Carlquist, *Hawai'i: A Natural History*, 1970.
Cox and Banack, *Islands, Plants, and Polynesians*, 1991.
Decker, Volcanoes, 1981.
Kay, *The Natural History of the Hawaiian Islands*, 1994.
Krauss, *Ethnobotany of Hawai'i*, 1974.
Kepler, *Hawaiian Heritage Plants*, 1998.
MacDonald and Abbott, *Volcanoes in the Sea: The Geology of Hawai'i*, 1983.
Palmiter, *"Geology of the Kōloa volcanic series of the south coast of Kauai, Hawaii,"* 1975.

Chapter Three

The Polynesians Arrive

Apple and Kikuchi, *Ancient Hawaiian Shore Zone Fishponds*, 1975.
Barrau, *Plants and Migrations of Pacific Peoples*, 1963.
Buck, *Explorers in the Pacific*, 1953.
________, *Vikings of the Sunrise*, 1959.
Chun, *Hawaiian Canoe Building Traditions*, 1995.
Cox, *Hawaiian Petroglyphs*, 1970.
Emory, Bonk, and Sinoto, *Fishhooks*, 1968.
Finney, *Hokule'a: The Way to Tahiti*, 1979.
Fornander, *Account of the Polynesian Race: Its Origin and Migrations*, 1961.
Golson, *Polynesian Navigation*, 1963.
Jennings, *The Prehistory of Polynesia*, 1979.
Kirch, *Feathered Gods and Fishhooks*, 1985.
________, *"Rethinking East Polynesian Prehistory,"* 1986.
Kirk and Szathmary, *Out of Asia: Peopling of the Americas and the Pacific*, 1989.
Krauss, *Ethnobotany of Hawai'i*, 1974.
Lewis, *We, the Navigators*, 1972.
________, *The Voyaging Stars: Secrets of the Pacific Island Navigators*, 1978.
Mitchell, *Resource Units in Hawaiian Culture*, 1982.
Pfeffer, *"Distribution and Design of Pacific Octopus Lures,"* 1995.
Schütz, *The Voices of Eden: A History of Hawaiian Language Studies*, 1994.

Chapter Four

Culture and Customs

Abbott, *La'au Hawai'i: Traditional Hawaiian Uses of Plants*, 1992.
Bennett, *Archeology of Kaua'i*, 1931.
Brigham, *Ka Hana Kapa: The Making of Barkcloth in Hawai'i*, 1911.
Bryan, *Ancient Hawaiian Life*, 1950.
Bazore, *Hawaiian and Pacific Foods*, 1971.
Ching, Palama, and Stauder, *The Archaeology of Kona, Kaua'i*, 1974.
Elbert and Mahoe, *Nā Mele o Hawai'i Nei*, 1970.
Gallagher, *Hawai'i and Its Gods*, 1975.
Goldman, *Ancient Polynesian Society*, 1970.
Gutmanis, *Kahuna La'au Lapa'au. The Practice of Hawaiian Herbal Medicine*, 1976.
Hammatt, *Archeological and Biological Survey of . . . Kōloa, Kaua'i Island, Hawai'i*, 1978.

Handy and Handy, *Native Planters in old Hawaii, 1972.*
Ii, *Fragments of Hawaiian History, 1959.*
Kamakau, *Ka Poʻe Kahiko: The People of Old, 1991.*
_________, *Na Hana a ka Poʻe Kahiko: The Works of the People of Old, 1976.*
_________, *Ruling Chiefs of Hawaii, 1961.*
Kikuchi, *Archeological Reconnaissance Survey of the Keoneloa Bay Area. 1980.*
_________, *"Archeological Survey and Excavations on the Island of Kauaʻi," 1963.*
Kirch, *Feathered Gods and Fishhooks, 1985.*
Landrum, *Archeological Reconnaissance of . . . Kōloa, Kauai, 1984.*
Malo, *Hawaiian Antiquities, 1971.*
McBride, *The Kahuna, 1972.*
Mitchell, *Resource Units in Hawaiian Culture, 1982.*
Sinoto, *"Archeological Reconnaissance Survey . . . at Kōloa, Poʻipu, Kauaʻi," 1975.*
Titcomb, *The Native Use of Fish in Hawaii, 1972.*
Williams, *From the Mountains to the Sea: Early Hawaiian Life, 1997.*

Chapter Five

Contact, Conquest

Beaglehole, *The Journals of Captain James Cook, 1967.*
Benenson, *Control of Communicable Diseases Manual, 1995.*
Bushnell, *The Gifts of Civilization: Germs and Genocide in Hawaiʻi, 1993.*
Cook and King, *A Voyage to the Pacific Islands, 1784.*
Cook and Price, *Explorations of Captain James Cook in the Pacific, 1768-1779, 1971.*
Haraguchi, *Weather in Hawaiian Waters, 1979.*
Joesting, *Kauaʻi: The Separate Kingdom, 1984.*
Judd, *Voyages to Hawaiʻi before 1860, 1974.*
Kamakau, *Ka Poʻe Kahiko: The People of Old, 1991.*
_________, *Ruling Chiefs of Hawaii, 1961.*
Kuykendall, *The Hawaiian Kingdom, 1778-1854, 1938.*
Malo, *Hawaiian Antiquities, 1971.*
Osler, *The Principles and Practice of Medicine, 1892.*
Papers by Lahainaluna Students after Interviews with Old Residents of Kauai, 1885.
Porteus, *Calabashes and Kings, 1970.*
Schmitt, *"The Okuu: Hawaii's Greatest Epidemic," 1970.*
Strickland, *Tropical Medicine, 1998.*
Vancouver, *A Voyage of Discovery to the North Pacific Ocean, 1798.*

Chapter Six

Sandalwood and Whales

Alexander, "Early Visitors to the Sandwich Islands," 1890.
Cajski, "The Ports of Kaua'i," 1964.
Chevigny, *Lord of Alaska: Baranov and the Russian Adventure*, 1961.
Daws, *Shoal of Time: A History of the Hawaiian Islands*, 1974.
Ellis, *Journal of William Ellis. Narrative of a Tour of Hawai'i . . . 1826*, 1963.
Hohman, *The American Whaleman*, 1928.
Hunt, *The Shenandoah*, 1867.
Jarves, *History of the Hawaiian or Sandwich Islands*, 1843.
Joesting, *Kaua'i: The Separate Kingdom*, 1984.
Judd, *Voyages to Hawai'i before 1860*, 1974.
Kuykendall, *The Hawaiian Kingdom, 1778-1854*, 1938.
March, *Eastern Destiny: Russia in Asia and the North Pacific*, 1996.
McCoy, *Archeological Research at Fort Elizabeth, Waimea, Kauai*, 1972.
Morgan, *Hawaii: A Century of Economic Change, 1778-1876*, 1948.
Pierce, *Russia's Hawaiian Adventure, 1815-1817*, 1965.
Starbuck, *History of the American Whale Fleet*, 1864.
Vancouver, *A Voyage of Discovery to the North Pacific Ocean*, 1798.

Chapter Seven

Puritans in Paradise

Ahana, "A History of Kōloa School," 1930.
Damon, *Koamalu, A Story of Pioneers on Kaua'i*, 1931.
__________, "The First Mission Settlement on Kauai," 1925.
Gulick, *The Pilgrims of Hawai'i*, 1918.
Halford, *Nine Doctors & God*, 1954.
Jarves, *History of the Hawaiian or Sandwich Islands*, 1843.
__________, "Sketches of Kaua'i," 1838.
Judd, "Kōloa: A Sketch of its Development," 1935.
Judd, *Pukui, and Stokes, Introduction to the Hawaiian Language*, 1945.
Kaua'i Historical Society, *The Kaua'i Papers*, 1991.
Kōloa School History, *Kaua'i's First Public School, 1877 to 1977*, 1977.
Loomis, *Grapes of Canaan: Hawai'i 1820*, 1966.
Missionary Album, 1969.
Missionary Letters, 1820-1900.
Piercy, *Hawai'i's Missionary Saga*, 1992.
Schütz, *The Voices of Eden: A History of Hawaiian Language Studies*, 1994.
Smith, *Journal*.
Smith Papers, *Kōloa, Kauai 1865-1900*.
von Holt, *Stories of Long Ago: Ni'ihau-Kaua'i-O'ahu*, 1985.
Whitney, *Journal*.

Chapter Eight

Tall Cane

Alexander, *Kōloa Plantation 1835-1935, 1985.*
Beechert, *Working in Hawai'i: A Labor History, 1985.*
Cajski, *"The Ports of Kaua'i," 1964.*
Char and Char, *Chinese Historic Sites and Pioneer Families of Kaua'i, 1979.*
Conde, *Sugar Trains, 1973.*
Damon, *Koamalu, A Story of Pioneers on Kaua'i, 1931.*
Dean, *The Story of McBryde Sugar Co., Ltd., 1899-1949.*
Hooper, *Diaries in the handwriting of William Northey Hooper.*
Iwai, *"The Rice Industry in Hawai'i," 1933.*
Joesting, *Kaua'i: The Separate Kingdom, 1984.*
Johannessen, *The Hawaiian Labor Movement — A Brief History, 1956.*
Jones, *Papers, 1928-1950.*
Judd, *"Kōloa: A Sketch of its Development," 1935.*
Kaua'i Historical Society. *The Kaua'i Papers, 1991.*
Krauss and Alexander, *Grove Farm Plantation, 1985.*
Miyamoto, *Hawai'i: End of the Rainbow, 1964.*
Moir, *A History of Kōloa District, 1995.*
Moke, *Interview with Kapa Moke and Mary Kawena Pukui, 1963.*
Morgan, Hawaii: *A Century of Economic Change, 1778-1876, 1948.*
Pukui and Elbert, *Hawaiian Dictionary, 1971.*
Pukui, Elbert, and Mookini, *Place Names of Hawai'i, 1974.*
Takaki, *Raising Cane: The World of Plantation Hawai'i, 1994.*
Tanimoto, *Return to Maha'ulepu: Personal Sketches, 1982.*

Chapter Nine

Sojourners and Settlers

Chan, *Asian Americans: An Interpretive History, 1991.*
Char, *The Sandalwood Mountains: Readings and Stories of the Early Chinese in Hawaii, 1975.*
Day, *Hawai'i And Its People, 1993.*
Estep, *Social Placement of the Portuguese in Hawai'i, 1973.*
Glick, *Sojourners and Settlers, Chinese Immigrants in Hawai'i, 1980.*
Kim, *"The Koreans in Hawaii," 1937.*
Kimura, *Issei: Japanese Migrants in Hawaii, 1988.*
Luomala, *Voices on the Wind, 1992.*
Moriyama, *Imingaisha: Japanese Emigration Companies and Hawai'i, 1894-1908, 1963.*
Nordyke, *The Peopling of Hawai'i, 1989.*
Okahata, *A History of Japanese in Hawaii, 1971.*
Pukui and Korn, *The Echo of Our Song, 1973.*
Reinecke, *Language and Dialect in Hawai'i: A Sociolinguistic History to 1935, 1939.*

Schmitt, *Demographic Statistics of Hawai'i 1778-1965, 1968.*
________, *Missionary Censuses of Hawai'i, 1973.*
________, *Historic Statistics of Hawai'i, 1977.*
Takaki, *In the Heart of Filipino America: Immigrants from the Pacific Isles, 1995.*
Teodoro, *Out of This Struggle: The Filipinos in Hawaii, 1981.*
Young, *Chinese in Hawai'i: An Annotated Bibliography, 1973.*

Chapter Ten

Plantation Life

Alexander, *Kōloa Plantation 1835-1935, 1985.*
Center for Oral History, *Kōloa: An Oral History of a Kaua'i Community, 1988.*
Estep, *Social Placement of the Portuguese in Hawai'i, 1973.*
Judd, *"Kōloa: A Sketch of its Development," 1935.*
Kodama-Nishimoto, *Hanahana: An Oral History Anthology of Hawai'i's Working People, 1984.*
Krauss and Alexander, *Grove Farm Plantation, 1985.*
Moir, *A History of Kōloa District, 1995.*
Murayama, *Plantation Boy, 1998.*
Schmitt, *Demographic Statistics of Hawai'i 1778-1965, 1968.*
________, *Historic Statistics of Hawai'i, 1977.*
Takaki, *Pau Hana: Plantation Life and Labor in Hawaii, 1835-1920, 1983.*
________, *Raising Cane: The World of Plantation Hawai'i, 1994.*
________, *In the Heart of Filipino America: Immigrants from the Pacific Isles, 1995.*
Wilcox, *The Kaua'i Album, 1981.*
Wright, *"Reminiscences of Līhu'e and Kōloa, Kaua'i," 1919.*

Chapter Eleven

By the Wind Grieved

Adams, *The Japanese in Hawaii, 1924.*
Alexander, *Kōloa Plantation 1835-1935, 1985.*
Allen, *Hawaii's War Years 1941-1945, 1950.*
Beechert, *Working in Hawai'i: A Labor History, 1985.*
Benedict, *The Chrysanthemum and the Sword: Patterns of Japanese Culture, 1989.*
Chang, *The Rape of Nanking, 1997.*
Conde, *Sugar Trains, 1973.*
Dean, *The Story of McBryde Sugar Co., Ltd., 1899-1949.*
Fuchs, *Hawai'i Pono: An Ethnic and Political History, 1961.*
Ienaga, *The Pacific War, 1931-1945, 1978.*
Iriye, *The Origins of the Second World War in Asia and the Pacific, 1987.*
Johannessen, *The Hawaiian Labor Movement — A Brief History, 1956.*
Klass, *World War II on Kaua'i: Historical Research, 1970.*

Knaefler, *Our House Divided*, 1991.
Krauss and Alexander, *Grove Farm Plantation*, 1985.
Lind, *Hawaii's Japanese*, 1946.
Tanaka, *Go For Broke*, 1997.
Teodoro, *Out of this Struggle: Filipinos in Hawaii*, 1981.

A Tour of Kōloa and Poʻipū Today

Ahana, *"A History of Kōloa School,"* 1930.
Anderson, *Historical Report (Kōloa Church)*, 1935.
Center for Oral History, *Kōloa: An Oral History of a Kauaʻi Community*, 1988.
Clark, *Beaches of Kauaʻi and Niʻihau*, 1990.
Cook, *The Kauaʻi Movie Book*, 1996.
Damon, *Koamalu, A Story of Pioneers on Kauaʻi*, 1931.
Donohugh, *Kauaʻi*, 1992.
Donohugh, *Touring Kōloa*, 1998.
Forbes, *Queen Emma and Lāwaʻi*, 1984.
Hoverson, *Historic Kōloa: A Guide*, 1985.
Hulme, *The Robert Allerton Story, 1873-1964*, 1979.
Judd, *"Kōloa: A Sketch of its Development,"* 1935.
Kauaʻi Catholic Mission Centennial. *St. Raphael's Parish 1841-1991*, 1991.
Kauaʻi Historical Society. *The Kauaʻi Papers*, 1991.
Kikuchi, *Archeological Reconnaissance Survey of the Keoneloa Bay Area*, 1980.
________, *"Rainbow Petroglyph Site,"* 1983.
________, *"Archeological Survey and Excavations on the Island of Kauaʻi,"* 1963.
Kōloa School History, *Kauaʻi's First Public School, 1877 to 1977*, 1977.
Landrum, *Archeological Reconnaissance of . . . Kōloa, Kauai*, 1984.
Leinenweber, *1984*.
Moir, *A History of Kōloa District*, 1995.
Muroda & Associates, Inc. *Kōloa-Poipu-Kalaheo Development Plan, Phases I & II*, 1978.
Papers by Lahainaluna Students after Interviews with Old Residents of Kauai, 1885.
Pukui, Elbert, and Mookini, *Place Names of Hawaiʻi*, 1974.
Roelofs, *Makawehi Dunes and Sinkhole*, 1993.
Sinoto, *"Archeological Reconnaissance Survey of . . .Kōloa, Poʻipu, Kauaʻi,"* 1975.
Smith, *Journal*.
Smith, William O. *"History of Kōloa,"* 1915.
Summers, *Hawaiian Fishponds*, 1964.
von Holt, *Stories of Long Ago: Niʻihau-Kauaʻi-Oʻahu*, 1985.
Wilcox, *The Kauaʻi Album*, 1981.
Wright, *"Reminiscences of Līhuʻe and Kōloa, Kauaʻi,"*

Bibliography

Abbott, Isabella A. *La'au Hawai'i: Traditional Hawaiian Uses of Plants.* Honolulu: Bishop Museum Press, 1992.

Adams, Romanzo. *The Japanese in Hawaii.* New York: The National Committee on American-Japanese Relations, 1924.

Ahana, Dora R. *"A History of Kōloa School,"* May 26, 1930. Kaua'i Historical Society. Typescript.

Alexander, Arthur C. *Kōloa Plantation 1835-1935.* 2nd ed. Līhu'e, Hawai'i: Kaua'i Historical Society, 1985.

Alexander, William D. *"Early Visitors to the Sandwich Islands."* Hawaiian Annual, 1890.

Allen, Gwenfread. *Hawaii's War Years 1941-1945.* Honolulu: University of Hawai'i Press, 1950.

Anderson, Eleanor Blake. *Historical Report (Kōloa Church), April 3, 1935.* Typescript.

Apple, Russell A. and William Kikuchi. *Ancient Hawaiian Shore Zone Fishponds.* Honolulu: Office of the State Director, National Park Service, U. S. Dept. of the Interior, 1975.

Armstrong, R. Warwick. *Atlas of Hawai'i.* Honolulu: University of Hawai'i Press, 1983.

Barrau, Jacques. *Plants and Migrations of Pacific Peoples.* Honolulu: Bishop Museum Press, 1963.

Bazore, Katherine. *Hawaiian and Pacific Foods.* New York: Gramercy Publishing Company, 1971.

Beaglehole, John C. *The Journals of Captain James Cook: The Voyage of the Resolution and Discovery, 1776-1780.* Cambridge, England: Cambridge University Press, 1967.

Beaglehole, John C. *The Life of Captain James Cook.* Stanford: Stanford University Press, 1974.

Beechert, Edward D. *Working in Hawai'i: A Labor History.* Honolulu: University of Hawai'i Press, 1985.

Benedict, Ruth. *The Chrysanthemum and the Sword: Patterns of Japanese Culture.* Boston: Houghton Mifflin Company, 1989.

Bennett, Wendell C. *Archeology of Kaua'i. Honolulu: Bishop Museum Bulletin No. 80,* 1931.

Bishop, Isabella Bird. *Six Months in the Sandwich Islands. Honolulu: University of Hawai'i Press, 1964.*

Blay, C., and R. Siemers. *Various Aspects of the Geology of Hawai'i and the Island of Kaua'i. Waimea, Kaua'i: TEOK Investigations, 1997.*

Brigham, William T. *Ka Hana Kapa: The Making of Barkcloth in Hawai'i. Honolulu, Bishop Museum Press, 1911.*

Bryan, E.H. Jr. *Ancient Hawaiian Life. Honolulu: Books About Hawai'i, 1950.*

Buck, Peter H. *Explorers in the Pacific. Honolulu: Bishop Museum Special Publication No. 43, 1953.*

________. *Vikings of the Sunrise. Chicago: University of Chicago Press, 1959.*

Bushnell, O. A. *The Gifts of Civilization: Germs and Genocide in Hawai'i. Honolulu: University of Hawai'i Press, 1993.*

Cajski, Thomas A. *"The Ports of Kaua'i." Master's thesis, University of Hawai'i, 1964.*

Carlquist, Sherwin J. *Hawai'i: A Natural History. Garden City, NY: National History Press, 1970.*

Center for Oral History, *Social Science Research Institute, University of Hawai'i at Mānoa. Kōloa: An Oral History of a Kaua'i Community. 3 vols. 1988.*

Certificates of Boundaries, *Department of Accounting and General Services, State of Hawai'i:*

    No. 8. Kalaheo, Kōloa, Kaua'i.

    No. 9. Wahiawa, Kōloa, Kaua'i.

    No. 10. Lāwa'i, Kōloa, Kaua'i.

Chan, Sucheng. *Asian Americans: An Interpretive History. Boston: Twayne Publishers, 1991.*

Chang, Iris. *The Rape of Nanking. New York: Penguin Books, 1997.*

Char, Tin-Yuke. *The Sandalwood Mountains: Readings and Stories of the Early Chinese in Hawaii. Honolulu: University of Hawai'i Press, 1975.*

Char, Tin-Yuke, and Wai Jane Char. *Chinese Historic Sites and Pioneer Families of Kaua'i. Honolulu: Hawai'i Chinese History Center, 1979.*

Chevigny, Hector. *Lord of Alaska: Baranov and the Russian Adventure. Portland, Oregon: Binfords and Mort, 1961.*

Chinen, Jon J. *The Great Mahele. Honolulu: University of Hawai'i Press, 1958.*

Ching, Francis, Stephen Palama, and Catherine Stauder. *The Archaeology of Kona, Kaua'i, Na Ahupua'a Weliweli, Pa'a, Maha'ulepu. Archeological Research Center Hawai'i, Lāwa'i, 1974.*

Chun, Naomi N.Y. *Hawaiian Canoe Building Traditions. Honolulu: Kamehameha Schools Press, 1995.*

Clark, John. *Beaches of Kaua'i and Ni'ihau.* Honolulu: University of Hawai'i Press, 1990.

Conde, Jesse C. *Sugar Trains.* Felton, California: Glenwood Publishers, 1973.

Cook, Chris. *The Kaua'i Movie Book.* Honolulu: Mutual Publishing Company, 1996.

Cook, James. and James King. *A Voyage to the Pacific Islands. 3 vols.* Dublin: Printed for H. Chamberlaine . . ., 1784.

Cook, James. *Explorations of Captain James Cook in the Pacific as Told by Selections of His Own Journals, 1768-1779.* Ed. A. Grenfell Price. Mineola, New York: Dover Publications, 1971.

Cook, James. *The Journals of Captain Cook on his Voyages of Discovery.* Ed. John C. Beaglehole. London: Boydell & Brewer, 1999.

Cook, James. *The Journals of Captain James Cook: The Voyage of the Resolution and Discovery, 1776-1780.* Ed. John C. Beaglehole. Cambridge, England: Cambridge University Press, 1967.

Cox, J. Halley. *Hawaiian Petroglyphs.* Honolulu: Bishop Museum Press, 1970.

Cox, Paul A, and Sandra Banack, eds. *Islands, Plants, and Polynesians.* Portland: Dioscordes Press, 1991.

Damon, Ethel M. *Koamalu, A Story of Pioneers on Kaua'i.* Privately printed, 1931.

__________. *"The First Mission Settlement on Kauai." The Garden Island,* June 16, 1925 *et seq.*

Daws, Gavan. *Shoal of Time: A History of the Hawaiian Islands.* Honolulu: University of Hawai'i Press, 1974.

Day, A. Grove. *Hawai'i And Its People.* Honolulu: Mutual Publishing Company, 1993.

Decker, Robert. *Volcanoes.* San Francisco: W.H. Freeman, 1981.

Denny, Jim. *The Birds of Kaua'i.* Honolulu: University of Hawai'i Press, 1999.

Donohugh, Donald, and Beatrice Donohugh. *Kaua'i.* 3rd ed. Portland, Oregon: Paradise Publications, 1992.

Donohugh, Donald. *Exploring Historic Kōloa.* Līhu'e, Hawai'i: Kaua'i Historical Society, 1998.

Elbert, Samuel H, and Noelani Mahoe. *Nā Mele o Hawai'i Nei.* Honolulu: University of Hawai'i Press, 1970.

Ellis, William. *Journal of William Ellis. Narrative of a Tour of Hawai'i . . 1826.* Honolulu: Advertiser Publishing Co., 1963.

Emerson, Nathaniel B. *Unwritten Literature of Hawai'i.* Rutland, Vermont: Charles E. Tuttle Co., 1991.

Emory, Kenneth P., W.J. Bonk, and Y. Sinoto. Fishhooks. *Bishop Museum Special Publication 47.* Honolulu: Bishop Museum, 1968.

Estep, Gerald Allan. *Social Placement of the Portuguese in Hawai'i as Indicated by Factors in Assimilation Honolulu: University of Hawai'i Press,* 1973.

Finney, Ben R. *Hokule'a: The Way to Tahiti.* New York: Dodd, Mead & Company, 1979.

Forbes, David. *Queen Emma and Lāwa'i.* Honolulu: Kaua'i Historical Society, 1984.

Fornander, Abraham. *Account of the Polynesian Race: Its Origin and Migrations.* *Rutland, Vermont: Charles E. Tuttle Co., 1961.*

Fuchs, Lawrence H. *Hawai'i Pono: An Ethnic and Political History. Honolulu: Bess Press, 1961.*

Gallagher, Charles F. *Hawai'i and Its Gods. Honolulu: Weatherkill/ Kapa, 1975.*

Glick, Clarence E. *Sojourners and Settlers, Chinese Immigrants in Hawai'i. Honolulu: University of Hawai'i Press, 1980.*

Goldman, Irving. *Ancient Polynesian Society. Chicago: University of Chicago Press, 1970.*

Golson, Jack, ed. *Polynesian Navigation. Wellington: The Polynesian Society Memoir No. 34, 1963.*

Green, R.C. *"Settlement pattern archeology in Polynesia." Studies in Oceanic Culture History. Eds. R.C. Green and M. Kelly, Honolulu: Department of Anthropology, Bishop Museum, 1970.*

Gulick, Rev., and Mrs. Orramel Hinckley. *The Pilgrims of Hawai'i. New York and London: Fleming H. Revell Company, 1918.*

Gutmanis, J. *Kahuna La'au Lapa'au. The Practice of Hawaiian Herbal Medicine. Honolulu: Island Heritage, 1976.*

Halford, Francis John. *Nine Doctors & God. Honolulu: University of Hawai'i Press, 1954.*

Hammatt, Hallett et al. *Archeological and Biological Survey of the Proposed Kiahuna Golf Village Area, Kōloa, Kona, Kaua'i Island, Hawai'i. Lāwa'i: Archeological Research Center Hawai'i, Inc., 1978.*

Handy, E.S. Craighill, and Elizabeth Green Handy. *Native Planters in Old Hawaii. Honolulu: Bishop Museum Press, 1972.*

Haraguchi, Paul. *Weather in Hawaiian Waters. Honolulu: Pacific Weather, Inc., 1979.*

Hawaiian Annual. *Ed. Honolulu: Thomas G. Thrum*

Hohman, Elmo P. *The American Whaleman. New York: Longmans, Green and Co., 1928.*

Hooper, William. *Diaries in the handwriting of William Northey Hooper. Photocopy of the original diaries and documents made in 1965 by Elsie Wilcox.*

Hoverson, Martha, ed. *Historic Kōloa: A Guide. Kōloa, Hawai'i: Friends of the Kōloa Community/School Library, 1985.*

Hulme, Kathryn C. *The Robert Allerton Story, 1873-1964. John Gregg Allerton, 1979.*

Hunt, Cornelius. *The Shenandoah. New York: G. W. Carleton & Co., 1867.*

Ienaga, Saburo. *The Pacific War, 1931-1945. New York: Random House, 1978.*

Ii, John Papa. *Fragments of Hawaiian History. Trans. Mary K. Pukui. Honolulu: Bishop Museum Press, 1959.*

Iriye, Akira. *The Origins of the Second World War in Asia and the Pacific. London: Addison Wesley Longman Ltd., 1987.*

Iwai, Charles K. *"The Rice Industry in Hawai'i." Master's thesis, University of Hawai'i, 1933.*

Jarves, James J. *History of the Hawaiian or Sandwich Islands*. Boston: Tappan Dennet, 1843.

__________. "Sketches of Kaua'i." *Hawaiian Spectator*, Jan. 1838, pp. 66-68.

Jennings, J. D., ed. *The Prehistory of Polynesia*. Cambridge, Massachusetts: Harvard University Press, 1979.

Joesting, Edward. *Kaua'i: The Separate Kingdom*. Honolulu: University of Hawai'i Press, 1984.

Johannessen, Edward. *The Hawaiian Labor Movement — A Brief History*. Boston: Bruce Humphries, 1956.

Jones, Stella M. Papers, *1928-1950*. Unpublished papers from Kaua'i field trips. Bernice P. Bishop Museum Library, Honolulu.

Judd, Bernice. "*Kōloa: A Sketch of its Development.*" Hawai'i Historical Society Report 44, 1935.

__________. *Voyages to Hawai'i before 1860*. Honolulu: University of Hawai'i Press, 1974.

Judd, Henry P., *Mary Kawena Pukui, and John F.G. Stokes. Introduction to the Hawaiian Language*. Honolulu: Tongg Publishers, 1945.

Kamakau, Samuel M. *Ka Po'e Kahiko: The People of Old*. Trans. Mary Kawena Pukui. Honolulu: Bishop Museum Press, 1991.

__________. *Na Hana a ka Po'e Kahiko: The Works of the People of Old*. Trans. M. K. Pukui. Honolulu: Bishop Museum Press, 1976.

__________. *Ruling Chiefs of Hawaii*. Honolulu: The Kamehameha Schools, 1961.

Kaua'i Catholic Mission Centennial. *St. Raphael's Parish 1841-1991. Kōloa, Hawai'i*: St. Raphael Church, 1991.

Kaua'i Historical Society. *The Kaua'i Papers*. Līhu'e, Hawai'i: KHS, 1991.

Kay, E. Alison, ed. *The Natural History of the Hawaiian Islands*. Honolulu: University of Hawai'i Press, 1994.

Keegan, John. *The Second World War*. New York: Penguin Books, 1990.

Kepler, Angela K. *Hawaiian Heritage Plants*. Honolulu: University of Hawai'i Press, 1998.

Kikuchi, William. *Archeological Reconnaissance Survey of the Keoneloa Bay Area*. Līhu'e, Hawai'i: Kaua'i Community College, May 14, 1980.

__________. *Assessment of Damage to Historical and Archeological Resources Resulting from Hurricane 'Iwa to Kaua'i County, 50-30-10-80, Po'ipu, Kōloa District, Island of Kaua'i*. Līhu'e, Hawai'i: Kaua'i Community College, 1983.

__________. *Rainbow Petroglyph Site. Archeology on Kaua'i, Vol. 10, No. 1* Līhu'e, Hawai'i: Anthropology Club of Kaua'i Community College, February, 1983.

__________. "*Archeological Survey and Excavations on the Island of Kaua'i, Kona District, Hawaiian Islands. Manuscript*, 1963.

Kim, Bernice B.H. "*The Koreans in Hawaii.*" Master's thesis, University of Hawai'i, 1937.

Kimura, Yukiko. *Issei: Japanese Migrants in Hawaii*. Honolulu: University of Hawai'i Press, 1988.

King, Josephine Wundenberg. *"Queen Emma on Kaua'i." Kaua'i Historical Society. Typescript.*

Kirch, Patrick V. *Feathered Gods and Fishhooks. An Introduction to Hawaiian Archeology and Prehistory.* Honolulu: University of Hawai'i Press, 1985.

_________. *Legacy of the Landscape.* Honolulu: University of Hawai'i Press, 1996.

_________. *The Wet and the Dry: Irrigation and Agricultural Intensification in Polynesia.* Chicago: University of Chicago Press, 1994.

_________. *"Rethinking East Polynesian Prehistory." Journal of the Polynesian Society* 95:9-40, 1986.

Kirk, R.E. and E. Szathmary, eds. *Out of Asia: Peopling of the Americas and the Pacific.* Canberra: Journal of Pacific History, 1989.

Klass, Tim. *World War II on Kaua'i: Historical Research.* Līhu'e, Hawai'i: Kaua'i Historical Society, 1970.

Knaefler, Tome Kaizawa. *Our House Divided.* Honolulu: University of Hawai'i Press, 1991.

Kodama-Nishimoto, Michi. *Hanahana: An Oral History Anthology of Hawai'i's Working People.* Honolulu: University of Hawai'i Press, 1984.

Kōloa Quadrangle. *Maps. U. S. Department of the Interior, Geological Survey, 1983.*

Kōloa School History, *Kaua'i's First Public School, 1877 to 1977. Kōloa, Hawai'i: Kōloa School, 1977.*

Krauss, Beatrice H. *Ethnobotany of Hawai'i. Honolulu: University of Hawai'i, Department of Botany, 1974.*

Krauss, Bob, and William P. Alexander. *Grove Farm Plantation. Palo Alto: Pacific Books, 1976. Updated to 1985 by the Kaua'i Historical Society.*

Kuykendall, Ralph S. *The Hawaiian Kingdom, 1778-1854. 3 vols. Honolulu: University of Hawai'i Press, 1938.*

Landrum, James L. *Archeological Reconnaissance of Alexander and Baldwin lands at Kukuiula, Kōloa, Kauai. Honolulu: Department of Anthropology, Bishop Museum, 1984.*

Leinenweber, Spencer. *"The Kōloa Story: Turning Historic Assets Into New Life for Old Town." Historic Hawai'i News, Vol 10, No. 8, September 1984.*

_________. *The Voyaging Stars: Secrets of the Pacific Island Navigators. New York: W.W. Norton & Company, 1978.*

Lewis, David. *We, the Navigators. Honolulu: University of Hawai'i Press, 1972.*

Lind, Andrew W. *Hawaii's Japanese. Princeton: Princeton University Press, 1946.*

Loomis, Albertine. *Grapes of Canaan: Hawai'i 1820. Honolulu: Hawaiian Mission Children's Society, 1966.*

Luomala, Katherine. *Voices on the Wind. Honolulu: Bishop Museum Press, 1992.*

MacDonald, Gordon A., and Agatin T. Abbott. *Volcanoes in the Sea: The Geology of Hawai'i. Honolulu: University of Hawai'i Press, 1983.*

Malo, David. *Hawaiian Antiquities*. Honolulu: Bishop Museum Press, 1971.

March, G. Patrick. *Eastern Destiny: Russia in Asia and the North Pacific*. Westport, Connecticut: Praeger Publishers, 1996.

McBride, Leslie R. *The Kahuna*. Hilo, Hawai'i: Petroglyph Press, 1972.

McCoy, Patrick C. *Archeological Research at Fort Elizabeth, Waimea, Kauai, Hawaiian Islands, Phase 1. Departmental Report Series 72-7*. Honolulu: Department of Anthropology, Bishop Museum, 1972.

Missionary Album. *Honolulu: Hawaiian Mission Children's Society, 1969.*

Missionary Letters, 1820-1900. *Honolulu: Hawaiian Mission Children's Society.*

Mitchell, D.D.K. *Resource Units in Hawaiian Culture*. Honolulu: Kamehameha Schools Press, 1982.

Miyamoto, Kazuo. *Hawai'i: End of the Rainbow*. Rutland, Vermont: Charles E. Tuttle Co., 1964.

Moir, Eric. *A History of Kōloa District*. (videotape recorded in Kōloa, July 25, 1995) *Kaua'i Historical Society Archives.*

________. *Lawa'i Interview*. (2 audiotapes recorded by the Kaua'i Historical Society, n.d.) *Kaua'i Historical Society Archives.*

Moke, Kapa. *Interview with Kapa Moke and Mary Kawena Pukui*. (audiotape recorded in Kōloa, July 19, 1963, in Hawaiian). *Bishop Museum Archives.*

Morgan, Theodore. *Hawaii: A Century of Economic Change, 1778-1876*. Cambridge, Massachusetts: Harvard University Press, 1948.

Murayama, Milton. Plantation Boy. *Honolulu: University of Hawai'i Press, 1998.*

Moriyama, Alan T. *Imingaisha: Japanese Emigration Companies and Hawai'i, 1894-1908*. Honolulu, University of Hawai'i Press, 1963.

Muroda & Associates, Inc. *Kōloa-Poipu-Kalaheo Development Plan, Phases I & II*. Honolulu: EDAW Inc., 1978.

Nordyke, Eleanor C. *The Peopling of Hawai'i*. Honolulu: University of Hawai'i Press, 1989.

Okahata, James, ed. *A History of Japanese in Hawaii*. Honolulu: United Japanese Society of Hawai'i, 1971.

Osler, William. *The Principles and Practice of Medicine*. New York: D. Appleton & Co., 1892.

Palmiter, Daniel Brian. *"Geology of the Kōloa volcanic series of the south coast of Kauai, Hawaii." Master's thesis, Mānoa, University of Hawai'i at Mānoa, 1975.*

Papers by Lahainaluna Students after Interviews with Old Residents of Kauai, 1885. Bishop Museum Archives.

Pfeffer, Michael T. *"Distribution and Design of Pacific Octopus Lures: the Hawaiian Octopus Lure in Regional Context." Hawaiian Archeology Vol. 4, Honolulu. Society for Hawaiian Archeology, 1995.*

Pierce, Richard A. *Russia's Hawaiian Adventure, 1815-1817*. Berkeley and Los Angeles: University of California Press, 1965.

Piercy, LaRue W. *Hawai'i's Missionary Saga*. Honolulu: Mutual Publishing, 1992.

Porteus, Stanley D. *Calabashes and Kings. Rutland, Vermont: Charles E. Tuttle Co.,* 1970.

Pukui, Mary Kawena, and Samuel H. Elbert, Hawaiian Dictionary. *Honolulu: University of Hawai'i Press, 1971.*

Pukui, Mary Kawena, Samuel H. Elbert, and Esther T Mookini. *Place Names of Hawai'i. Honolulu: University of Hawai'i Press, 1974.*

Pukui, Mary Kawena, and Alfons L. Korn. *The Echo of Our Song. Honolulu: University of Hawai'i Press, 1973.*

Reinecke, John E. Language and Dialect in Hawai'i: *A Sociolinguistic History to 1935. Honolulu: University of Hawai'i Press, 1939.*

Roelofs, Faith. Makawehi Dunes and Sinkhole. *Honolulu: Moanalua Gardens Foundation, 1993.*

Schmitt, Robert C. *Demographic Statistics of Hawai'i 1778-1965. Honolulu: University of Hawai'i Press, 1968.*

________. *Historic Statistics of Hawai'i. Honolulu: The University of Hawai'i Press, 1977.*

________. *Missionary Censuses of Hawai'i. Honolulu: Bishop Museum Press, 1973.*

________. *"The Okuu: Hawaii's Greatest Epidemic." Hawai'i Medical Journal 29 (5): 359-364, 1970.*

Schütz, Albert J. *The Voices of Eden: A History of Hawaiian Language Studies. Honolulu: University of Hawai'i Press, 1994.*

Sinoto, Aki. *Archeological Reconnaissance Survey of Knudsen Trust Lands at Kōloa, Po'ipu, Kaua'i. Manuscript. Honolulu: Dept. of Anthropology, Bishop Museum, 1975.*

Smith, James W. Journal. *Honolulu: Hawaiian Mission Children's Society.*

Smith Papers, Kōloa, Kauai 1865-1900. Honolulu: *Hawaiian Mission Children's Society. Manuscript.*

Smith, William O. *"History of Kōloa." The Garden Island, March 30, 1915 et seq.*

Starbuck, Alexander. *History of the American Whale Fleet. 2 vols. New York: Argosy-Antiquarian, 1864.*

Strickland, G. Thomas. *Tropical Medicine. Philadelphia: W.B. Saunders Company,* 1998.

Summers, Catherine C. *Hawaiian Fishponds. Honolulu: Bishop Museum Press, 1964.*

________. *In the Heart of Filipino America: Immigrants from the Pacific Isles. New York: Chelsea House, 1995.*

Takaki, Ronald. *Pau Hana: Plantation Life and Labor in Hawaii, 1835-1920. Honolulu: University of Hawai'i Press, 1983.*

________. *Raising Cane: The World of Plantation Hawai'i. New York: Chelsea House,* 1994.

Tamura, Eileen H. *Americanization, Acculturation, and Ethnic Identity: The Nisei Generation in Hawaii. Chicago: University of Illinois Press, 1994.*

Tanaka, Chester. *Go For Broke. Novato, California: Presidio Press, 1997.*

Tanimoto, Charles Katsumu. *Return to Maha'ulepu: Personal Sketches.* Honolulu: Fisher Printing Co., 1982.

Teodoro, Luis V., ed. *Out of this Struggle: Filipinos in Hawai'i.* University of Hawai'i Press, 1981.

Tyler, Varro E. *The Honest Herbal: A Sensible Guide to the Use of Herbs and Related Remedies.* New York: Haworth Press, 1993.

Vancouver, George. *A Voyage of Discovery to the North Pacific Ocean . . . (6 vols.)* London: G.G. Robinson, J. Robinson, and J. Edwards, 1798.

Von Holt, Ida Knudsen. *Stories of Long Ago: Ni'ihau-Kaua'i-O'ahu.* Honolulu: Daughters of Hawai'i, 1985.

Whitney, Samuel. Journal. Honolulu: Hawaiian Mission Children's Society.

__________. *Sugar Water. Hawaii's Plantation Ditches.* Honolulu: University of Hawai'i Press, 1996.

Wilcox, Carol. *The Kaua'i Album.* Līhu'e, Hawai'i: Kaua'i Historical Society, 1981.

Williams, Julie S. *From the Mountains to the Sea: Early Hawaiian Life.* Honolulu: Kamehameha Schools Press, 1997.

Wright, Anna W. "Reminiscences of Līhu'e and Kōloa, Kaua'i." Kaua'i Historical Society. Typescript, 1919.

Wyngaarden, James B., *Lloyd H. Smith, and J. Claude Bennet. Cecil's Textbook of Medicine.* Philadelphia: W. B. Saunders, 1998.

Young, Nancy. *Chinese in Hawai'i: An Annotated Bibliography (Social Science and Linguistic Institute Special Publication).* Honolulu: University of Hawai'i Press, 1973.

Zimmerman, Elwood C. Introduction. *Insects of Hawai'i. vol. 1.* Honolulu: University of Hawai'i Press, 1948.

Index

A

African-Americans,121, 123, 183
Ahukini Landing, 74
ahupua'a (land division), 22-23, 269-270
Alaka'i, 1, 5, 270
Alexander & Baldwin (A&B), 182, 187, 225, 258
Allerton Garden, 269, 271-272
American Board of Commissioners for Foreign Missions (ABCFM), 66-67, 71-72, 76, 82, 201
Americans, 20, 43, 48, 55-56, 59-60, 62, 64, 72, 80, 116, 120-121, 130, 133, 176
Annexation 1898, 98, 127, 133, 137, 180
Archeology, x, 9-10, 12, 14, 16-17, 21, 23, 114, 231, 257, 262

B

Bacle, William, 252-253
bāngo (numbered tag), 154-155, 160, 216
Baranoff, Alexander, 58-59, 62
Beaglehole, J.C., 17, 35
Bering (ship), 58-60
Bingham, Reverend Hiram, 67-68, 70-76, 82
Bishop Museum, 108, 144, 147-148, 150-151, 256
Brennecke Beach, 241, 251, 253
British, 35, 42-43, 48, 55-56, 58-60, 80, 124, 129-130, 132, 178

C

Canoes
    Outrigger, x, 2, 10, 12, 22, 30-31, 35, 50, 106
    Voyaging, x, 11-14, 17-18, 22, 27
    Double-hulled, ceremonial or war (peleleu), x, 11, 17, 22, 43-44, 256-257
Canton, China, 56, 124-125, 127, 129
Catholic Church, 82, 138, 164, 237-239
Chants (mele), x, 1, 20, 24, 112-113, 126-128
Chinese, 55-56, 71, 79, 86-88, 92, 109, 116, 122, 124-126, 127-129, 131-134, 136, 140-143, 153, 157, 159,
    161, 166, 176-178, 250-251, 270
Clerke, Captain Charles, 27, 33, 41, 55
Cook, Captain James, x, 2, 17, 27, 31-42, 50-51, 55, 71, 79-80, 114, 248

D

Diseases
    Cholera, 47-48
    ma'i 'ōku'u, 45-46, 48
    Leprosy, 79, 202
    Measles, 49-79
    Sexually transmitted, 41
    Smallpox, 45, 79
Dixon, Captain George, 51
Dole, Reverend Daniel, 77-78, 80, 82, 197-198, 200, 215, 258

E

Easter Island, 12, 231
'Ele'ele, 100, 101, 187, 248, 265
Electricity, 100, 161, 163, 171, 184, 214-216, 219
Ellis, Dr. William, 35
Ellis, Reverend William, 20, 72-73, 75, 115
Emma, Queen, 99-100, 204, 228, 270-271

F

Farley, John K., 202, 254-255
Filipinos, 102, 116, 137, 139-143, 146, 149, 155, 159, 166-170, 172, 210, 216, 219, 227, 239
Fishponds, 15, 17, 30, 71, 77, 253
Fort Elizabeth, 49, 61, 70
Fur trade, 50, 54-56, 58-59, 62-63, 106, 124, 130

G

Germans, 119, 180
Glottal stop, (see 'okina)
Government Road, 102, 144-145, 194, 224
Great Britain, 42-43, 56, 80, 124, 129, 178
Greeks, 52, 74, 120
Grove Farm Plantation, 99-101, 109, 119, 146, 159, 171, 184-185, 187, 189, 191, 194, 204, 219, 224, 226,

235-236, 250, 255, 258
Gulick, Reverend Peter J., 57, 75-78, 82, 197, 201

H

Ha'ikū (ahupua'a), 101, 187, 189, 236
Hanalei, 5, 16, 60, 62, 64, 100, 113
Hanamā'ulu Bay, 94
Hanapēpē, 23, 31, 49, 53, 64, 71, 100, 170-171, 194, 248

Hā'upu Range, 23, 35, 101
Hawaiian culture, 15-32, 69, 76, 83, 88, 90, 111-113, 231, 235, 243
Hawaiian language, 8, 15, 36, 40, 71-74, 76, 79, 85, 116, 125-126, 130-131, 152, 155, 197
Hawaiian Sugar Planters' Association (HSPA), 98-99, 121, 137, 152
heiau, 15, 17, 24-25, 37-38, 224-225, 227-228, 235, 252-253, 257
Hōkūle'a, 17
Holman, Dr. Thomas, 67-70, 74
Hooper, William, 87-89, 90, 92-93
Hula, 31, 112-113, 187, 250
Humehume, Prince, 67, 69, 49
Hurricane 'Iniki, 79, 187, 202, 251, 254, 271
Hurricane 'Iwa, 191, 204, 222, 230, 236, 253-254, 265

I

ILWU, 171, 182, 184-185, 219, 225
imu, 25, 29
International Longshoremen's and Warehousemen's Union, (see ILWU)
Inter-island Steamship Company, 108
Iron, 36-39, 50-51, 59, 88, 106, 159-160, 174, 230-231, 254
Irrigation systems, 2, 15, 21-23, 26, 29, 53, 87, 97-100, 128, 149, 152, 157, 187, 215, 253, 262, 269-270

J

Japanese, 99, 102, 106, 116, 120, 123, 132-137, 140-143, 146, 149, 150, 154-155, 159-161, 163, 165-167, 169, 170-183, 205, 212-217, 221-222, 226, 229, 230-231, 234-236, 250, 252, 265-266, 270
Issei, 170-171, 175-178, 180-181, 183, 212, 225
Nisei, 169-170, 175, 180, 181-183, 212, 225
100th/442nd Regimental Combat Team, 181-182
Jarves, James, 90-91, 94
Joesting, Edward, 31, 44-45, 59, 63, 88

K

Ka'ahumanu, Queen, 48-49, 60, 68, 75, 238
kahakō, (see macron)
Kāheka Beach, 261
kahuna, 15, 23-25, 38, 69
Kaikio'ewa, Governor, 49, 57, 88, 92, 94
Kailua, 60, 68-70
Kalāheo, 23, 99, 106, 227-229, 234-235
Kalaniana'ole, Prince Jonah Kūhiō, 260
Kamakau, Samuel, 19-20, 38, 45-48, 57
Kamehameha, 41-46, 48-49, 53-54, 56-62, 68, 113, 118, 255-256, 261
Kamehameha II, (see Liholiho)
Kamehameha III, 49, 88, 93, 239, 269
Kamehameha IV, 115, 270
Kamehameha V, 115, 120, 270
Kanaloa (Hawaiian god), 24
kānāwai (secular decrees), 23
Kāne (Hawaiian god), 24, 112, 253
kapu system, 23-24, 54, 68, 114-115, 238
Kapule, Chiefess, 70, 77
Kaua'i Fruit and Land Company, Ltd. ("Kaua'i Pine"), 225, 228-229
Kaumuali'i Highway, 188-189, 191, 194, 227
Kawailoa Bay, 255
Kealakekua Bay, 41, 63
Keiki Beach, 261, 265
Keoneloa Beach, 253-255, 257
King, James, 31, 55, 114
Kīpū (ahupua'a), 187, 189
Knudsen Trust, 190-191, 194-195, 250, 252, 245, 249
Kōloa (ahupua'a), 2, 3, 16, 23, 26, 83, 149, 191, 239-241
Kōloa Church, 76, 78-80, 197, 200-202
Kōloa (District), 23, 28, 32, 35, 50-51, 53, 63-64, 83
Kōloa Gap, 23
Kōloa Landing, 51-54, 56, 61-64, 119, 145, 197, 200, 214, 216, 238-239, 241, 244, 246, 248, 265, 267
Kōloa Mills
First and second at Mauhili, 88-90, 197, 221, 251
1841 "Old Mill" in Kōloa, 101, 106, 195, 202, 208
Mill in Pa'a, 101, 106, 159, 167, 197, 222
Kōloa Missionary Church, 198, 202, 204
Kōloa Plantation, 63, 142-143, 146-147, 152, 154-155, 158-159, 163, 165, 167, 189, 191, 195, 203-205, 208, 213, 216, 219, 224, 236, 248-249, 250, 265
Kōloa Plantation Hospital and Dispensary, 163, 203

Kōloa Plantation camps, 106, 120, 135,
149, 152, 156-161, 164-165, 167,
175, 179, 265, 267, 269
Kōloa Plantation life, xi, 141-167
Kōloa Plantation Railroad, (see railroads)
Kōloa Road, 143-144, 190, 191, 195,
197, 204, 205, 208, 210, 212-213,
215-216, 219, 222, 224, 235
Kōloa School, 164, 195-198, 200,
202, 222
Kōloa (tour), 188-239
Kōloa Town Associates, 191, 194, 208,
213-215
Koreans, 123-124, 142-143, 146, 159,
164, 174, 176, 215
KTA, (See Kōloa Town Associates)
Kū (Hawaiian god), 24, 227
kukui, 22, 26-27, 74, 100, 111, 265
Kukui-o-Lono, 224, 227-229, 235
Kukuiʻula Harbor, 197-198, 212, 246,
265, 267
Kuroshio Current, 39

L

Ladd & Company, 76, 80
Lahaina, 44, 63-64, 70
Lahaina luna, 19, 38, 75, 256
lau hala, 25-26, 29, 88
Lāwaʻi (ahupuaʻa), 99, 204, 224-226, 228,
270, 272
Lāwaʻi Beach, 197, 246, 258, 261, 265,
267-272
Liholiho (Kamehameha II), 20, 48-49, 57,
68-69, 70, 239
Līhuʻe, passim 5-6, 23, 30, 64, 94, 100-
101, 106, 119, 161, 165, 171, 182,
188-189, 194, 197-198, 208, 212,
214
Līhuʻe Plantation, 94, 100, 109, 119,
184, 187, 219
London Missionary Society (LMS), 20, 72
Lono (Hawaiian god), 24, 37-38, 41, 224,
227-229, 234
luna (foreman), 22, 117, 149, 152, 155,
216

M

Macron, 74
Māhāʻulepū, 23, 86-87, 97-98, 106, 109,
152, 189, 224, 246, 250, 255-
258
Mahele, 190, 252, 269
Makahiki (festival), 24, 31, 88
Makahūʻena, 2, 35, 50, 52, 241, 244,
246, 252
makaʻāinana (commoners), 24, 54, 90,
114, 262
Malo, David, 19, 38
Maluhia Road, 102, 194-195, 214, 224,
228

mana (spiritual power), 15, 25
Manō-ka-lani-pō, 253
Marquesas, 12-13, 28
Maui, 14, 17, 19, 21, 28, 38, 41, 44, 49,
62, 70, 75, 269
Maulili, 75-76, 88-90, 197, 221, 251
McBryde, Alexander, 100, 270-271
McBryde Plantation, 99-100, 106, 109,
161, 171, 187, 191, 198, 227-228,
234, 248, 262, 265, 267-268, 270
McBryde, Walter, 99-100, 194, 224-228,
230-232, 234-235, 270
mele, (see chants)
menehune, 15, 16, 30, 43
Missionaries, xi, 2, 20-21, 42, 58, 64,
66-82, 88, 91, 93, 100, 113-115,
121, 123, 146, 166, 189, 190, 197-
198, 202, 204, 238-239, 241, 257,
268
Moir Garden, 232, 249-251

N

Nāpali Coast, 5, 6, 22,
National Tropical Botanical Garden
(NTBG), 269, 271-272
Nāwiliwili, 61, 64, 76, 94, 106, 189,
216, 251
Niʻihau, 2, 5-6, 21, 34, 41, 43, 48-49, 53,
79, 131, 191, 234, 243
Northwest Passage, 2, 33, 55
Numila, 100, 161, 187, 267

O

Oʻahu, xi, 16, 21, 31, 34, 43-45, 49, 60-
62, 69, 94, 98, 170, 180, 183, 185,
228, 235, 238, 256, 262
ʻokina (glottal stop), 74
ʻŌmaʻo Stream, 93, 100, 195
Organic Act of 1900, 98, 116, 137

P

Pāʻā, 23, 101, 255
Petroglyphs, 17, 225, 254, 255-257
Pidgin, 117, 129, 141, 164
Pīhākekua, 244, 252, 254
poi (taro paste), 30, 92, 213
Polynesians, x, 2, 8-16, 27-29, 31, 73,
231
Port Allcn, 61, 101, 171, 216, 248
Portuguese, 117-118, 130, 141-143, 145-
146, 155, 157, 159, 164, 167, 215,
229, 239
Poʻipū, 188, 191, 213-215, 222, 236,
239-272
Poʻipū and environs, tour of, 239-272
Poʻipū Beach, 197, 238, 244, 246,
248, 251, 258, 245
Poʻipū Beach Park, 167, 241, 243,
246, 251-252
Poʻipū Road, 195-198, 200, 202, 204-
205, 213, 224, 238, 244,
258,

Puerto Ricans, 120-121, 142-143, 157, 239
Pukui, Mary Kawena, 85, 87, 189
Pu'u-o-hewa, 195

R
Raiatea, 14-15, 17, 33
Railroads, 97, 100, 102, 106, 109, 157, 198, 216, 236, 248, 262, 265
Reciprocity treaties, 97, 125
Rice, 64, 99, 125-128, 132, 136, 138, 164, 166, 214, 250, 270
Ruggles, Samuel, 67-71
Russia, 54-55, 58-62
Russian-American Company, 55, 58-60, 62
Russians (immigrant workers), 118

S
Saint Raphael Church, 117, 237-238
Salt, 16-17, 26, 31, 41, 47, 53-54, 58, 64, 161, 261
Sandalwood, 50, 56-58, 60, 62-64, 106, 124
Scheffer, Georg Anton, 59-62
Schmitt, Robert, 45, 132
Scots, 121
Sitka, 55, 59
Smith-Waterhouse Family Partnership, 190-191, 195, 202, 204
Society Islands, 16-18, 28, 72
Spain, 55, 58, 139
Spanish, 40, 55, 113, 120-121, 130, 138, 140, 142, 157, 167, 254
Spanish galleons, 34, 39-40, 254
Spanish immigrant workers, 106, 120-121, 142, 157
Spouting Horn Park, 267-269
Statehood 1959, 80
Strikes, 92, 99, 133, 137, 159, 204, 215, 219, 225-226
Sugar cane and sugar industry, xi, 2, 22, 26, 28, 36, 50-51, 53, 63-64, 71, 76-77, 79, 83-110, 115-116, 118-119, 121, 124-128, 133, 137-138, 152, 161, 168-171, 183-185, 187, 195, 225-226, 228, 248, 250-251, 268-270
Sweet potatoes, 12, 22, 29, 50, 53

T
Tahiti, 11, 15-18, 28, 33-35, 72
Tahitian, 15-17, 20, 26, 28, 36, 38, 40, 71-73
tapa (barkcloth), 26-27, 31-32, 56, 91, 112
Taro, 12, 22, 23, 26, 28-30, 38, 48, 51, 53, 57, 77, 88, 90-92, 113, 128, 132, 157, 225, 234-235, 262, 269
Telephones, 161, 208
ti (plant), 25, 29, 165, 213

Tree Tunnel, 194, 224, 228

U
United States, 48, 55, 58, 71, 76-77
United States and Chinese Exclusion Act, 127
United States and Gentleman's Agreement of 1908, 102, 133
United States and Restriction on Japanese immigration 1924, 102, 133-134

V
Vancouver, Captain George, 42-43, 56

W
Wahiawa ahupua'a, 23, 99-100, 228, 233-234
Waihohonu Stream, 88, 93, 195
Waikomo Road, 197, 200, 204, 221, 238
Waikomo Stream, 93, 97, 100, 159, 195, 210, 215, 248, 252
Waila'au Road, 106, 157, 214, 235-236
Wailua, 42, 64, 75, 79, 94, 201
Waimea, 2, 34, 37-42, 48-49, 51, 55, 57, 59-63, 67, 69, 71, 87, 92, 113, 161, 165, 214, 253
Waimea Bay, 34, 37, 40-41, 51-52, 248
Waimea Bay and kona storms, 51-52, 59, 248
Waimea Canyon, 1, 5
Waimea River, 5, 37, 43, 61, 71
Waimea and missionaries, 70-71, 75, 77-78, 79, 91, 197, 201
Waitā Reservoir, 99, 101, 106, 164, 235, 263
Wai'ale'ale, Mount, 1, 5, 188, 194
Wai'ohai, 221, 241, 244, 246, 251-253, 245
War of 1812, 43, 48, 56, 58-59
Waterhouse, Dr. Alfred Herbert, 162-164, 167, 190, 202, 204-205, 210, 253
Waterhouse, Jack "Keaka", 190, 261
Waterhouse Trust, (see Smith-Waterhouse Family Partnership)
Weliweli Road, 197, 214-215, 221-222, 236, 238
Whaling industry, 2, 50, 63-65, 87-88, 106, 200, 215, 248, 250, 267
Whitney, Reverend Samuel, 67, 69-71, 75, 77, 86
Wilcox, George Norton, 82, 100, 145, 161, 184, 199, 202, 208, 236
Williamson, Lieutenant John, 36-37, 41
World War II, 109, 130, 135, 139, 146, 169, 171, 173, 182-183, 267

Y
Yams, 22, 29, 41, 53, 91